Washington County Tennessee Wills

1777-1872

by

Goldene Fillers Burgner

SOUTHERN HISTORICAL PRESS, INC.
c/o The Rev. Silas Emmett Lucas, Jr.
275 West Broad Street
Greenville, South Carolina 29601

Reprinted 1992

ISBN 0-89308-285-6

INTRODUCTION

WASHINGTON COUNTY was erected* by the General Assembly of North Carolina in November, 1777. It was formed from Washington District which had been detached from Wilkes and Burke Counties and included all the present State of Tennessee, although a part of it was thought at the time to belong to Virginia. This county has the distinction of being the first political division in the United States which was named in honor of George Washington. From it all the other counties in Tennessee have been carved. It is, therefore, the oldest county in the state and was the theatre of the important events which occurred in its early history.

At this session of the Legislature provision was also made for opening a land office in Washington County, permission being given that each head of a family might take up six hundred and forty acres, his wife and his children one hundred acres each, all at the rate of forty shillings per hundred acres. The facility with which settlers might obtain lands caused a large influx of pioneers immediately, although no wagon road had been opened across the mountains.

At least eight years prior to the formation of this county permanent settlers had taken up their abodes on the Watauga, as we have seen. The Watauga Association was formed in 1772, and Henderson's Purchase of the Transylvania Country was made from the Indians by treaty signed in 1775 on the Watauga.

John Carter, who had been chairman of the court of the Watauga Association, was appointed colonel of Washington County.

The county was organized on February 23, 1778, with the following named magistrates in attendance: John Carter, chairman, John Sevier, Jacob Womack, Robert Lucas, Andrew Greer, John Shelby, George Russell, William Been, Zachariah Isbell, John McNabb, Thomas Houghton, William Clark, John McMahan, Benjamin Gist, John Chisholm, Joseph Wilson, William Cobb, James Stuart, Michael Woods, Richard White, Benjamin Wilson, James Robertson, and Valentine Sevier. On the next day the officers were elected as follows: John Sevier, clerk; Valentine Sevier, sheriff; James

Stuart, surveyor; John Carter, entry-taker; John Mc-
Mahan, register; Jacob Womack, stray-master; John
McNabb, coroner.

The first courhouse was built by Charles
Robertson. Andrew Jackson lived in Jonesboro when
he first came to Tennessee and boarded with Mr. Chester

Jonesboro, the oldest town in the state, was
selected for the county seat. It was named for Willie
(pronounced Wylie) Jones, who had shown himself
friendly to the Watauga settlers when they had sent
delegates to Halifax, N. C., to see the governor.
Jonesboro was laid off in 1779. The first and the
last Legislatures of the State of Franklin met at
Jonesboro. Many noted men have lived in this historic
place. Among them were: David Nelson, author of
"The Cause and Cure of Infidelity"; B. F. Lundy,
publisher of an abolition paper; W. G. Brownlow,
before he moved to Knoxville; Landon C. Haynes, uncle
of Robert L. and Alfred A. Taylor; Judge T. A. R.
Nelson; and Chief Justice J. W. Deaderick.

*Chapter XXXI of the Laws of N.C. Iredell's Revisal, page 346.
By this act the County of Washington was "declared to be part
of the District of Salisbury."

*From Austin P. Foster's COUNTIES OF TENNESSEE
(THE FORMATION OF), which is being reprinted
by Southern Historical Press, Inc., in 1984.*

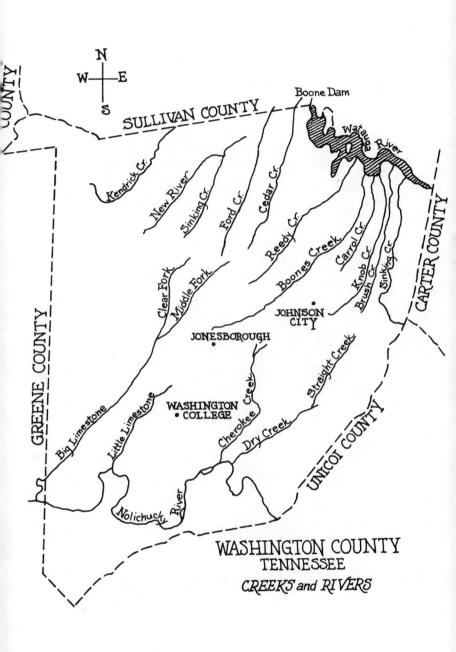

WASHINGTON COUNTY
TENNESSEE
CREEKS and RIVERS

istopher Taylor, early pioneer of Washington County, and town of Jonesborough.
is house was built before Jonesborough was a town. Andrew Jackson lodged here in
98.

In 1771 Jacob Brown from South Carolina settled on the Nolachucky River. He p
chased 2 tracts of land from the Cherokee 25 Mar. 1775. Jacob died 25 Jan. 1785.
grandson Bud Brown built this house about 1800.

Old Millhouse across road from the house built by Bud Brown.

Brick house on original Brown Purchase. It is near the house built by Bud Brown

Chimney at Plum Grove, home of John Sevier (Nolachucky Jack).

Site of Old Dutch Church (Lutheran).

... memory of an American Revolutionary War soldier who brought his family to ...ennessee from Virginia in 1778.

Thomas West Died Jan. 1796	His wife	Rachel Died April 1814
Their son Edward West and wives October 29, 1766 —	Lydia Died —	Elizabeth — —

Cassimore May
Pvt.
Rev. War
1752-1836
In Old Dutch Cemetery

REBECCA VANDERPOOL   May 12, 1779
To Teter Nave, husband of dau. Ann, 6 head of meat cattle with a swallow
fork in ear. Son Abraham Vanderpool has money in his hands. Executor:
Peter Nave. Teste: Thomas Houghton, James Grayson, Elizabeth Grayson.
Proven August Sessions, 1779.   her
                              Signed: Rebecca X Vanderpool
                                               mark

JOAB MITCHELL   October 7, 1779
Wife, Mary Mitchell, sole heir. Teste: John Coulter, Richard Mitchell,
Jane X Coulter. Recorded May Sessions, 1780.   his
                              Signed: Joab X Mitchell
                                               mark

NATHANIEL DAVIS   February 21, 1781
To brother, Robert Davis, my blacksmith tools, 100 Acres, Stallion colt
and take care of Mother, then money to go to Manumission Society. To
sister, Ann, my bay mare. To sister, Elizabeth, 100 Acres land at Bethel
Springs. Sister, Mary. Bro. Robert's sons, James and Esa. Executors:
Bros. Robert and Isaac. Teste: Robert Davis, Mary Davis. Recorded May
Sessions, 1781.
                              Signed: Nathaniel Davis

AARON BURLESON   November 16, 1781
To son, John, rifle gun. To son, Joseph, rifle gun. Son, Jonathan.
Daughter, Elizabeth. To son, Thomas, one shilling sterling. Daughter,
Sarah. To son, Aaron, one shilling sterling. To daus. Rachel and
Nancy, one shilling sterling each. To daus. Abigail, Mary, Rhoda, one
cow each. Remainder to son, James, at death of my wife. Executors:
Wife and son Aaron. Teste: Thomas Williams, Patrick X Shields, Henry
Clark. Recorded May Sessions, 1782.
                              Signed: Aaron Burleson

JOHN PAVELEY   April 12, 1781
"Of Chucky, in County of Washington." Wife, Elizabeth, lands during her
life. Son, William, a cow called Cherry and her increase. Son, Elijah,
150 Acres. Son, James, 100 Acres. Son Jeremiah. Daughters: Mary,
Frances, Lucia, Elizabeth, Eysa and Margaret. Eldest son Lewis. Teste:
George Mooney, Charles X Dotson, John Powers, Jonathan Currier. Recorded
May Sessions, 1782.
                              No Signature

WILLIAM BEAN
To wife, Liddy, negro girl "Grace", horses, cattle, household goods, land
and mill during her natural life, at her decrease to son Russell. RE-
mainder of estate to be divided amongst my surviving children. Sons
William, Robert and George, Executors. Teste: Thomas Hardeman, John X
Callihan, Robert Stone. May Sessions, 1782.   his
                              Signed: William X Bean
                                               mark

ADAM BROYLES   April 19, 1782
To eldest son, Moses, 200 Acres bought of Joseph Bullard southside Little
Limestone. To sons, Aaron and Joshua, land where I live. To dau. Milla
Panther, 200 Acres I bought of George Doherty. To dau. Mima Broyles, 60
Lb. currency. To dau. Anne Brown, 5 shillings. To dau. Mary, 50 Lb.
currency. Negroes and Kentucky lands. Friends: Joseph Brown, Moses
Broyles and William Moore, Executors. Teste: John X Waddle, Coonrod
Willpightle, Mathias Broyles. May Sessions, 1782.
                              Signed: Adam Broyles

JOHN NODDING   November 6, 1782
Wife, Priscilla - Slaves and land. Slave "Prince" to have her freedom
at my wife's death. Teste: Samuel Wood, James Scott. February Sessions,
1783.   his
                              Signed: John X Nodding
                                           mark

PETER KUYKENDALL   February 6, 1783   Wash. Co., N.C.
To son Jesse, slave and land. To dau. Jane, slave and land. To son
Adam, 5 shillings. To dau. Elizabeth, 1 shilling. To son Matthew, 1
shilling. To son Peter, 1 shilling. Children: Mary, Ruthy, Rebecca,
Offay. Brother Abraham, executor. Teste: Andrew Thompson, John
Kuykendall, Robert Irwin. May Sessions, 1783.
                              Signed: Peter Kuykendall

BAPTIST McNABB   January 4, 1784   Washington Co., N.C.
Dau. Isabella McNabb. Sons: John, David, Jonathan. Daus. Mary,
Margaret, Jane & Katrin, 5 shillings each. Sons John and David,
executors. Teste: William McNabb, Agness Campbell, John Campbell.
May Sessions, 1784.   his
                              Signed: Baptist B McNabb
                                           mark

THOMAS MITCHELL   June 14, 1784   Washington Co., N.C.
To son, James, and daus., Margaret McAdow and Elizabeth Thompson, 5
shillings each. Son Thomas and dau. Sarah Mitchell to get remainder.
Teste: Robert Irwin, Mary Irwin. August Sessions, 1784.
                              Signed: Thomas (X) Mitchell

RANDOLPH CRECELIAS   January 7, 1787
Wife, Elizabeth. Son John, ½ land. Sons: Isaac, Cuthart, John, Jacob.
Daughters: Elizabeth, Barberry, Catherine, Dolly, Margaret, Grace.
Teste: James Cash, Abraham Riffe, Philip X Coussions. November Sessions,
1787.

ANDREW TAYLOR   May 22, 1787   Washington Co., N.C.
Wife, Ann. Sons Isaac, David McNabb, Andrew Taylor, Nathaniel Taylor,
Matthew Taylor - land I purchased from Isaac Taylor. "Till youngest
child Rhoda comes of age." Dau. Rebecca. Slaves to each child. Teste:
John Hyder, William English. November Sessions, 1787.
                              Signed: Andrew Taylor

JOHN FAIN   July 15, 1788
Wife, Agnes and sons to share equally. To dau. Ruth Fain, negro "Punch".
Teste: Rosannah X Fain. November Sessions, 1788.
                              Signed: John Fain

JOHN BULLARD   October 20, 1780   Washington Co., N.C.
(Noncupative Will) Wife, Mary Bullard. Teste: Joseph (X) Nation,
Elinor (X) Nation, Ann (X) Bullard. No date of probate.
                              No Signature.

JOHN COX   October 19, 1777
To sons, Abraham and William, 2 negroes and land I possess. To daus.,
Jane and Agnes, 50 Lb. Va. money, slaves I should have had from my
father's estate, all stock and movable estate. Executors: Sons Abraham
and William, and John Sevier. Teste: John Carter, Christopher
Cunningham, Emanuel Carter. No date of probate. his
                              Signed: John X Cox
                                           mark

CHRISTOPHER CUNNINGHAM   November 10, 1782
Wife, Mary. My fifteen children: Elizabeth Gatril, Susannah Robertson,
Lyddia Cunningham, John Cunningham, Mary Job, Ann Orr, Sarah Cunningham,
Jane Cunningham, Jacob, Joseph, Matthew, Moses, Aaron, Elinor, David.

Daus. Elizabeth Gatril and Susannah Robertson to have no part in legacy
that John Musgrove left Mary, my wife. Executors: Mathew Talbot and
Joseph Tipton. Teste: Robert Orr, Isaac Taylor. May Sessions, 1783.
                                                    his
                    Signed: Christopher cc Cunningham
                                            mark

ROBERT FOWLER   September 22, 1784
Wife, Agnes Fowler, to have what her father gave her and 1/3 of my
estate. Mother Ann Fowler. Child, Esther Fowler. Executors: William
Fowler and Wife, Agnes Fowler. Teste: Abednego Inman, Adam Willson,
Molly Inman. August Sessions, 1785.   his
                    Signed: Robert X Fowler
                                       mark

THOMAS DILLARD   May 13, 1784
Wife, Martha, to have one half of slaves. To son, Benjamin, Virginia
land warrant for 1000 Acres land. Children: Benjamin, Winnesophia,
Mary Ann, Thomas, Stacy, Martha, Amy, John, Rebecca, Elizabeth Hutchings.
Executors: Wife, Martha and son-in-law, Robert Love. Robert Love
guardian for minor children, Sept. 23, 1784. Teste: Edmond Samms,
John Samms, John Webb. _____ Sessions, 178_.
                    Signed: Thomas Dillard

WILLIAM CARSON   March 10, 1790
Wife, Margaret. Oldest dau., Jennet. Dau., Mary. Oldest son, William.
Son, John, to have English schooling. Executors: David Carson, John
Strain. May Sessions, 1790.

JOHN POTTER   November 18, 1789   Washington Co., N.C.
Wife, Hannah. Sons, John, Johnston, Abraham. To son-in-law, Adam
Rainbolt, land on Progres Creek where George Miller now lives.
Children: Nancy, John, Elizabeth, Johnston, Sarah. Executors: Wife,
Hannah and friends Cornelius Bowman and Thomas Whitson. Teste: William
Moreland, John (X) Grindstaff, Isaac Grindstaff. May Sessions, 1790.
                                          his
                    Signed: John O Potter
                                     mark

WALTER BAYLEY   June 10, 1790   Washington Co., N.C.
My wife to have land in Sussex County, Virginia, in care of Thomas
Whitfield. Wife and daus., Mary and Lucy, to have slaves. To Sarah
Maggot, dau. of Mary Maggot, land in Sussex Co., Va. Executors: Joseph
Greer of Washington Co., N.C. and Etheldred Davis of Sussex Co., Va.
Teste: Thomas Reneau, Archer Evans, Charlot Evans. August Sessions,
1790.

                    Signed: Walter Bayley

DAVID MATLOCK   March 15, 1790   Washington County, N.C.
Wife, Margaret. Three daughters, Sarah, Elizabeth and Catherine. Sons:
George, David and Gideon. Executors: Son David and Joseph Greer.
Teste: Moses Humphreys, Peter Parkson, Andrew (X) Sholdy. August
Sessions, 1790.

                    Signed: David Matlock

MICHAEL HIDER   May 28, 1790
To wife, Elizabeth, plantation with orchards and houses, also household
furniture and stocks during her life. To sons John, Michael, Adam,
Jacob and Joseph, 100 Acres I bought of Matthew Talbot. Executors: Wife
and son John. Teste: Edmond Williams, Robert English, Henry (X) English.
August Sessions, 1790.

                    Signed: Michael (X) Hider

BENJAMIN BLACKBURN   August 10, 1786
"of the State of Franklin and county of Washington, farmer." Wife Mary
"good sufficient genteel and handsome, maintaince during her life of all

3

things necessary." To son Benjamin "my Great Bible". To each grandson named Benjamin "a good school Bible". To son John, my shoe buckles. To sons Robert and Benjamin, bond on Hiram Gerim for 300 pounds. Son Samuel. Daughters Ann and Elizabeth Bay. Archibald's bond to Thomas Bay. Executors: Son Archibald and John Wear. Teste: James Cunningham, Jeremiah Robinson, Andrew Hannah. August Sessions, 1791.
                                No Signature

JAMES GALLEHER   Sept. 22, 1791   Wash. Co. of the Western Waters
Wife, Sarah, sons George, Thomas, James "having got their share". Son
John. Youngest son David "when comes of age". Executors: Wife Sarah
and sons George and John. Teste: George Gillespie, John Allison,
Robert McFarland. February Sessions, 1792.
                            Signed: James Galleher

ROBERT YOUNG   February 8, 1792
"County of Washington, Territory of the United States of America, South
of the Ohio River." Wife, Mary. To son Joseph, 600 Acres where I live.
Children: Elizabeth Gillaland, Marth Cashedy, John, William, Robert,
Thomas, Charles, Jane Long, Margaret Bates, Mary Dugless, Agnes Henry.
Grandsons: Joseph Young, son of deceased son James, Robert Gillaland
and Robert Cashedy. Executors: Wife Mary and son Joseph. Teste:
Thomas Gourley, James Gunnon, Absolem Scott. May Sessions, 1792.
                            Signed: Robert Young

THOMAS BELL   March 19, 1792
Wife, Elizabeth. Children: John, David, Sarah and Mary to be taught to
read God's word distinctly and taught to cypher to the rule of three.
Brother, John Bell, guardian. Executors: Wife Elizabeth and brother
William Bell. Teste: Robert Carson, James Bell. May Sessions, 1792.
                            Signed: Thomas Bell

ROBERT ALLISON   April 26, 1792
"Washington County, Territory in the United States of America, South of
the Ohio River." Wife, Ann. Two youngest daus. Jane and Polly. Dau.
Ann. Youngest son Robert. "My married children." Executors: Ann
Allison and Robert Allison. Teste: John Anderson, George Bell. May
Sessions, 1792.
                        Signed: Robert (X) Allison

WILLIAM SHEALDS   February 10, 1791
Wife to have 15 bushels Indian corn yearly. Son Joseph, rest of children
equally. Executors: Son Joseph and Andrew Thompson. Teste: John
Campbell, David Brown, Robert Bleakly. November Sessions, 1792.
                            Signed: William Shealds

CHARLES HAY   December 23, 1792
"of Washington County in the Ceded Territory Southwest of the Ohio River."
To wife, Rebecca, household goods and the following books - her Bible,
Boston Fourfold State of Man, Erskin's Gospel Sonnets, a book entitled
A Dead Faith Anatornized. To nephew Charles Greer, my dictionary with an
old book of Arithmetic. To nephew Charles Hatcher, 2nd volume of
Baxter's Philosophical Inquiry in the Nature of the Human Sole. To
nephew David Greer, my Bible. To sister Hulda Grier, the 4th Volume of
Dr. Doddridge's Family Expository. To sister Sarah Hatcher's daughter
Anna, 2nd volume of Family Expository. To Charles H. Nelson my wife's
sister's son, ten dollars. To brother Reuben Hay. To Wife's sister
Sarah Robinson, one new Bible. To sister Hulda Grier's youngest dau.
Mary Grier. To Jamiston Hatcher's youngest daus. Sarah and Rebecca. To
Harris Hatcher, son of James Hatcher. To Charles Hatcher and James
Hatcher, sons of Jameson Hatcher. $195 of estate of James Grier, decd.,
put to interest May 19, 1779. Executors: Wife Rebecca, Capt. James
Scott, Nathaniel Davis. Teste: Henry McMullen, Agness (X) Davis, Mary
McMullen. February Sessions, 1793.
                            Signed: Charles Hay

                                4

WILLIAM NODING, JUNR.   September 15, 1792
Nephew Charles McCray. To sister Elizabeth Calvert, negro "Adam". To
nephews Charles McCray and John Calvert, land on Camp Creek if my father
William Noding obtains a deed for it. Sisters Sarah McCray, Mary Bayles,
Elinor Hill and Alis Brown's, decd. children, Mill seat where bro. John
Noding lived. Executors: Daniel McCray and William Calvert. Teste:
Samuel Wood, Senr., James Wood, Samuel Wood Junr. May Sessions, 1793.
                              Signed: William Noding

JOSEPH BARRON   August 2, 1793
Wife, Ann. Five children: John, Joseph, William, Henry, James. Daus.:
Sarah Dotson, Mary Ford, Walker Barron. Executors: Sons Joseph and
William. Teste: John Kinchloe, Margaret (X) Barron. August Sessions,
1793.
                                        his
                         Signed: Joseph (X) Barron
                                        mark

JOSEPH TROTTER   January 8, 1794
Wife, Jenny. Brothers Alexander and James to get my clothes. "Chest at
Col. Roddie's." Executors: Jenny Trotter, Alexander Trotter. Teste:
John Carmicle, Isabella Trotter, Margaret Carmicle. February Sessions,
1794

                    Signed: Joseph Trotter

GEORGE GILLESPIE   December 14, 1794
"of Green County, Territory South of Ohio River." Wife, Martha. To son
Thomas and his son George, 20 lb. currency Virvinia count. To daughter
Martha Jack and her son George Jack, if he arrives at age 15, horse, 15
lb. Va. Count. To son John and his son George Gillespie, land where he
lives in Green County mouth of Big Limestone. Dau. Jane Gillespie.
Dau. Elizabeth Hays and her son Charles Hays. Three sons George, Allen
and James. Slaves to each. Executors: Wife & Sons George and Allen.
Teste: F. A. Ramsey, George Galleher, Henry Earnest. February Sessions,
1794.

                    Signed: George Gillespie

SAMUEL SHAW   July 29, 1794
"of Washington County in the ceded Territory." To wife, Margaret, while
living at my plantation, her bed, clothing and her mare. Sons Francis
and Samuel. Married daughters. Executors: Sons Francis and Samuel.
Teste: Margaret Spear, Samuel Brison, William Purselly. Proven
November Sessions, 1794.

JAMES ALLISON   September 21, 1794
Wife, Jane. To Elizabeth Scott, Hannah Scott, Rachel Sharp, Esther
Allison (relationship not given). To dau. Elizabeth Allison. Real
estate to be disposed of. Executors: Robert Allison, Nathaniel Davis,
James Chastin. Teste: Frank (X) Allison, John Adams, Michael Harrison.
Proven May Sessions, 1795.

                    Signed: James Allison

ISAAC DENTON   July 14, 1795
To wife, Ann, 20 lb. or $66. To sons Isaac (infirm) and Jeremiah Denton,
all my lands equally divided. Daughters Martha, Agge, and Elizabeth
Denton. To Susanna Rider, 10 lb. Executors: David Job, Jesse Whitson.
Teste: Jesse Whitson, David Job. Proven May Sessions, 1795.
                         Signed: Isaac Benton (Denton)

ALEXANDER TROTTER   April 24, 1795
Wife, Isabella. To sons, David and Joseph, my clothes. Daughter,
Susanna. Executors: Wife Isabella and James Carmicle Senr. Teste:
Alexander Stuart, Abigail Carmicle. November Sessions, 1795.
                         Signed: Alex Trotter

EDMUND WILLIAMS   September 16, 1795
Territory of United States, Washington County. Wife, Lucretia. To sons

                              5

Joshua and Samuel, negroes, money Matthew Bass owes me. To son George,
turning and joining tools. Son Archibald. Daughters Levina Tipton,
Terphena Williams and Sarah Adams Williams. To son John Lindsey Williams,
land on Buffalo Creek granted to Edmund Williams by state on N.C. To
daughters, negroes. Executors: Son Joshua Williams of Boncomb Co., N.C.
and son Archibald Williams of Washington Co. Teste: William Davis,
Charles Whitson, William Whitson. November Sessions, 1795.

Signed: Edmund Williams

JOSHUA WOOD   June 11, 1773
Wife, Agnes. Daughters: Wineford Wood, Milly Wood and Elizabeth Wood,
5 shillings each. Sons: Richard, Elijah, John, Henry. 159 Acres to be
sold to pay debts. Executors: Robert Donald and William Armstrong.
Teste: Robert Ewing, Robert Irwin, Barbary (X) Mayberry. Proven May
Sessions, 1780.

Signed: Joshua Wood

WILLIAM WHITSON   October 16, 1783
"of Washington County, State of North Carolina." To son, Jesse Whitson,
whole estate. Daughters, Susannah Eajan and Lydda McKay. Executors:
Sons Joseph and Jesse. Teste: Henry Nelson Junr., William Wood, Reuben
Rider. November Sessions, 1783.

Signed: William Whitson

JAMES IRWIN
Wife, Mary. Sons: Benjamin and Robert. Daughters: Lettice, Ellenor,
Mary, Eliza. To Ellnor's child, Rose, account against Neil McFall whose
estate is in the hands of William Duffle in Pennsylvania. My small
children. Executors: Son Benjamin and wife Mary. Teste: Richard
Jones, Samuel (X) King. February Sessions, 1796.

Signed: James Irwin

GEORGE KINDAL   November 18, 1795
Wife Barbary and children. Executrix: Barbary Kindal. Teste: Samuel
Wood, Martin Sidner, Michael Harmon. February Sessions, 1796.

Signed: George Kindal

JOHN WHITE   May 14, 1796
"of Washington County in the territory of the United States South of the
river Ohio (alias Tennessee)." Wife, Ann. Children as they come of age.
Executrix: Ann White. Teste: Joseph Brittin, John (X) Hill, Ellinor
Hill. May Sessions, 1796.

Signed: John White

ROBERT HAMPTON   March 29, 1796
Wife, Mary. Sons: John, George, Robert, William and Jesse. Executor:
oldest son John. Teste: Reubin Bayles, Mary (X) Eton. August Sessions,
1796.

Signed: Robert Hampton

JAMES BOREN   October 14, 1795
Wife, Sarah. Sons: William, Absolem, Chaney, James and John Dopon
Boren. Daughters: Rachel Price, wife of Mordiciai Price, Abrrodla
Moore, Tempereace Boren, Martha Ball and Frances Downing. Executor:
son Chaney. Teste: Horatio Ford, Edward (X) Smith. August Sessions,
1796.   his
                         Signed: James (X) Boren
                                        mark

CHARLES ROBERTSON, SENR.   August 31, 1798
"of County of Washington, State of Tennessee." To wife, Susannah,
negroes "Peter" and "Poll". To son William, negro "Kate." To Rosamond
Beane, negro "Rhoda". To Kesiah Sevier, "a likely negro girl". To
Sarah Cox, $10. Real estate 2000 acres lying at Mussel Shoals to be
taken out of 8000 acre tract, 1000 acres to James Gordon and 1000 acres

to Charles Sevier. Executors: Charles Robertson, Junr. and James Gordon. Teste: Henry Taylor, Abraham Hartsell, Era Witt. November Sessions, 1798.

Signed: Charles Robertson Senr.

SAMUEL CULBERTSON   December 24, 1798   Wash. Co., Tenn.
Wife, Jane. Children: Andrew, Josiah, Samuel, Joseph, James, Mary Weakfield. Executors: Robert Love and Daniel McCray. Teste: James Deakins, John Young, Holland Hyggins. February Sessions, 1799.

Signed: Samuel Culbertson

JOHN CARMICLE   February 27, 1799
To wife, Isabella, ½ of plantation. To son James, 20 shillings. To my oldest daughter Mary Moore, £5. To daughter Jenny, 2 cows and calves. Daughter Margaret Carmicle. Sons George Pumry and Archibald to divide land in Grassy Vally, George to have improvements on part next to Knoxville. To sons John and Daniel, plantation on Tennessee River. To son David, home plantation after wife's decease. To son William, the mill. Youngest dau. Elizabeth. Executors: David Thompson and wife, Isabella. Teste: Peter Smetzer, John Adam. May Sessions, 1799.

Signed: John Carmicle

LILES BROOKS   February 17, 1799
Wife, Jane. Children as they come of age. Executors: Wife and John Bayles. Teste: Daniel Bayles, Colvin Finch, Ann Bayles. May Sessions, 1799.

Signed: Liles Brooks

JAMES HENLEY
Son John, heir to my land and livery. Wife. Father. Teste: John Hendley, Caty Hendley. May Sessions, 1799.

Signed: James (X) Hendley

CHARLES LONGMIRE   October 28, 1797   Codicil July 17, 1799
To wife, Lucy, a negro named "Beck". To son John, 285 Acres I bought of James Stuart. To son William, land I purchased of Charles McCrary on Indian Creek, branch of Nolachucky River. Sons Joseph and George. Daughter Sarah Longmore. Other children. Executors: sons John and Joseph Longmore. Teste: Peter Brown, John Brown. November Sessions, 1799.

Signed: Charles Longmire

JONATHAN WATSON   October 15, 1796
Wife, Martha and Children. Goods and chattels to be sold and money equally divided. Executors: Wife and Major John Sevier. Teste: Samuel Wood, David Smith, William Wood. November Sessions, 1799.

Signed: Jonathan Watson

JOHNSON WHITAKER   October 24, 1799
Wife, Sarah and Children. Executrix: Sarah Whitaker. Teste: Mark Whitaker, Jonathan Tullis. February Sessions, 1800.

Signed: Johnson Whitaker

JAMES CARUTHERS   February 13, 1799
To daughter, Jane Smith, "all my books" and a legacy willed to her mother by her grandfather. Executor: Richard Smith. Teste: John Bleakley, John McCall, Jane McCall. February Sessions, 1800.

Signed: James (X) Caruthers

WILL WATSON   March 9, 1800
To wife, Nancy, 200 Acres. To daughter, Susannah, 100 Acres land adjoining Robert Young. Sons: William, Jonathan. Daughters: Mary, Elizabeth, Hannah and Abigail. Executors: Wife, Joseph Young and Jonathan Tullis. Teste: John Parker, Thomas Linville, Robert (X) Cashedy. May Sessions, 1800.   Signed: William (X) Watson

SAMUEL WOOD   April 26, 1800
Wife, Sarah. Eldest son William. Son James. To son Samuel, Big Bible.
To son Thomas, cow and feather bed. Sons Abraham, John and George.
Daughter Mary Hendricks. Executors: Wife and sons Abraham and John.
Teste: William Carlvert, Martin Sidner, Colvin Finch. August Sessions,
1800.

                         Signed: Samuel Wood

WILLIAM DANIEL   May 23, 1794
Wife, Ann. Son John. To son, William, my rifle gun. Five daughters,
Mary, Ann, Phebe, Jemima and Alice Daniel. Executor: friend Joseph
Crouch. Teste: David Job, Philemon Lacy. August Sessions, 1800.
                         Signed: William Daniel

SAMUEL SHERRILL   June 4, 1800
To daughter, Catherine Sevier, wife of John Sevier, Senr. - "a negro
wench named Rachel and her youngest child about ten weeks old". Sons
Uriah and John Sherrill. To daughter, Mary Jones, wife of Littlepage
Simons - two slaves. To sons, George and William - land on which I now
live being 200 acres purchased from John Sevier on Nolachucky River
adjoining land of John Sevier. Son, Adam. Executors: John Sevier,
Senr. and William Sherrill. Teste: Benjamin Were, George Were. August
Sessions, 1800.   his
                         Signed: Samuel (S) Sherrill
                                        mark

JOHN WEIR   January 7, 1800
Wife, Agnes. Three youngest daughters, Nancy, Phebe and Susannah. Two
daughters, Betsy and Jane. Sons, Benjamin, George, John and Hugh when
he comes of age. Daughters, Mary Cunningham and Margaret Wilson.
Executors: Wife, Agnes, son Benjamin and son-in-law John Wilson.
Teste: John Nelson, Reuben Payne, Allen Mathis. August Sessions, 1800.
                         Signed: John Weir

THOMAS RODGERS   April 10, 1800
To son, Samuel, "mansion house and plantation adjoining where Andrew
Rodgers now lives". Son, William. To son Andrew, land to Joseph
Metcalf's line. Three girls. Executors: Sons Moses and James Rodgers.
Teste: James Rogers, Thomas Biddle. August Sessions, 1800.
                         Signed: Thomas Rodgers

JAMES MARTIN   January 6, 1801
Wife, Elizabeth and Children. Executor: Samuel Denton. Teste: John
Carr Junr., Jonathan Mulkey, Joseph Britten. February Sessions, 1801.
                         Signed: James Martin

HENRY STEVENS   January 10, 1801
Wife, Margaret. Stepson, James Barnes. Sons, David and Isaac Stevens.
Step daughters, Jenny, Polly and Peggy Barnes, and Nancy, William,
Betsy, Thomas, John and Henry Stevens to share equally. Executors:
Wife Margaret and William Ward. Teste: Henry King, James Morrison,
James Barnes. May Sessions, 1801.   his
                         Signed: Henry (H) Stevens
                                        mark

FREDERICK SANDERS   June 10, 1801
Wife, Margaret. Son, Frederick. "What doctor's drugs are on hand to be
sold." Executor: Jacob Simmerly of Washington County, Virginia.
Teste: J. Brittin, Thomas Enson. August Sessions, 1801.
                         Signed: Frederick Sanders

ROBERT BLAIR   April 6, 1801
Wife, Jean. Children: Mary, John, Martha, Anna, Isabel and David "until
they are of age", James Buoin, my loving boy to stay with them. All to
be schooled. Executors: Friend Robert Allison and bros. John and

William. Teste: Brue Blair, Alexander McLin, John Cunningham. February Sessions, 1802.

Signed: Robert Blair

ADAM MITCHELL   April 3, 1802
Wife, Margaret. Daughter, Margaret. To son John, land adjoining John Fair. Son, Robert. To son William, land in Guilford Co., N.C. To son, Adam, land purchased of James Witherspoon. To sons Samuel, David, James and Hezekiah, remaining lands. Daughters, Ibby, Rebecca, Jenny. Teste: Nicholas Fair, John Hammer. August Sessions, 1802.

Signed: Adam Mitchell

BENJAMIN SHIPLEY   April 2, 1802
Wife, Elizabeth. Sons: Nathan, James. Grand-daughter, Rebecca, dau. of son Nathan. "all my children". Executor: Nathan Shipley. Teste: Joseph Brittin, James Chamberlain. February Sessions, 1803.

Signed: Benjamin (X) Shipley

JAMES SEHORNE   March 1, 1803
Wife, two daughters and two sons. Executor: Samuel Davis. Teste: James McWherter, Polly Reaney McWhorter. May Sessions, 1803.

Signed: James Sehorne

ALEXANDER JERVIS   April 10, 1803
Wife, Ellenor. Daughters, Rebeccah and Ellinor. Son, William. To Isaac McInturff for use of his oldest son. To George Clouse Senr. for his son Jacob. Executors: Wife and son William Jarvis. Teste: Aaron (X) Clouse, Joel (X) Parker, R. Love. August Sessions, 1803.

Signed: Alexander (C) Jervis
his
mark

JOHN BLAIR   September 17, 1803
Wife, Jenny Blair. Adopted son, James Moore. Brothers, James and Samuel Blair. Executrix: Jenny Blair. Teste: John Strain, James Tweddy. November Sessions, 1803.

Signed: John (X) Blair

JESSE CLARK   October 5, 1801
Wife to get 1/3. Children not named. Executrix: Wife Nancy. Teste: James Sevier, Thomas Brown, Mary Clark. November Sessions, 1801.

Signed: Jesse Clark

WILLIAM CARSON   January 21, 1804
Wife, Polly. Children: Susanna, Ann, Robert, William, Polly. "When William comes of age". I want my family to have sufficient water. Executors: Wife Polly Carson, David Wilson and Samuel Davis. Teste: Ellenor (X) Humphrey, William Caruthers, Jenny Caruthers. February Sessions, 1804.

Signed: William (C) Carson
his
mark

THOMAS GRESHAM   October 5, 1803
Wife, Dorcas. Children: Fuller, John, Betsy, Rhoda, Susannah, Preon, Simeon, Thomas, Anna. "Anna, my youngest daughter, to be equal with others." Wit.: Jonathan Walker, John Crouch. February Sessions, 1804.

Signed: Thomas (X) Gresham

JOSEPH BOOTH   December 30, 1804
Wife, Sarah. To son, Joseph, plantation I bought of Henry Slyzer. To son, John, 1/3 this present improvement when 21 years. To son, David, land I bought of Benjamin Brown. To daughters, Elizabeth, Jemima, Phebe, Rachel, Sarah and Jane - $250. Executors: Son David, son-in-law John Million and Eli Edwards. Teste: Isaac Hair, Isaac Ember, Elihu Embree. May Sessions, 1805.   Signed: Joseph Booth

THOMAS MURREY   September 5, 1802
Grandson Thomas Murrey, son of son Shadrack. Grandson Jabez Murrey, son
of son Thomas. Sons Christopher, Shadrack and Thomas. Son, Morgan
Murrey, has his part. Daughters: Elizabeth Philips, Uroth King, Ann
Doty, wife of Joseph Doty, Mary Barron, wife of William Barron, Sarah
Barron, wife of Joseph Barron. Executors: Shadrack and Thomas Murrey.
Teste: Joseph Brittin, Enoch Kinchloe, Jemima (X) Kinchloe. Proven
May Sessions, 1805.   his
                              Signed: Thomas (T) Murrey, Sr.
                                                      mark

GEORGE HALE SENR.   April 30, 1805
Wife, Anne. Granddaughter Susannah, daughter of son George Hale. Son
Samuel. Daughters Elizabeth and Ann to have $33. "all my children."
Executors: Anne Hale and George Hale. Teste: Nicholas Hale Senr. &
Jesse Crouch. August Sessions, 1805.
                              Signed: George Hale

CATHERINE ROBERTSON   July 27, 1796
"of Sullivan County, State of Tennessee." "only son Jacob Robinson."
Executor: Jacob Robertson. Teste: John Chester, Daniel Duff.
November Sessions, 1805.
                              Signed: Catherine Robertson

ROBERT YOUNG   October 19, 1804
Wife, Phebe. To son William, 100 acres on Harpeth in Williamson Co. To
son John, land in Williamson Co. Sons: James, Jonathan, Thomas, Joseph,
Robert. Three young daughters to have schoolhouse and spring.
Executors: Jonathan Duglas, Phebe Young. Teste: William Young,
Abraham Job, Joshua Job. May Sessions, 1806.
                              Signed: Robert Young

MICHAEL BRICKER   December 21, 1805
To wife, Barbary, 150 lb. pork, 25 lb. beef, 8 bu. wheat, 8 bu. corn,
6 lb. sugar. Daughters: Betsy Oberboker, Christiana Oberboker. Sons:
John, Michael, Jacob, William. Other children. Executors: Son John
and Thomas Telford. Teste: John Nelson, James Houston, Alex. M.
Nelson. May Sessions, 1806.   his
                              Signed: Michael (X) Bricker
                                                      mark

ALEXANDER MATHIS SENR.   June 3, 1806
Wife, Anne. To son, Alexander, "plantation adjoining Mr. Doak, and
while there is a college kept at Salem Church he is to allow 50 acres
for its use." Children: George L., Jeremiah, John, Grace Patton,
Rachel Mathis, Miriam Telford, Allen Mathis, Alexander Jr., Ebenezer L.
Executors: Sons Alexander and George. Teste: John Nelson, Andrew
Hannah, Thomas Telford. August Sessions, 1806.
                              Signed: Alex Mathis

WILLIAM KELSEY   July 8, 1805
Son, John. Granddaughter, Agnes Goudy Kelsey. Dau., Susannah Blair.
Dau., Margaret Adams. Granddaughter, Agnes Adams. Grandson, William
Adams. Granddaughter, Nancy Blair. Dau., Elizabeth Davis. Dau., Ann
McCracken. Granddaughter, Agnes Kelsey McCracken. Dau., Mary Patton.
Executors: John Kelsey and son-in-law John Blair. Teste: Henry
Nelson, Ann Nelson, Robert Patton. August Sessions, 1806.
                              Signed: William Kelsey

JANE NELSON   November 4, 1799
Deceased husband, Henry Nelson. To daughter, Jemima Tyler, all wearing
apparrel. Four sons, William, Henry, John and Charles Nelson.
Executor: Son John. Teste: Adam Lowry, Zadock Willet, Jesse Payne.
February Sessions, 1807.   her
                              Signed: Jane (X) Nelson
                                                      mark

JAMES CASH   April 10, 1806
Wife, Margaret. To eldest son, James, $100 with part of my books. To
son, John, 50 acres. To dau., Sally Thomas, $3. To grandsons, William
and Isaac Thomas, sons of dau. Sally, $5. Sons, William, Leonard,
Thomas, Zachariah, Asbury, Benjamin. Daughters, Margaret Cash, Patsy
Anderson. Executors: Wife, son Benjamin and William Colvert Senr.
Teste: Joseph Keher, Samuel Berryman. May Sessions, 1807.
                              Signed: James Cash

JOHN FERGUSON   July 29, 1806
Wife, Jane. Sons, Samuel and John. Dau., Betsy Hodge, Ester Oar.
Executors: Wife and son Samuel. Teste: James Kennedy, Joseph Duncan,
George Bell. May Sessions, 1807.
                       Signed: John Ferguson

JOHN ENGLISH SENR.   December 20, 1798
To wife, Agnes, 1/3 of all movable property. To son, Thomas, ½ plantation.
To son, John, other half plantation. Two grandsons, John and Thomas, sons
of son Andrew English, decd. Daughters, Jane English, Elizabeth English,
Sarah Dodridge, Agnes English. Executors: Thomas and John English.
Teste: Isaac White, Thomas Robison, Andrew English. August Sessions,
1807.   Signed: John English

JOHN McCLURE   January 9, 1808
Wife, Rebecca. Sons, Robert, Ewin, James, William. Daughters, Mary &
Nancy. Executors: William Bayles, William & John McClure. Teste:
William Crabtre, Thomas Macy, Samuel Cloyd. February Sessions, 1808.
                       Signed: John McClure

ROBERT MITCHELL   November 7, 1808
To wife, Elizabeth, land adjoining Adam Rader on Knob Creek, land ad-
joining Christopher Taylor and Samuel Broyles. Son, James. Daughters,
Jenny and Eliza. Executors: Robert Allison and William Fain Senr.
Teste: John C. Harris, Sarah Fain, William Robison. February Sessions,
1809.   Signed: Robert Mitchell

MICHAEL INGLES   December 13, 1808
Wife, Mary. Wife's son, Jacob Varner. Son, John. Children. Executors:
Alexander Mathis, Adam Slyger. Teste: Abraham Williams, Simon Hart,
Adam Inglis. February Sessions, 1809.
                       Signed: Michael (X) Ingle

WILLIAM ELLIS   September 11, 1809
Wife, Martha. Dau., Margaret Beane and Edmund Beane, her husband. Three
sons, James, William & John have their part. Sons, Jacob, Clark, Elijah.
Dau., Martha. Executors: sons James and Jacob and Daniel Bowman.
Teste: Joseph Brittin, James Crabtree, Michael Crouse. November
Sessions, 1809.   Signed: William Ellis

PHEBE YOUNG   February 26, 1810
Daughters, Phebe and Anna. Sons, Joseph and Robert. Children: Joseph,
Robert, Amy, Phebe, Anna, Polly, Jemima, Jenny, Betsy. Executors: James
Young, Jonathan Young. Teste: Edward Treewits, James Young. May
Sessions, 1810.   Signed: Phebe Young

ABRAHAM SMITH   June 25, 1810
Wife, Martha. Children except Isaac and George, are to have "land they
live on in Blount County." Daughters, Rachel and Hannah, equal with
others. Executors: Closson and Isaac Hammer. Teste: Thomas and
Samuel Stenfield. August Sessions, 1810.
                       No Signature

MARY YOUNG   March 29, 1808
To son, James, "Jane Davis's part of land (340 acres) I bought that fell
to her as legatee of Thomas Young, decd. James to pay his son, Thomas

Young and Thomas Rutledge Davis. Daughters, Polly & Caty. Son, William.
Negro woman named "Amy" to be set free. Sons, Joseph and James, Exe-
cutors and trustees for William & Caty. Teste: John Parker, Barnet
Bowman. August Sessions, 1810.   Signed: Mary (X) Young

JOSEPH BARNES   November 23, 1810
Wife, Mary, and children. Executors, Wife and Joseph Kenner. Teste:
John White, Jacob Holt. February Sessions, 1811.
                              Signed: Joseph (X) Barnes

CHRISTIAN WHITE   May 9, 1810
To wife, Elizabeth, whole estate. Executrix: Elizabeth White. Teste:
William Sands, Christian Zetty. February Sessions, 1811.
                              Signed: Christian (X) White

JOHN COSSON   September 24, 1810
Wife, Margaret. Children: John E., Isaac N., Selina Johnston, Matilda
Helm, Delilah, Abbinah, Serinah, Cynthia, Maria and Mercy Cosson. Wife
and sons, Executors. Teste: John Helm, Samuel Davis, Henry French.
November Sessions, 1811.   Signed: John Cosson

SUSANNAH WOODROW   May 5, 1810
"of Jonesboro, Washington County." Land and real estate in city of
Philadelphia, Pennsylvania, daughter Elizabeth Jackson. To David
Deaderick, of Jonesboro. To grandson, Henry Jackson of Davidson Co.
To James V. Anderson of Jonesboro. Daughter, Elizabeth Jackson, wife
of Samuel Jackson and their following children: Eliza, Caroline,
Harriet and Alfred E. Jackson. Executrix: Elizabeth Jackson. Teste:
William Roddman, John Adams, Joseph Brown, Hugh Brown. February
Sessions, 1812.   Signed: Susannah Woodrow

JAMES COX   November 13, 1810
Children: George, Mayberry T. Cox, Susannah, Dorcas, James, Mary Hale,
wife of Nicholas Hale, John, Sarah Strong, wife of Obediah Strong, Fanny
Hale, wife of Gideon Hale. Executors: Jacob Hoss Senr., Joseph Crouch
Senr. & Charles Daryworth. Teste: Peter Hoss, Henry Bowers, Thomas
Buckingham. February Sessions, 1812.

E. JOHN CUNNINGHAM   March 5, 1812
Wife, Martha. Son, Samuel B. Cunningham, "to be put to college until he
obtains a degree." Children: Jenny, John Whitfield Cunningham,
Alexander Newton Cunningham, William Madison Cunningham, Martha Rowe
Cunningham. Executors: Martha Cunningham, Nathan Stephenson, William
McLin. Teste: John Nelson, John Helm, John Jordan. May Sessions, 1812.
                              Signed. E. J. Cunningham

WILLIAM NODDING   October 4, 1804
Wife, Mary. Children: Sarah McCray, Mary Bayles, Elizabeth Calvert,
Ellenor Hill. John Brown's orphan children. My smallest still.
Negroes to be set free. Executors: Daniel McCray, William Calvert.
Teste: William Bayles, Reuben Bayles, Hannah Bayles. May Sessions,
1812.   Signed: William (X) Nodding

ADAM RADER   September 4, 1807
Wife, Ann, to have everything during her life. Daughter, Elizabeth
Cashady. Grandson, John Rader Cashedy. Executors: Ann Rader.
Teste: Peter Bowman, Jonathan Mulky. August Sessions, 1812.
                              Signed: Adam Rader

ANTHONY GOTT   October 7, 1807
Children: John, Ruth, Richard, Caleb, Joshua, Sarah, other children.
Executor: John Gott. Teste: Nathan Shipley, George Fitzgerrels.
August Sessions, 1812.   Signed: Anthony Gott

ROBERT ALLISON   July 18, 1812
My father, Robert Allison Senr. Wife, Jane. Children: Nany, Rachel,
Polly Anna, Hannah Elya. Executors: Jane Allison, John Stephenson,
Joseph Darean. Teste: William Walker, George Kirk, Elizabeth Mitchell.
November Sessions, 1812.   Signed: Robert Allison

ALEXANDER McKEE   July 10, 1812
Children: Robert, William. Brother, John McKee's children should
William have no heirs. Executors: William Slemmons, Robert McKee,
Jane Nelson. Wit.: Hugh Weare, William McCloud. November Sessions,
1812.   Signed: Alex McKee

WILLIAM INGLE   April 7, 1807
Wife, Margaret. Children: Adam, Michael, Caterina Wartebarger, Mary
Frum, Elizabeth Slyger. Executors: Margaret Ingle & Adam Ingle.
Wit.: Jacob Brown, Nicholas Lineberge, William Laikbrooks. April
Sessions, 1807.   Signed: William (X) Ingle

PETER HOSS   April 30, 1807
Wife, Sarah. To son, John V. Hoss, ½ plantation. To son, Jacob Hoss,
other half of plantation. To daughters, Mary and Elizabeth Hoss, $25
each. Executors: Sarah Hoss, Henry Hoss. Wit.: Henry Hoss, Isaac
Hoss. November Sessions, 1812.   Signed: Peter Hoss

THOMAS McADAM   December 3, 1811
To oldest son, John, plantation, 100 acres on Mill Creek. Son, Hugh.
To youngest son, Robert, $50. Executors: Sons John, Hugh & Robert
McAdam. Wit.: John Gilworth, Hugh Campbell, Nathan Shipley. August
Sessions, 1818.   Signed: Thomas McAdams

KINDLER HAZLET   September 9, 1813
To wife, Nancy, all property forever, my pensions and 100 acre land
warrant in care of John Rhea Esqr. for my services in Revolutionary
War. Executor: James Moore, brother to my present wife. Wit.: Henry
Hartman, Levi Hartman, Hugh Allison. Proven November Sessions, 1815.
                                 Signed: Kindler (X) Hazlet

ROBERT FORBES   July 28, 1813
Child, Polly. Executor: Adam Wateenberger Sr. Wit.: William Bayles,
George Swingle, John Gott. Proven November Sessions, 1815.
                                 Signed: Robert (X) Forbes

JOHN COWAN   August 13, 1813
To Elizabeth Cowan. To Richard Carr, relationship not mentioned. To
Jacob Ellis, relationship not mentioned. Brothers, Jonus Cowan, Thomas
Cowan. Nephew, James Crabtree. Sisters. Executors: Elizabeth Cowan,
Jacob Ellis, Richard Carr. Wit.: George Humphrey, William Carr,
Samuel Denton. Proven November Sessions, 1813.
                                 Signed: John Cowan

HENRY POWELL   November 24, 1812
To wife, Elizabeth, 1/3 of land and movable affects. To sons, John and
Joseph, plantation on Lick Creek. Three youngest sons when they reach
21 years. Executors not given. Wit.: Levi Beele, Amon Hale, Elijah
Matheny. Proven November Sessions, 1813.
                                 Signed: Henry Powel

SAMUEL DENTON   January 11, 1814
To wife, Martha, 198 acres land on Cherokee Creek, at her death to be
equally divided between my 5 sons, also land in Cocke County on Causby
Creek. Children: Thomas, John, Jonathan, David, Samuel, Jonas, Louisa,
Levina, Tabetha, Abigail, Martha, Anne. Executrix: Martha Denton.
Wit.: Henry King, John Carr, John Miller. Proven February Sessions, 1814.
                                 Signed: Samuel Denton

                                13

JOHN McALISTER   July 30, 1812
Wife, Fanny. To son, John, my silver watch and 4 silver spoons. To
son, Charles, 4 silver spoons and 1 set coat buttons. To son, James,
225 acres I bought of Robert Blackburn. Sarah Squart to have cabbin
and garden. 500 Acre grant from state of N.C. Executors: John
McAlister, James Aiken, Sarah Squart. Wit.: William Roadman, Joseph
Brown. Proven February Sessions, 1814.
                              Signed: John McAlester

SIMON HUNT   January 13, 1814
Children: Sally, Charles Wesley and Samuel. Executors: My sons,
Samuel Hunt and Charles Wesley Hunt. Wit.: John Nelson, Robert McKee,
John Gilbert. Proven May Sessions, 1814.
                              Signed: Simon Hunt

JOHN M. SMITH   December 12, 1812
About to leave home and join troops of Col. Williams. Wife of William
Anderson. Mother. To sister, Mary Smith, my breast pin. To brother,
William M., my watch. Brother, V. Casper Smith. Sister, Margaret
Branson, wife of William Branson. I am due a balance on my brother
David, decd., estate. Wit.: John Blair Jr., James Anderson, David
Deadrick, John A. Aiken. Proven May Sessions, 1814.
                              Signed: John M. Smith

LEWIS TADLOCK   May 13, 1815
To wife, Jane, 518 acres. To son, John, 346 acres. To son, James, $10.
Son, Edward. Two youngest son, Sevier and Carter. Son-in-law, Jesse
Mullens. Michael Masters. 5 youngest children. Executors: Jane
Tadlock, John Tadlock. Wit.: John Strain, Francis Erwin, Benjamin
Archer. Proven August Sessions, 1815.
                              Signed: Lewis Tadlock

RICHARD BASKET   September 31, 1814
Wife, Rachel. Children: Michael, Charles, Polly, Rachel, Nancy, John,
William. Wit.: William Basket, Charles Jones, Joseph Clark. Proven
August Sessions, 1815.   Signed: Richard Basket

THOMAS KING   May 8, 1812
Wife, Elizabeth. Children: James, Henry, Mary McKenny wife of James
McKenny, Elenor Calhoon wife of David Calhoon, Betsy Fulkerson wife of
John Fulkerson, Sarah McCoy wife of John McCoy, William King, Margaret
Waddell wife of Charles Waddell. Grandsons, John and Henry, sons of
Henry King. Son, John King's widow, $1. Grandson, George King. Grand-
son, Thomas King Waddell, son of William King, 100 acres. Granddaughter,
Mary Fulkerson. Executors: James King, Henry King, Charles Waddell.
Wit.: John Hoss, Jonathan Caruthers. Proven November Sessions, 1815.
                              Signed: Thomas (X) King

ABSOLEM BOREN
Wife, Nancy. Nancy Miller, relationship not given. Greene Boren
(relationship not given) to have contract on land. Wit.: Horatio
Ford, John Sailor, Catherine Coon. Proven January Sessions, 1816.
                              Signed: Absolem (A) Boren

THOMAS ENGLISH   October 23, 1815
Wife, Elizabeth English, and son, Alexander. Executor: Alexander
English. Wit.: Alexander Whitlock, Abra Deatherage, John English.
Proven January Sessions, 1816.   Signed: Thomas English

WILLIAM FAIN   December, 1815
(William Fain was acting Court Clerk in Pulaski Co., Ky. at time of
writing will - Recorded in Book 1, Page 202.) Son, Eberneza Fain.
To son, John Fain, land with 4 apple trees. Son, Samuel, to care for
mother and grandmother. To son, David, $200 in silver. Five daus.,
Rosanna Young, Sally, Betsy Gray, Nancy and Polly Ann. Executors:

Samuel Fain, Robert Gray. Wit.: Thomas Pashal (Dashal), Andrew Erwin, William Ovens. Proven April Sessions, 1816.
Signed: William Fain

THOMAS TELFORD   February 6, 1816
Wife, Marian. Children: George, Betsy, Grace. Executors: Marian Telford, Ebernger L. Mathes. Wit.: John Nelson, John S. Telford, Patsy Telford. Proven April Sessions, 1816.
Signed: Thomas Telford

JACOB HOSS   February 20, 1816
Eldest son, John Hoss. Second son, Abraham Hoss. Other children: George, Isaac, Henry, Catherine Nave wife of Jonathan Nave, Mary Bowman wife of Joseph Bowman. Grandchildren: John, Mary, Elizabeth, Jacob, children of Peter Hoss, decd. Grandchildren: Nath, George Henry, Frederick, Jacob, James, children of Elizabeth Nelson, wife of James Nelson. Granddaughter, Elizabeth Hoss, daughter of Jacob Hoss, decd. Grandchildren: Mary, William, Calvin, children of Isaac Hoss. Executors: John Hoss, Abraham Hoss, George Hoss. Wit.: Joseph Melven, George Jenkins, John Jenkins. Proven April Sessions, 1817.
Signed: Jacob Hoss

JOSEPH MELVIN
Wife, Hannah. Children: Joseph, John, Rheba (or Rhoda) Melvin. Executors: Hannah Melvin, James Melvin. Wit.: Ed G. King, John Range, William Duncan. Proven April Sessions, 1817.
Signed: Joseph Melvin

JOHN HAMMER   November 12, 1817
Wife, Margaret. To eldest son, John, my Bible. Children: Jacob, Isaac, Jonathan, Joseph, John, Barbary Range, Elizabeth Kelly, Mary Bogart. Executors: Samuel Bogart, James White. Wit.: John Range, William White, Anne Hammer. Proven January Sessions, 1818.
Signed: John (X) Hammer
The following agreed with the will:
    Margaret Hammer   Mary Bogart
    Barbara Range   Isaac Hammer
    Jacob Hammer   John Hammer
    Elizabeth Kelly   Jonathan Hammer

PETER RANGE   August, 1817
Wife. Children: Jacob, Peter, Isaac, Barbara, Sarah, Rachel, John. Executors: John Range, Jacob Range. Wit.: John Melloner, Jonathan Hammer, Mark Mears. Proven January Sessions, 1818.
Signed: Peter (X) Range
The following agreed to the will December 7, 1817:
    Elizabeth Range   Elizabeth Miller
    John Range   Susan Devault
    Jacob Range   Margaret Devault
    Peter Range   Barbara Range
    Isaac Range   Sarah Range
    Rachel Range

HENRY BOWERS   February 8, 1818
Wife, Nancy. Children: Levi, Joshua, Abraham, Leah, Lourane. Executors: John Bowman, Nancy Bowers. Wit.: Joseph Melvin, Hezekiah Boren, Joshua Hunt. Proven April Sessions, 1818.
Signed: Henry Bowers

JOHN BLAIR SENR.   July 12, 1818
Wife, Susannah and 8 children. Executor: John Blair Junr. Wit.: Henry Nelson, Alex Mathes, John Blair Junr. Proven July Sessions, 1818.
Signed: John Blair

JOHN CARR SENR.   July 24, 1811
Children: John, James, Richard, William, Hannah, Louise, Sarah, Mary,
Elizabeth, Isabelle. Executors: Richard Carr, William Carr.
Wit.: Samuel Denton, Martha Denton, Tabitha Denton. Proven July
Sessions, 1818.   Signed: John Carr, Sr.

CHARLES DUNCAN   April 14, 1817
Wife, Susannah. Children: John, William, Robert, Sarah, Mary, Stacy,
Elizabeth, Margaret, Lovarry, Raleigh. Executors: Susannah Duncan,
William Duncan. Wit.: T.V.Y. King, Richard Carr, William Carr.
Proven July Sessions, 1818.   his
                              Signed: Charles (V) Duncan
                                             mark

NICHOLAS HALE SENR.   July 20, 1807
Children: Richard, William, Nicholas, Nathan, Amon, Joshua, Elizabeth,
Cage. Ruth Hale and Sarah Gray, heirs of John Hale, decd. Mullato man
"Bob" to be set free. Executor: Richard Hale. Wit.: Loyd Ford,
George Jacksin, Ordena Bray. Proven July Sessions, 1818.
                              Signed: Nicholas Hale, Sen.

JOHN SLYGER   April 18, 1817
Wife, Catrena. Children: Mary Ingle, John Slyger, Henry Slyger, Adam
Slyger, Catherine Brown, Christian Slyger. Executors: Alex Mathes,
Adam Slyger. Wit.: Jacob Brown, Nicholas Puny. Proven July Sessions,
1818.   Signed: John (X) Slyger

ANTHONY McNUTT   April 10, 1818
Wife. Wife's daughter, Jane Russell. Polly Furgeson, wife of Alexander
Furgason. Servant, Dinnah, to have freedom. Executors: Thomas
Furgeson, David Russell. Wit.: William Russell, Isaac Hair, John
Stuart. Proven October Sessions, 1818.
                              Signed: Anthony McNutt

ROBERT ALLISON   March 19, 1818
Children: Hannah Carmicle, Rachel Thompson, Polly Duncan, Ann Thompson.
Granddaughter, Polly Anna Ellison. Executors: Joseph Duncan, John
Stephenson. Wit.: Nathaniel Davis, Elias Owens, John McCall. Proven
April Sessions, 1819.   Signed: Robert (X) Allison

ABIGAIL JOB   March 8, 1819
Children: Abraham Job, Sarah Humphreys, Phebe Gibson, Joshua Job,
Rebecca Carr, John Job. Executor: Joshua Job. Wit.: Abraham Hoss,
Elijah Boren, Isaac Little. Proven April Sessions, 1819.
                              Signed: Abigail (X) Job

AARON JENKENS   March, 1819
Wife, Elizabeth. Children: George, Joseph, William. Executors: John
Jenkens and George Jenkens, my brothers. Wit.: Henry Hoss, William
Houston, Jacob Miller. Proven April Sessions, 1819.
                              Signed: Aaron Jenkens

WILLIAM ILES   May 16, 1815
Wife, Jane Isles. Eldest son, Thomas Iles. Eldest daughter, Polly
Barnet. Children: Hannah Overholtzer, Sarah Perkins, William Isle,
Jr. Executor: Jane Ingle. Wit: John Helm, Samuel Overholtzer, Ann
Helm. Proven July Sessions, 1819. Signed: William (X) Isle

HENRY MARTIN   September 15, 1819
Wife, Cloe Martin. Children: Richard Martin, Betty Jones, Other
children. Executors: Abel Wyley, John Martin. Wit.: John Strain,
Harry March, Joe Duncan. Proven October Sessions, 1819.
                              Signed: Henry (X) Martin

WILLIAM CARSON   October 24, 1812
Wife, Sarah. Executors: Wife Sarah, George Bell, John Strain.
Wit.: Alexander Campbell, Robert W. Strain. Proven October Sessions,
1819.   Signed: William Carson

ISAAC WHITE   May 5, 1819
To wife Sarah, my negro woman "Beck." Children: Terry, William,
Stephen, Richard, Mary wife of Thomas Gibson, Susannah wife of Daniel
Denton, Anna wife of Elijah Keen - $100 each. Other sons have been
given. Executors: Wife and son Terry. Wit.: Nathan Shipley, William
Grimsley. Proven October Sessions, 1819.
                                 Signed: Isaac White

ANDREW THOMPSON   March 13, 1818
Wife, Elizabeth, 1/3 price of all salable property and use of black boy
during her widowhood. Eldest son, John, $1. Children: Adam, Moses,
Betsey, Amey, Jenny, Thomas. Slave, Ben, to be sold and money divided
between last 6 children mentioned. Executors: Sons Adam and Moses.
Wit.: John Strain, Benjamin Sands. Proven October Sessions, 1819.
                                 Signed: Andrew Thompson

JOHN BLAIR
Wife, Martha. To daughter, Martha, negro named Tom. To son, Joseph, ½
of all land I posess. To son, William, my bound boy Robert Dennis.
Executors: Son-in-law Alexander McLin, son John. Wit.: William
Montgomery, Lewis Jordan.   his
                         Signed: John ⌂ Blair
                                             mark

JOHN BLAIR   November 1, 1819
To wife, Hannah, all household furniture during her lifetime at the end
of which she shall dispose of at her pleasure. Children, Polly and
Rachel to receive equal with those married. Sons, Hugh and Thomas to
have 1 equal part. Sons, Samuel and John. Grandson Jonah Blair. Five
daughters. Have sale when William Nelson's time is out with the mill,
then Jonah Blair to take mill and get 1/3 proceeds. Son John Blair, to
get his grinding free of toll. Executors: William Carmack, son John,
wife Hannah. Wit.: John Strain, Joseph Nelson, John Robinson.
Probated January Sessions, 1820. Signed: John Blair

ANN McKILLOP (McCALEB?)   May 8, 1808
Son, John McKillop. Daughters Ann Nefs?, Mary Purroll, Peranah McKaleb.
Son, Isaac, the sum of ½ a dollar. Wit.: Will Taylor, Joseph Tucker?.
Probated January Sessions, 1820.   her
                         Signed: Ann ⌂ Kellop
                                           mark

CASPER LOTT   December 18, 1819
Wife, Rhoda Lott. Children: John, Betsey. Seven youngest children:
Daniel, Sally, Martha, Samuel, Kitty, Rachel and Mary. Executors:
Montgomery Stuart, wife Rhoda. Wit.: Jona Collum, John Bricher?,
William O. McGee. Probated October Sessions, 1820.
                         Signed: Casper (X) Lott

DANIEL MOORE   May 12, 1820
Wife, Rebecca, all real and personal estate during widowhood or until
death. Son, James, draws a childs part of the land only. Daughter,
Basheba, $1. Executors: Sons James and Stephen Moore. Wit.: Alex
Prethero, Margaret A. Bitner. Probated October Sessions, 1820.
                         Signed: Daniel Moore

JOHN W. DOAK   August 23, 1820
To wife, Jane, the northend of my house or tenement in which I now live
from the entry both upstairs and downstairs, to her and my children till
the youngest comes of age - comfortable support. Two eldest sons,

Samuel Harvey and John Newton Doak, land in Kentucky, and to get two plantations on Little Limestone where I now live. Line to be run by John Nelson - land adjoining Nathan Barnes, Henry Nelson, James Gray. Two other sons, Archibald Alexander and James Witherspoon Doak, my land on northside of Nolachucky River adjoining Montgomery Stuart, William Tyler, John Gott, also education at Washington College. To four daughters, Sophia Doak, Esther Montgomery Doak, Eliza Smith Doak, and Jane Doak, proceeds of land in Kentucky on waters of Lukey? River - divided equally. My 2 oldest sons to furnish Mother and Sisters with wool, flax and cotton to make their summer and winter clothing until they have wives of their own. Having experience myself the bad effects of having to cloth a family with store goods. Executors: William Mitchell Esq., John Nelson Jr. and Ebenezer Mathes. Wit.: John McAlister, John Patton, James S. Johnston.

Signed: Jn⁰. W. Doak

WILLIAM TYLER   August 13, 1820
To wife, Nancy, where I live and land I purchased from Hugh Wees. To daughter, Melinda, bureau and book case. Son, William - dest and featherbed. Dau., Phebe Tyler - featherbed. Dau., Minerva Tyler - featherbed and bureau. Dau., Betsy Tyler - bureau. Nancy had Melinda before our marriage. Melinda to get ½ as much as others. Dau., Polly, to live with my widow. Ira, a boy of color that I raised, to have 9 months schooling and $110 when he becomes of age. Executors: William Wilson, Joseph Crouch, wife Nancy. Wit.: Edwin West, Baly Phillips, Edwin West Jr., James McCarroll.   Signed: William Tyler

ELIHU EMBREE   January 21, 1820
My blac, Nancy to have her freedom with her children. All other black, yellow etc. persons to be equally emancipated and free as soon as they can, when the note of Godfrey Carriger, decd. has on them can be extinguished and papers signed by myself and Godfrey and Christian Carriger his executors. Each child to receive $40 and schooling. My brother, Elija, to let Nancy settle on our land, rent free, her life-time. One tenth of my estate above $10,000 to go to Abolition of Slavery in the United States by the Manumission Society of Tennessee. Property to go to legal heirs. Sell moveable property to pay debts of E & E Embree. My children to be educated. Executor: My only brother and business partner, Elijah Embree. Wit.: John McCarele, Southwell Vincent. Probated January Sessions, 1821.

Signed: Elihu Embree

JOHN McCALL SENR.   March 5, 1821
To wife, Jenny, the Mansion House except 1 clock and a case of drawers. To son, William, 250 acres I bought of Henry Tiffen. To son, John McCall, balance of land and premises. To son, Robert, half my home plantation. To son, James, other half of home plantation. To daus., Margarim Armstrong and Margaret Blair - $5 each. Executors: Sons, William and James. Wit.: William B. Odenol?, Jno. Blakely, Uriah Hunt.   Signed: John McCall

JOSEPH HALE   March 4, 1817
Brother, Henry Hale, has title to land. Sister, Elizabeth Hale. Slaves to have their freedom. To Elizabeth Chennett, dau. of Nicholas Chenneth, residue of my estate after brother and sister decease. Executors: Nephew, Nicholas Chenneth, James and Robert Gray. Wit.: John Gott, George Gresham. Proven January Sessions, 1822.

Signed: Joseph Hale
Henry Hale
Elizabeth Hale

HENRY HALE   October 11, 1820
After death of sister, Elizabeth, I give and bequeath to free persons of color: Maria, Lydia, Thomas, John, Stephen, Solomon, Canda and Lucy, who call themselves by the surname Hale, and have been liberated at the July Sessions of our County Court - 610 acres land. To Joseph, Henry and Nicholas Chenneth, several tracts of land. Executors: Nicholas

Chenneth, James Gray. Wit.: Henry Hoss, James Ellis, John Gott.
Proven January Sessions, 1822.   Signed: Henry (X) Hale

POINTEN CHARLETON   June 3, 1821
To wife, Rebecca, all moveable property, her hay to be put up by son,
John Charleton, who gets the plantation where I now live. To son,
Thomas, 200 acres land on Kendrick's Creek. To daughter, Polly Snapp,
a slave girl. To son, Simpson, balance of debt owed me by my son
Pointon Jr. To son-in-law, James Mathes, 200 acres. To Lawrence
Snapp - $125. Land on Muddy Fork of Big Limestone. Executors:
Matthew Stephenson, Hugh Campbell. Wit.: John Strain, John McCrehan,
John Kelsey. Proven January Sessions, 1822.
                              Signed: Pointen Charleton

ALEXANDER M. NELSON   December 17, 1821
Of Greeneville, County of Greene, State of Tennessee. Wife, Pamela H.
Nelson. Two children, Nancy and Alexander Nelson, to receive 1/3 part
each of my lands and personal property when become of age. Executors:
Valentine Sevier of Greeneville, Bro. John Nelson and Matthew Stephenson
of Washington Co. Wit.: Ewing McClure, John D. Hannah, E.L. Mathes.
Proven January Sessions, 1822.   Signed: Alex M. Nelson

JOSEPH YOUNG   17 _____ 1822
To wife, Esther. Youngest daughter, Elizabeth - where I now live.
Daughters: Jenny, Peggy and Elizabeth, to get equal to what my oldest
daughter, Polly's got. Polly wife of Samuel B. Love - 450 acres adjoin-
ing Daniel Bayles. Jenny wife of Jonathan Dugless - land adjoining
Reuben Bayles. Four daughters to get Flag Pond Tract. Executors: James
W. Young, wife Esther. Wit.: Henry King, William D. Jones, Chaney
Boren, Robert Cashedy. Proven April Sessions, 1822.
                              Signed: Joseph Young

DAVID GRATES   June 9, 1822
Jane Scott is my sole heir. Executors: John Walker, Jane Scott.
Teste: John Parker, Thomas Cooper, Mary Scott. Proven October Sessions,
1822.   his
                         Signed: David ⊕ Grates
                                           mark

CHARLES BACON   October 26, 1821
To my 2 sons, Charles and Jacob, all my lands and give Polly and
Catherine 9 months schooling, and Catharine one $25 saddle, also $1500
in Jonesboro Bank when of age. To daughter, Elizabeth, $575. To
daughter, Nancy, $20 and her husband is to lift his note I have on him
for $430 at my death. Executors: Sons Charles and Jacob Bacon. Wit.:
William Jackson, Elizabeth Bacon, Samuel Duglas.
                                           his
                         Signed: Charles 3 Bacon
                                           mark

ZADOCK WILLET   March 26, 1821
Wife, Ann. Son, Washington. Grandson, Joseph Willet. Daughters, Betsey
and Fanny Willet. Son, Francis, decd. Daughter, Polly Marshall. Grand-
son, Zadock W. Moyan. Daughters: Peggy Clawson, Nancy Hendly, Letty
Simpson, Sally Morgan. Son, Zadock Jr. Executors: Betsey Willet,
Zadock Willet. Wit.: John Link, Jacob Whistler, William L. French.
Proven January Sessions, 1823.   Signed: Zadock Willet

JOHN BAYLIS   December 21, 1816
To wife, Ann, a riding horse, saddle and bridle. Two youngest sons,
Rees and Samuel. Children: Daniel, John, George Bayles, Anna Jones,
Martinen Morgan. Executors: sons Daniel and Rees Bayles. Wit.:
Calvin Finch, Samuel Bayles, Sarah ◯ Bayles. Proven April Sessions,
1823.   Signed: John Bayles

JAMES ADAIR SENR.   July 13, 1822
To wife, Jane, part of my plantation to support on and if required
medical aid and sickness. Youngest son, James Adair, plantation at his
mother's decease. Other children: Hannah Robinson, Jane Alexander,
John Adair, Polly Lyon. Ezekiel Lyon and Polly to be their mother's
guardian as long as she lives in this country. Executors: James Adair,
Jane Alexander. Wit.: Samuel Robeson, James Alexander. Proven July
Sessions, 1823.
                                                 his
                          Signed: James *ʃ* Adair
                                                 mark

JOHN HUNTER   February 25, 1809
To wife, Barbary, necessary maintenance. Children: Isaac Hunter,
Barbary Rubb. The rest of my children have received 100 pounds each.
Executors: William Calvert, Joseph Hunter. Wit.: William Bayles,
Hezekiah Bayles.   his
                          Signed: John *FFF* Hunter
                                                 mark

(Codicil I guess – G.F.B.)   January 27, 1819
   To set slave "Bet" free and give her clothes and bed. Executors: John
C. Harris, William Bayles. Teste: Nat Kelsey, Crampton J. Harvey, John
K. Balch. Proven July Sessions, 1823.

ARCHIBALD BLACKBURN   August 4, 1823
Wife, Isbell. To son, William, slave "Jim". To son, Nathaniel, $100.
To son, Benjamin, $20 in property. To son, Samuel, 100 acres adjoining
Michael Woods. To daughter, Rosannah Mathis, $150 in property. To
daughter, Polly Hoss, $50. To son, Thomas, horse, saddle and $70. To
daughter, Betsey, cattle etc., $500. To son, Archibald, horse, saddle,
$75. Executors: son William, John Mathis, son-in-law Henry Hoss.
Wit.: John Nelson, David Nelson, David Brown. Proven October Sessions,
1823.   Signed: Archibald (X) Blackburn

JACOB KEPLINGER   February 11, 1817
To wife, Mary, all my estate during her life. Children: Samuel and
John have gotten $500 each. Daughters: Katy Stonecypher, Mary Kiker,
Susannah Cresileus. Executors: James and Samuel Keplinger, sons.
Wit.: John Nelson, John May, John Starnes. Proven January Sessions,
1824.   Signed: Jacob (X) Keplinger

DAVID DEADERICK   September 4, 1821
To wife, Margaretta, house and lot, storehouse and all it contains and
all debts due me, all personal property, horses, cattle and slaves.
Youngest sons, Joseph A. and John F. Deaderick to be supported and
completely educated, also son, James William, until they are 21 years
of age. I have 300 Acres in Greene County on Cove Creek, and interest
in a store Deaderick & Sevier, also 60 Acres on Lick Creek, land in
Hawkins and Jefferson Counties known as Cheeks Cross Roads. Land in
Washington County adjoining Peter Miller, Hezekiah B. Mitchell and
others. Daughters: Elizabeth R. Deaderick and Amanda F. Nelson.
Executors: Wife Margaretta, son David A. and James V. Anderson.
Wit.: John McAlister, William T. Anderson. Probated January, 1825.
                          Signed: David Deaderick

JOSEPH MARTIN   December 30, 1823
To son, Samuel Martin, all the plantation. To son, Michael H. Martin,
my Maple Shoals lands. Executors: son Samuel Martin and John Stephenson.
Wit.: Samuel Kennedy, John Blakely, Francis Ross. Proven April Sessions,
1824.   his
                          Signed: Joseph *ʓ* Martin
                                                 mark

MARTHA CUNNINGHAM   November 8, 1823
All worldly property to support my 3 youngest children, Alexander Newton,
William Madison and Martha Rowe Cunningham until they be taught and
educated. Other children: Samuel B., John W., Jane McLin. Husband,

E.J. Cunningham, decd. Executor: Son Samuel B. Cunningham. Wit.:
Matthew Stephenson, Susan Wear. Proven April Sessions, 1824.
                              Signed: Martha Cunningham

NATHAN NELSON
Son John has received $300. Son Isaac to have $300 and the mill until
the youngest child comes of age. Daughter Rachel, wife of Charles
Deakins. Youngest daughter Hannah. My sons, Nathan, Levi and James
are under age, also daughters Thurza and Ruth. Executors: James
Deakens, my sons John Nelson and Isaac Nelson. Teste: William Smith,
Benja. Jackson, Jacob Taylor. Proven July Sessions, 1824.
                              Signed: Nathan Nelson

REBECCA CHARLTON
Three dear sons: Pointen, John and Thomas Charlton. To Thomas, the
first and second volume of my large Bible. Daughters Margaret Mathes,
Mary Snapp the Third Volume of my large Bible with Illustrations.
Executors: Hugh Campbell and Methias Stephenson. Wit.: Samuel
Biddle, William Likens, Elias Rodgers. Proven October Sessions, 1824.
                              Signed: Rebecca (X) Charlton

ROSEANNAH STEPHENSON   March 15, 1825
John Duncomes Will (my first husband) dated 17 July 1776, 2nd husband
now in possession of John Duncome land. To be divided between Joseph
Duncome Jr. of Rice Duncome; Rice Duncome and Mowel Duncome sons of
Joseph Duncome Sr., bro. to the said John Duncome. To Stacy Duncome
Melven, daughter of Charles Duncome, bro. to the above named John
Duncome. Executors: James Melvin. Wit.: William Grimsley, John
English, Joseph Crouch. Proven July Sessions, 1825.
                              Signed: Roseannah (X) Stephenson

ADAM WATTENBARGER SENR.
Wife, Elizabeth. Sons: William, Adam, Jacob and Peter - to have horse,
saddle and bridle worth $60. Other sons: Solomon, Michael, Frederick,
George and Samuel - to have same. Daughters: Elizabeth and Sally
Wattenbarger. Son Solomon has body infirmity. Son Peter is a black-
smith. Money due me from sale to John Aiken. One note on George Hinkle
Senr. Executors: Frederick Fensler, Christian Getty Senr. Teste:
John Link, L.B. Cunningham, Christian Getty. Proven July Sessions, 1823.
                              Signed: Adam Wattenbarger

SAMUEL BAYLES   August 5, 1825
To wife, Susannah, ½ land (220 Acres) to include house and barn, small
pot, large oven and skillet. To son William - surveying instruments.
To son Daniel - price of a cow he owes me for. Children of my daughter
Polly Brown, decd. - 150 Acres where Samuel Brown and John Helibe? now
live. Samuel to pay his brothers, Hezekiah and Henderson $94, and
sisters Elizabeth Brown, Polly Rice, Matilda Slyger, Hannah Brown,
Martena Brown. To Reuben Brown. To Reese Brown. To John Bayles -
oldest note he owes me. To daughter Hannah Hoss - land adjoining John
Lamons and David Lamons (200 Acres) out of which is to come 1¼ Acres
for Meeting House and Burying Grounds. My son Reuben Bayles, the
youngest. Daughters Phebe White, Martena Hunts, Alice Tabor.
Executors: John and Reuben Bayles. Wit.: Henry McCray, William
Thompson, John McCrary. Proven October Sessions, 1825.
                              Signed: Samuel Bayles

JOHN SMITH, son of John Smith   May 28, 1825
To my wife - all property, then to my 6 daughters. Executors: My wife
and Abraham Fine. Wit.: Benjamin Drain, Henry E. Ruble. Proven
October Sessions, 1825.   Signed: John (X) Smith

HENRY KING   September 30, 1825
Daughter Mary Harrington, wife of Peter Harrington - $1. To Mary Barnes,
daughter of James and Elizabeth Barnes - $5. To son Thomas - my foot
adz. To son William - $1. To daughter Sarah Mares, wife of Mack Mares -

$1. To son John - 24 Acres. To grandsons Albert and Billy F. King, sons
of Billy F. King and Ruth - $5. Sons Henry and John. Executors: Wife
Sarah, sons Thomas and Henry. Wit.: James Fulkerson, Thomas Stevens,
James Barnes. Proven October Sessions, 1825.
                            Signed: Henry King

THOMAS ELSEY   September 14, 1825
Son, John. Executors: Son John and George Crow. Teste: James P.
Hale?, Charles Cox. Proven April Sessions, 1826.
                            Signed: Thomas (X) Elsey

JOHN SNAPP SENR.   October 9, 1818
To wife, Mary, household and kitchen furniture with buildings and land.
To son John Junr, land. To son Joseph, $1000. To daughter Margaret
Spangler - $1000. Daughter Susanna, married to George Huston. Land
on Mill Creek, Rockingham Co., Va. - sold to George Huston. Land I
sold to P. Kyle on Great Road leading from Staunton to Winchester by
way of Keizletown. David Kyle's meadow. Executor: John Snapp Junr.
of Greene County. Wit.: John Doan, Daniel Yeager, Robert L. Kennedy,
David Walles, Susanna Yeager. Proven January Sessions, 1819.
                            Signed: John Snapp Senr.

ALEXANDER WHITLOCK   January 1, 1822
To wife, Jennet, all property her lifetime. Three sons: John, Charles
and Samuel Whitlock - to have all at her death. Executors: Son John
and wife Jennet. Wit.: Charles Dungworth, Stephen L. Keen, Lofton
Grimsley. Proven April Sessions, 1826.
                            Signed: Alexander (X) Whitlock

ANN MILLER   March 23, 1795
To Ann Hunter - 2/3 of remaining estate, the rest to Margaret Leach.
Executors: Robert Macklin, James Carmule. Wit.: William Montgomery,
Abraham Campbell, Mary Campbell. Proven (no date given).
                            Signed: Ann (X) Miller

JOSEPH WHITSON
To my sisters son, Joseph Peyton - the plantation. To my brother,
Thomas Whitson - my negro man. To my brother, William Whitson - my
negro woman. To my brother, John Whitson - my negro woman. To my
brother, Jesse Whitson - my negro man. Three sisters: Sarah Nelson,
Susannah Eagan and Lydia McCoy. Executors: Brothers Jesse and John.
Wit.: Thomas Gourley, William Wood, Henry Nelson. his
                            Signed: Joseph   Whitson
                                           mark

SAMUEL KELSEY   February 23, 1795
To my sister, Ann Nelson's sons, Samuel Kelsey Nelson and Henry Nelson -
2 tracts of land on Boon's Creek, Washington Co. To Ann's son, Samuel
R. Nelson - 25 lb. Va. Currency. To three brothers, William, Moses and
John Kelsey and to sister, Margaret Roples - 2 last tons of iron from
Henry Herklbarea? of Sullivan Co. To brother, David. To two neices,
Elizabeth and Mary Pooples? - 16 lb. of Va. Currency due from their
father, Nathan Pooples?. To Moses' sons, John and Samuel. Executors:
William Kelsey, Brother-in-law Henry Nelson. Wit.: Adam Loury, Lewis
Jordan, William Whitson. No proven date given.
                            Signed: Samuel Kelsey

JOHN MOORE   October 20, 1797
Wife, Ann. Son, Samuel. Executor: son Samuel. Wit.: Zachariah
McCulbee, Samuel Hall, Antipas Thomas. Proven _____ Sessions, 179_.
                            Signed: John (X) Moore

PETER MILLER   November 14, 1801
To son Jacob Miller - all my possessions and give daughter, Margaret, 1
horse, a good cow and calf when she comes of age. My wife and all my

children. Mary Miller and Barbary Miller, Mary Painter and Elizabeth Schiles, Jacob and Margaret Miller. Executor: Michael Broyles Senr. Wit.: Felix Earnest, Elizabeth (X) Broyles, Michael (X) Broyles. No proven date given. Signed: Peter (X) Miller

PETER WALTER   August 19, 1809 - One day after his decease. Wife, Clary, to retain all property for herself and maintenance of her children. Two sons to pay others and keep land. Wit.: Conrad Kiker, Margaret (X) Kiker, George Bible. Probated.
                              Signed by Jacob Brown, Justice
                                      of Peace.

DANIEL McCRAY   March 1, 1819
Jane Jenkins shall have my 3 beds, furniture, pots and pans and $40 for Sally Hains. All my children to receive equally. Executors: Henry and Thomas McCray. Wit.: George Hayes, Charles Jenkins, Joseph Jenkins of Mark. Proven (date not given).   his
                              Signed: Daniel ⨏ McCray
                                       mark

ALEXANDER McLIN   September 23, 1819
To wife, ½ my mansion house and $40 from Joseph McLin. To Benjamin, my son, desk and bookcase. To daughter Isabella - $5, her son Alexander $20, same for daughter Polly and her son Alexander. Children: Martha and her son Alexander, son John, son Alexander, son Robert and his son Alexander. Sons Joseph, Benjamin, James and Richard to stay in college. Executors: Sons Robert and Benjamin. Wit.: Samuel B. Cunningham, William B. Helm, William Crookshank. Proven January Sessions, 1820.
                              Signed: Alexander McLin

DAVID RUSSELL   November 27, 1821
Eldest son David - 74 Acres where he now lives, by survey of Mathew Stephenson. To 2 sons William and James - all of land on which Anthony McNutt, decd. resided. To son Robert - 50 Acres adjoining land of Isaac Beals and Isaac Hair it being part of 100 Acres granted to me. To daughter Jane and sons George and Andrew and 2 grandchildren Matilda Hair and Eliza Jane Hair - the residue of my estate. Daughter Sarah, mother of Matilda and Eliza Jane Hair. Executors: Sons David and William. Teste: James Adair, Joseph Beals, Solomon Bales. Probated October Sessions, 1825.   Signed: David (X) Russell

DAVID CRAWFORD   October 7, 1787
To daughter, Sarah Evans, 5 shillings lawful North Carolina money. To daughter, Mary Riggs, 5 shillings lawful North Carolina money. To son, John, 10 shillings of like money. To my wife ? her lifetime. Son, William. Executors: Wife and Reuben Riggs. Wit.: Reuben Riggs, Shadrach Hale, William Crawford.   Signed: David (X) Crawford

HUGH CAMPBELL   October 12, 1790
Sons: Hugh, Robert. My wife to be supported by Hugh. Daughter, Sarah. To son, Samuel, sorrel horse and bay filly, to live with his mother and at her death to have a plantation of his own. Executors: John Alexander, Thomas Rogers, John Campbell.   his
                              Signed: Hugh Hugh Campbell
                                       mark

ANDREW DUNCAN
Wife, Jane. Son, Samuel, has his part. Child Andrew to care for Jane and have oversight of younger children. Married daughters have their part. Non-Cupative Will. Proven by oaths of Joseph Duncan and George Bell.

WILLIAM STEPHENSON   June 15, 1796
To wife Alice - 1/3 of my personal estate and plantation her widowhood or lifetime. I give to Ralph Loftes power of attorney to sell land in

Rockingham Co., Va. To son Matthew, where he now lives. Daughter
Elizabeth is to live with Matthew while she is single. To son, John,
land I purchased of William Houston adjoining lands of Robert Allison.
To daughter, Elizabeth, ½ money from sale of land in Rockingham Co. To
son John, 2/3 money from sale of land in Rockingham Co., Va. To Philip
Hooper, Indenture, if he stays dutiful and obedient. Executors: Wife
Alice, son Matthew and Bro. David Stephenson of Augusta Co., Va.
Wit.: Vance Aiken, George Crookshanks, Patrick (X) Shields.
Signed: William Stephenson

HENRY ISENBERGER   October 20, 1809
Wife, Sarah, to have my land while she is my widow then to my father or
his heirs. Executor: Daniel Bowman. Teste: Nicholas Isenberg, Jacob
(X) Isenberg, Rebecka (X) Bowman. Signed: Henry (X) Isenberger

JOHN ADAMS   No date
Daughter, Mary Hanley. To my son, Samuel Hanly, daughter Jannet Scott,
daughter Mary - each a common Bible. To son, William - 180 Acres on
Big Limestone where I now live. I gave to James Moore 2 years schooling
he is now at school. Wife, Agnes, to have 1/3 of estate. Executors:
Son Samuel Hanly, James Montgomery, William Adams. Wit.: Alex Mathes,
Jeremiah Mathes, John McConnell. Signed: John Adams

ALEXANDER McEWEN   No date
To wife, Margaret, 1/3 of land and personal property. To son, John, the
land where I now live. To son, Ebenezer, 195 Acres. Sons Samuel and
Robert to be paid by John. Daughter, Sarah McEwen. A son or daughter
yet unborn to share equally. Executors: Alex Mathes, Andrew Hannah,
my wife Margaret. Wit.: James Montgomery, John Milliken. Proven 179_.
Signed: Alexander McEwen

JOHN YOUNG   June 1, 1796
Wife Isbell - a child's share of movable property and 1/3 land for 5
years, then son John ½ plantation and to son, Thomas, the other half
when he comes of age, so they both can have timber and good spring water
200 Acres on Third Creek, Knox Co. to son, John. Executors: wife
Isbell, Jonathan Coruthers my son-in-law. Wit.: Thomas Gibson, John
Carr. Signed: John Young

CHARLES YOUNG   March 28, 1796
To wife, Rebecca, until my 2 sons, Wilkins and Ervery Young comes of
age - to have land and negroes. To daughter, Jinny, as executors see
fit - raise and school my family. Executors: wife Rebecca and George
Gillespie. Wit.: John Gilliland, Elisha Rhodes.
Signed: Charles Young

ISAAC BACON   June 3, 1826
To 3 sons: Jonathan, Charles and John Bacon - my plantation of 286 acre
with all buildings, furniture, negroes and cattle, equally divided.
Charles and John to be guardian for Jonathan. They shall care for my
wife, Abigail. I have given to 3 sons, Thomas, Joseph and Isaac Bacon
and daughter, Nancy Hunt. Executors: sons John and Charles. Wit.:
Jacob Taylor, Thomas Hunt, Henry Deakins. Probated July Sessions, 1826.
Signed: Isaac Bacon

THOMAS LITTLE
To wife, Mary, everything where I now live. Wit.: Barbary (X) Seller,
Margaret (X) Parrot and a Dutch name.
Signed: Thomas Little

WILLIAM RUSSELL   March 18, 1826
Black girl, Bloo?, to be emancipated when she is 28. To daughter, Amanda
Jane, land on Big Limestone adjoining Henry Richards and others - when
she is 18, also my part in land joined jointly with my brother, James.
My bed and bedding to be kept by Jane Allison. Brother David and I own

stud horse. I have a debt due me in Ohio to be collected and divided
to daughter Jane and ½ to my fathers heirs and Aunt Polly Ferguson.
xecutors: Brothers James and Robert Russell. Wit.: Isaac Horton,
achel Russell, Polly Ann Allison. Proven July Sessions, 1826.
                              Signed: William Russell

OBERT STUART   Not dated
o brother, John Stuart, where I now live adjoining Isaac Smith, Nelly
erguson, Samuel Greer. To sister, Nancy Conley, land with buildings,
nd her son, Josiah Conley, a negro to be emancipated. To my nephew,
amuel Conley, $50. To my nephew, David Stuart son of John, my black
olt. To nephew, Robert son of John, my sorrel colt. To brother,
lexander Stuart, sisters Margaret Allen and Susan Ferguson - $15. Our
ather, David Stuart, deceased. Executors: John Stuart, brother and
ephew, Josiah Conley. Wit.: John Stephenson, Matthew Stephenson,
saac Smith. Probated October Sessions, 1826.
                              Signed: Robert Stuart

ONATHAN MULKEY   August 3, 1826
o wife, Anna, her choice of personal property and clothing she has made
ince she has lived with me. To son, Isaac, all my land I now live on
180 Acres), at his death to be divided between his children. To
aughters, Rebecca Slaughter, Elizabeth Murry. Other children: John
ulky, Philip, Jonathan Mulky, Mary Mares, Nancy Billingsley, Sarah
arres - have received their sums. Executors: Nathan Shipley and 2
ons-in-law William Slaughter and John Murrey. Wit.: Thomas Galloway,
anly Allgood, Duke Ruble.   Signed: Jonathan (X) Mulky

ONRAD KICKER SENR.   January 16, 1826
o wife, Mary, loose property as long as she is my widow. Anna Lolwasser?
o have what I promised her. Executors: Son Conrad Kecker and George
alters. Wit.: Daniel M. Deakens, John Critselous. Proven October
essions, 1826.   Signed: Conrad Keicher

EUBEN BAYLES   July 26, 1826
o wife, Margaret, personal property of her choosing, 12 sheep, flock of
eese, land etc. Children: Luthy Broyles, Rebecca Bayles. Children of
on Reuben decd. Land in Carter County where John Hampton lives to be
old and get what he owes me ($600). Executors: Son Daniel, James
hite, Isaac Hindley?. Wit.: Daniel O'Donnel, James Sevier, Isaac
illiams. Probated January Sessions, 1827.
                              Signed: Reuben Bayles

ICHAEL BROWN   1826
ife, Elizabeth. Children: Michael, Joseph, Sarah Shawley, Hannah
ellour, Catharine Falls, John Brown and George Brown. Jacob Brown is
o be guardian of my son Michael. Executors: Henry Earnest Esqr.,
ichael Hoyle. Wit.: John Fellour, Michael Hoyle.

AVID MITCHELL   August 27, 1826
ife and children to live as close to my father as possible. Willis
cGlaughlin owes me, so does Higgins Coppery. Executors: Thomas J.
rown, Jacob Gyme, Bro. William Mitchell. Teste: Charles Quillen,
ohn Coppinger, Elijah Embree. Proven January Sessions, 1827.
                              Signed: David (X) Mitchell

HOMAS BIDDLE   January 5, ____
ife, Sarah. Sons: James, John, Samuel. Heirs of son Thomas, decd.
owit: Sons John Biddle, Hugh and James Biddle. Daughter-in-law
lizabeth, wife of Thomas Biddle, decd. To daughter, Nancy Stroun,
nd adjoining Lesly Humphrey. Daughters: Elizabeth Holt, Peggy
ampbell. Land adjoining Samuel Biddle, Thomas Brabson. Executors:
on James and wife Sarah. Wit.: Jacob Whistler, Samuel M. Graybeal,
ohn Strain.   Signed: Thomas (X) Biddle

                              25

HENRY NELSON   April 2, 1785
Wife, Jane. Sons, Henry, John. Son, Charles, to live with my wife. To
son, William, 5 shillings in order to cut him off from any other. Grandson, Joel Nelson. Granddaughter, Nancy Nelson. Daughter, Jemima. Money
in Virginia to sons, John and Charles, to pay my debts. Executors: sons
John and Charles. Wit.: James Reed, William Wood, Isaac Denton. Proven
_____ 178_.   Signed: Henry Nelson

WILKINS YOUNG   April 8, 1824
To my sister Jane White - at her death it is to go to my mother. To
William Erwin, my mare to justify a debt I owe him. Executrix: My
Mother. Wit.: James W. Young, Elijah Boren, William H. Young.
Rebecca Erwin qualified as executrix. Probated April Sessions, 1827.
                              Signed: Wilkins Young

PHILIP McCARDEL   April 17, 1826
Daughter, Esther Thornburgh, and her children. Daughter, Rebecca Tucker.
Son, John McCardel. Daughters, Nancy Miller, Hannah Speek. Rebecca
Tucker to have $43 more than Hannah Speek and Hannah $43 less than the
other legatees on account of Ruse Tucker paying that amount to Matthew
Stephenson for and on an account of Hannah Speek. Executor: Jesse
Smith. Wit.: Matthew Stephenson, James Payne. Probated April Sessions,
1827.   Signed: Philip (X) McCardel

MARGARET HAMMER   August 24, 1826
Sons, Jacob and John - to divide jointly the proceeds of a certain horse
beast willed to me by my husband, John Hammer, decd. To my son, Isaac
Hammer, one large German Bible and other book. Sole Executor: Jonathan
Hammer, my son. Wit.: Henry Hoss, Lemuel Bogart. Probated April
Sessions, 1827.   Signed: Margaret Hammer

ISABELLA BURRIS   May 27, 1823
To Sarah Isabella Beard, daughter of William Beard - one brown mare.
Wit.: John Bollen. Probated July Sessions, 1827.
                                                her
                    Signed: Isabella ₁S Burris
                                              mark

ELIZABETH HALE   October 11, 1820
To Elizabeth Hale, wife of Thomas Hale and to Henry Hale, son of Thomas
Hale - my bed and bedding. To Lucy Chenith, wife of Nicholas Chenith -
set of china. To Richard Chenith - two boys of color. Executor:
Nicholas Chenith. Wit.: Henry Hoss, John Gott, James Ellis. Probated
September Sessions, 1827.   Signed: Elizabeth T. Hale

THOMAS BALL   August 30, 1827
To daughter, Rebecca - 40 Acres. To son, Joseph - 40 Acres, not to
include new house built by Conrad Brown. Daniel Salts and Joseph Ball
to pay Samuel Ball $50. Elizabeth Brown to have balance of land. My
cow to Emily McCardel. Executors: Daniel Salts, Nathan Barnes.
Wit.: Robert Gray, Daniel Salts. Probated January Sessions, 1828.
                              Signed: Thomas (X) Ball

JONATHAN HAMMER   August 27, 1827
To daughter, Elizabeth - bed and bedsheets, bed clothes and side saddle
with twenty dollars and a spinning wheel. To Sarah, my wife, all re-
maining movable estate to raise and school my children who are under
age. Four youngest children: Deborah, Samuel B., Catharine and
Jonathan M. Eleven children: Rachel Bogart, John Hammer, Anna Range,
Margaret Cook, Mary Booth, Elizabeth, Isaac C., Deborah, Samuel B.,
Catharine and Jonathan M. Executor: Henry Hoss. Wit.: John Range,

Jacob Range.   Probated January Sessions, 1828.
                         Signed: Jonathan Hammer

JOHN WADDELL   May 23, 1823
Wife, Susannah - $250. Grandson John Waddell Jr., whom I have raised
and now lives with me - land where I live (150 acres). Sons and Daus.:
John Waddell, Sith que Waddell, Hester Shields, Charles Waddell, Peggy
Gann, Samuel D. Waddle, Jonathan Waddle, Rachel Shields and Abigail
Wilson. Executor: James Broyles Senr. Wit.: Daniel Yeager, Peter
Earnest, Isaac Earnest. Probated January Sessions, 1828.
                         Signed: John (X) Waddell

ROBERT BLAKELY   May 9, 1828
To son, Daniel, a large Bible to give to son Thomas if at all possible.
A book of Gospel Sonnets to dau. Martha. Daughter, Lydia, to have ½ of
all that remains. Other half to go to sons, Daniel, John, William and
daughter, Martha Crawford and son, Thomas. Executors: Sons Daniel,
John and James Blakely. Wit.: James and Robert Blakely, Nathaniel
Sands.

JONATHAN TUCKER   January 8, 1828
Wife, Mary, to raise my 2 youngest children Jonathan and Catharine. To
daughter, Mary, a mare she now claims. To daughter, Eliza, a young
horse and cow. To son, Joseph, my stud horse. To son, George, $134 in
property. Other children not named in will. Land adjoining John
Duglas and John Ford decd. Executors: Son George and daughter Mary.
Wit.: Nathan Shipley, Jesse Jones, Mary Jones. Probated July Sessions,
1828.   Signed: Jonathan Tucker

NATHANIEL SMITH   November 8, 1824
Wife, Susannah. To dau. Ann - $1, dau. Lucy - $1, dau. Jewly - $1, son
Ezekiel - $1, Charlotte, Betsey, Solomon, Jewria - $1 each. Executors:
Wife Susannah and son Solomon. Wit.: John Blakely, Levi Hartman.

JOSEPH TUCKER   January 1, 1827
Wife, _____. Two daughters: Patience Marrs, Elizabeth Brown. Sons:
John, Abraham, Rees. Two sons, James and Joseph - 200 Acres on Lick
Creek. Land adjoining Thompson. Tuckers Grant from North Carolina.
Granddaughter, Ruth Murr - $18 in furniture delivered at his ship.
Grandsons Reese Murr and David Murr. Executors: Sons John and Abraham.
Wit.: David Beals, Samuel Beals, Caleb Beals, Elizabeth Beals.
Probated July Sessions, 1828.   his
                         Signed: Joseph ⏜ Tucker
                                         mark

CATRINA GYRE
To daughter, Sarah Eliza Gyre, my tin plate stove. Executor: friend
John Copley. Wit.: Sarah Brown, James Robinson. Probated _____
Sessions, 1828.   Signed: Catrina Gyre

GEORGE PURSELL SENR.   June 8, 1826
Granddaughter, Elizabeth Purcell. Son, John. Daughter, Elizabeth
Kennedy. To grandchildren: Elizabeth McPheron, daughter of William
M. and Elizabeth Kennedy; George Jr. and Sarah Pursell, children of my
son John Purcell. Executor: Isaac McPheron. Wit.: Mathew Stephenson,
Hiram Glass, Thomas Collins. Probated April Sessions, 1829.
                         Signed: George Purcell

DAVID WILSON   July 14, 1828
Wife, Phebe. Son, Robert C. Rest of my children, $1 apiece.
Executrix: Wife Phebe. Wit.: Hugh Campbell, Brookins Campbell.
Probated July Sessions, 1829.   Signed: David Wilson

ELIZABETH WEBB   December 23, 1827
Black woman, Hannah, to be set free, to be her own guardian in financial
matters. All property to be divided equally among my children. Wit.:
John Ross, Allen T. Ross. Proven July Sessions, 1829.
                              Signed: Elizabeth (X) Webb

THOMAS BROWN   April 22, 1829
Wife, Ann. Children: Jacob, Gabriel, Lemander Bayles, William.
Executors: Son Jacob and Samuel Baylis. Wit.: George Hendry, John
Bottles, George Murr. Probated July Sessions, 1829.
                              Signed: Thomas Brown

ABRAHAM ODELL   March 28, 1829
Wife, Mary. Children: James, David and Jeremiah Odell, Rebecca Kenner,
Margaret, Mary, Samuel. Executors: Samuel and John Odell. Wit.: J.W.
Whetsel Reeves, Clayton Reeves.   Signed: Abraham Odell

WILLIAM NELSON
Wife, Mary. Son, Mark W. Nelson. Six daughters: Jane wife of William
Dugan, Lydia wife of William Colyer, Edia wife of James Beard, Jemima
wife of Robert McCall, Polly and Susan Nelson. I have an Entry Claim
in Shenandoah Co., Virginia. Thomas Stuart is to recover said claim
for ½ the value. Executors: William and Mark W. Nelson. Wit.: Reuben
Carr, Jacob Klepper, Peter Kughn. Probated July Sessions, 1829.
                              Signed: William Nelson

WALKER BARRON   July 4, 1829
To wife Peggy and daughter Polly - plantation where I now live. Other
children. Executor: Friend, Thomas Barnes. Wit.: Nathan Shipley,
Peter Jacks, William Jackson. Probated October Sessions, 1829.
                              Signed: Walker (X) Barron

THOMAS LACKEY   No date
To son Joseph - 100 Acres land in Court of Chancery in Rogersville. To
Thomas Felts, son of William and Peggy - 50 Acres of above tract in
Rogersville as long as Peggy lives. To daughter Elizabeth V. Hendley
and Christian Grove and his wife Jane. To grandson William, son of my
son John - the house occupied by his father as a hatters shop. To
daughter Nancy Waldron - $1 which is all I allow John Waldron. I order
that the charges of the suit with Thomas Stuart about the tract of land
bequeath to my son Joseph and Thomas Felts be paid. Other children.
Executors: Joseph Lackey and Christian Grove. Wit.: John Blair, John
E. Cosson, Thomas Lackey. Probated October Sessions, 1829.
                              Signed: Thomas Lackey

THOMAS GIBSON   November 14, 1829
Wife, Polly. 446 Acres to go to 2 sons Thomas and Daniel Gibson by
their paying to their brothers and sisters $30 in trade each.
Executors: Wife Polly and son Thomas. Wit.: John Chester, John
Fulkerson. Probated January Sessions, 1830.
                              Signed: Thomas Gibson

DAVID LAMON   August 17, 1826
Sold land to sons John and Jacob Lamons. To son, Joseph Lamons - $15.
To son Abraham Lamons - $140. To Jacob Varners wife, Elizabeth - $130.
Sons David, John and Jacob, have their parts. John Coles wife and
Jacob Varners wife to take pay for land. John Cole has paid Christian,
Manuel and Samuel Lamon and Fanny Click. Executor: John Million.
Wit.: Jacob Brown, Daniel Davis, John Criselious. Probated January
Sessions, 1830.   Signed: David Lamons

CALVIN FINCH   August 14, 1829
At wife's death all property to be divided equal between my 4 children,
Thomas and Aaron Finch, Sarah Bewley and Mary Baylis. Jane, a bound girl,
to receive a heifer and a feather bed when she is 18. Wit.: William
Doper, Andrew Lilburn. Probated April Sessions, 1830.
                              Signed: Calvin Finch

FREDERICK ANDES
My seven only daughters: Elizabeth Hammil, Catharine Pruet, Barbary
Fine, Hally Bell, Ann Frances, Deborah Blye and Phoebe Brown. Wife,
Barbary. Wit.: W.E. Lister. Probated April Sessions, 1830.
                              Signed: Frederick (X) Andes

JOHN BROWN   March 15, 1830
Wife, Jane. Daughters, Elizabeth and Fanny. Executors: Wife Jane,
Nathaniel McNabb. Wit.: George Swingle, William Tilson, Colwell
Brown.

JOSEPH CROUCH   September 3, 1830
Sons: George, Joseph. Wife, Margaret. Mary, wife of John Crouch decd.
Mariah Hunt, daughter of John Hunt decd., her brother Samuel Hunt and
Sarah Bright. Joseph Hunt, son of Samuel Hunt. My daughter, Martha
Devault. Executor: Son George. Wit.: George Crouch, Jesse Crouch,
Jewel? Douge.

MARGARET McADAMS   June 19, 1832
Brother, Thomas McAdams. Father, Hugh McAdams, decd. When Thomas
McAdams started to the Sequatchie Valley last fall I put $40 in his
hands. He is to make two good bureaus and give one to Cynthia and one
to Mary Stephenson. I hold a $40 note on Joseph Haile. My two bros.,
Thomas and Samuel McAdams. My mother, Isabella Haile. Two sisters,
Polly Ellis and Jane Ellis. Executor: Bro. Thomas McAdams. Wit.:
John Stephenson, William Hope, William B. Strain.
                              Signed: Margaret McAdams

FRANCIS REGISTER   September 16, 1834
Son Gregory - 150 Acres when he is 21. Land adjoins William Craddock,
Isaac Horton, John and Carter Tadlock and Jesse Mullins. Wife, Jemima,
to have good and decent support. Children: James Archibald, Gregory,
Sarah, Lucinda and Hannah Eliza to have support until they come of age.
Lucinda and Deborah Martin to have $20 next Christmas. Executor:
Brother-in-law John Robertson. Wit.: Isaac Horton, Joseph Horton,
Jacob Hacker. Probated _____.

JESSE PAYNE   February 28, 1829
Wife, Mahaly. Children: Jesse, Hannah Earnest, Robert - $1 each. To
son, Henry - 325 Acres in Greene County where he now lives. Son, Joseph.
Daughter, Polly Payne. Son, William - $1. Elizabeth Mansfield - $1.
Daughter, Patsy Payne. Daughter, Els Barns - $1. Granddaughter, Polly
Earnest, daughter of Wesley and Polly Payne Earnest, under age. Dau.,
Sarah McCleary. Executors: E.L. Mathes, James McAlister, John Nelson
Junr., Jacob Whistler. Wit.: John Lenk, Alexander Mathes, Richard Gray.

MARY CATHARINE KUHN   May 22, 1828
Children: Elizabeth Williams, Jacob Kuhn, Christopher Kuhn, Mary Kirk,
Margaret Rogers, John Kuhn, Katherine Ruble, Nancy Jones and Peter Kuhn
who now lives with me and has labored with me and improved my farm and is to
have farm 2 years after my decease - then it is to be sold and divided
among my 9 children, Peter having 2 parts, making 10 parts in all.
Executors: Jacob Klepper, son John Kuhn. Wit.: William Dugan, Jacob
Klepper, James Dugan.   Signed: Mary Katherine (X) Kuhn

JOHN McCRACKEN   January 8, 1820
To wife, Margaret, house and lot where we live in Jonesborough. Land
adjoining John Kennedy and Samuel Bayles. Sons: John, Samuel, Robert,
Henry. Daughters: Mary Kelsey, Catharine Greer. Grandsons: John M.
Kelsey, John son of Samuel, John son of Robert, John B. son of Henry,
William son of John. Granddaughter, Mary B. McCracken. Debts due me
in Pennsylvania from the estate of Alexander Adams decd. Executors:
Son John, wife Martha. Wit.: John Patton, Sam G. Chester.
                         Signed: John McCracken

JAMES McWHORTER   February 10, 1831
Beloved wife. Two daughters: Suzy Campbell, Polly Seehorn. Executors:
Samuel Crawford, John M. Crawford. Wit.: Abraham Lane, John Wooten.
                         Signed: James McWhorter

JOHN HALL   December 21, 1830
Wife, Elizabeth. Son, James, to take care of his mother. Five daughters:
Polly, Peggy, Lucinda, Eliza, Nancy - to have land I own in Hiwassy
Purchase. Land in Jonesborough. Executors: Son Thomas, son-in-law
William King. Wit.: Nathan Shipley, John Robinson.
                         Signed: James (X) Hall

JOHN SLYGER   November 16, 1830
Wife, Mary Magdalene. Sons, John, Adam. Land about Jacob Hedrick's
cabin which I give to Jacob Hedrick. Daughter, Sarah Long. Mary Anna
Nelson. Executors: Sons Adam and John Slyger. Wit: Jacob Brown,
John Bacon, Humphreys West.

PATRICK ELLET   January 19, 1831
Wife, Mary. Children: Sarah Irvine, Mandy, John and George Ellet,
Margaret Canaser, Jane Harne, Mary Primmer. Sarah Irvine to stay with
Mary. Executors: James Bird?, Peter Miller. Wit.: John Stout, Lydia
Weire.   Signed: Patrick (X) Ellet

JOHN SHANNON   September 6, 1831
Wife, Rebecca Shannon. Three youngest sons, William, James and Joshua
to get plantation at wife's death. Daughters: Elizabeth, Pamelia,
Rebeckah, Nancy Bayles. What Jesse Bayles owes me. Elijah Embree and
John Tilson owe me. William Erwin owes me. Sons Elijah and Samuel
Shannon and daughter Mary Ann Fox. Executors: Wife Rebecca, son Elijah,
brother-in-law William S. Ervine. Wit.: James Sevier, S.E. Shannon,
William S. Shannon.   Signed: John (X) Shannon

WILLIAM SMITH   July 16, 1834
202 Acres I own on Cassi Creek in Washington County, southside Nolachucky
River, adjoining Godfrey Mock and the Big Survey to my sons John and
David Smith. Executor: Michael Capp.
                         Signed: William (X) Smith

HENRY SLYGER   March 20, 1834
Wife, Elizabeth. Seven children. My wife may have executors sell my 50
acre Winkle Tract and her part of William Ingle Tract. Executors: Sons
Adam and William Slyger. Wit.: Joseph Kyker, James B. Cloyd, Enos
Campbell.   Signed: Henry (X) Slyger

DANIEL YEAGER   June 13, 1834
Wife, Susannah, to keep family together and have control of property
coming to me from my father-in-law, Cornelius Yeager. Children: Eliza
Reser, Elijah F. Yeager, Martha E.F. and Susannah M. Yeager. Executors:
Solomon N. Yager and Jonah J. Yager, sons. Wit.: Jno. Link, Enos
Pickering, Henry Coile. Signed: Daniel Yager

JAMES P. YOUNG   March 20, 1834
To son William H. Young - 100 Acres I bought of Alexander McBride. Son
Thomas R. Young. When youngest daughter, Elizabeth, is 21. Land owned
by Joseph Young, adjoining Dillon Love, John Porter. I made an entry
adjoining Elijah Barnes. Son Joseph L. Young - 98 Acres on Cherokee
Creek. Five daughters: Sarah wife of James H. Gillespie, Jane Eliza
Young, Catharine Emily Young, Margaret Caroline Young and Elizabeth
Young. 114 Acres in Hawkins County conveyed to me by Robert Young for
the benefit of my Uncle Joseph Young's heirs. Sell land of James and
Thomas Price for heirs of Thomas Price decd. Executors: Son William
and James H. Gillespie. Wit.: John Kennedy, Benjamin Drain, Elijah
Boren.   Signed: James W. Young

JACOB ELLIS   July 19, 1834
Wife, Letitia. Land I own on Little Limestone, where Clark Ellis lives,
to be sold, provided he does not pay his debt due me. Sons: William,
Robert, John and Jacob to have where I now live. Daughters - $250 each.
Executors: Wife Letitia, son William. Wit.: George Crouch, William
Crouch, John N. Clark.   Signed: Jacob Ellis

ULLRICH KEENER   March 18, 1828
Plantation to my children: Rebecca, George, John, Jonathan, Joseph,
Peter Keener and dau. Hannah Cumtable. Hannah's part to be divided 3
ways, herself, her son Elkanah and her son William. The heirs of my
son, Daniel Keener, are not to share because I gave him his part in his
lifetime. Executors: Sons George and John Keener. Wit.: George and
Leonard Swingle.   Signed: Ullrich Keener

WILLIAM THOMPSON   February 7, 1829
Wife, Margaret. Children: (dau.) McClees, Ann Brown, John, Isaac
decd., Jesse M., William, Joseph, Mary Thompson. Sons Ebenezer A. and
Evan T. Thompson are idiots, to be well taken care of with 2/3 of the
land. Executors: John G. Earnest, Daniel Barkley. Wit.: Robert Gray,
Robert _____.   Signed: William Thompson

THOMAS HAMMONDS   January 14, 1835
Wife, Elizabeth. Son Thomas to build a house in orchard above the big
spring. Land Joseph Brown cleared. Thomas to care for his mother and
brothers. Sons John, Jacob and George. Daughters, Lydia Brown, Mary
Bottles, Catharine Murr. Executors: Sons John and Jacob Hammond.
Wit.: Matthew Stephenson, John Cowan, Stephen Brown.
                                Signed: Thomas (X) Hammond

WILLIAM B. STRAIN   June 17, 1833
Wife, Martha Alice. Both my parents. Father, John Strain Senr. to reside
on land adjoining John Campbell and William Smith. Executor: John A.
Strain, my brother. Wit.: Matthew Stephenson, William Hop, Solomon
Beals (of David), John Stephenson. Signed: William B. Strain

REBECCA IRVINE   February 20, 1834
To daughter, Jane wife of Thomas White, ½ money my son, William Young,
left me by his will. Other ½ I give to my grandchildren of Jane and
Thomas White. To son, William Young, if he ever returns. Executors:
Joseph L. Burtts, James W. Young. Wit.: Benjamin Drain, John C. Haws.
                                Signed: Rebecka Irvine

JOHN GATES   September 9, 1835
Wife, Elizabeth. Children: Richard Gates, Ann Carr, Jacob Gates, Jane
Wadley, William Gates. Brothers and sisters to get balance of my
personal estate. Executors: George Crouch, Jacob Ellis. Wit.: A.
Horton, John Bowman, Jeremiah Hale, James White.   his
                                Signed: John ⟩⟩ Gates
                                           mark

31

JACOB KEENER   July 13, 1832
Wife, Rebecca Keener, to take money and buy a farm. Money from my father
decd. Executrix: Wife Rebecca. Wit.: J.M. Jackson, Jacob Lonebarger.
                          Signed: Joseph Keener

SAMUEL CRAWFORD
All property to go to wife and children until youngest child comes of
age, then to be divided equally.

SAMUEL GREER SENR.   April 8, 1826
To son, John, land I purchased from John Kennedy adjoining David
Russell's heirs, Isaac Haite and others. After John's decease property
is to go to my 2 sons Samuel Greer and Thomas D. Greer. Executors:
sons Samuel and Thomas. Wit.: T.G. Chester, Nemrod C. Willet.
                          Signed: Samuel Greer Senr.

WALTER CHASE   January 12, 1836
Wife, Elizabeth. All my children. Wit.: Nathan Shipley, John Murry,
Shadrach Murry.   Signed: Walter (X) Chase

LEROY TAYLOR   March 17, 1834
To granddaughter, Margaret Irvin, my pensions due me 4 March 1834 - 4
September 1834. Wit.: Leroy C. Irvine, Anderson Miller.

ROBERT MOORE   March 3, 1834
To sister Sally Moore and brother William Moore, all of my estate.
Executor: John M. Crawford. Wit.: Van S. Miller, Alexander Miller.
                          Signed: Robert Moore

ROBERT BEARD   May 7, 1831
Wife, Marth Bear, to have full possession. To son, James, $5. To
daughters Betsy, Mattie, Sally, Esther and Isabella, heirs of my dau.
Nancy, $70. To son, William, $5. Sons Joseph, Robert, Samuel, $5 each.
Executors: Son James and Daniel Deaken. Wit.: G.A. Deadrick, ?
                          Signed: Robert Beard

ABRAHAM SNAPP . July 8, 1833
Children: Lawrence, Sarah McGhee, Joseph, Peter, Christina Ghrale?,
Catharine Broyles, George - to receive $1 to be paid one year after my
decease - I have already provided for them. To daughter, Elizabeth
McCune, who went to Indiana and married - $50. To son, Abraham Snapp -
land which I deeded to son Jacob and from him to Abraham - also my
farming utensils, household and kitchen furniture of every description.
Abraham has paid $300 of my debts and had given his oblication for my
maintenance during my natural live - Obligation dated 6 September 1831.
I give to daughter, Margaret Richards, son Jacob, dau. Mary Ann Prather,
dau. Florain Henly, dau. Mary Jane Doak - $1. I gave dau. Bathseba her
portion during my lifetime. Executor: Son Abraham. Wit.: William
Patton, John Link, E.L. Mathes.   Signed: Abraham Snapp

ANDREW BUCHANAN   October 13, 1832
Wife Margaret to use property to support my daughters while they are
single and to have $200 I have on interest. Son Henry Buchanan to have
plantation after the death of his mother. To three daughters: Sarah
Jane, Matilda and Lucinda - each a horse and bridle worth $100 in trade,
also $150 each when Henry can sell the land he has in Kentucky. Property
to stay in family - not to be sold. Executors: Son Henry and John
Stephenson. Wit.: John Milburn, Elizabeth Stephenson, Jonas Marsh.
                          Signed: Andrew Buchanan

JEREMIAH BOGART   January 24, 1837
Wife, Elizabeth, to have control of all property and raise and school
children. Executor: John Wright. Wit.: George Williams, Isaac C.
Hammer.   Signed: Jeremiah (X) Bogart

WILLIAM CROOKSHANKS   September 21, 1836
Wife, Sarah. Thirty negroes to be sold and money to be put on interest
for support of family if necessary. Daughter Eliza (now Mrs. Willet).
Aged father, George Crookshanks, to remain with my family. Children:
Samuel McSpadden, William Boule, George Campbell, Montgomery Henderson,
Sarah Keyes and Nancy Ann Crookshanks and Eliza Montgomery Willet.
Executors: George W. Willet, John Cowan Senr. and Matthew Stephenson.
Wit.: William Humphreys, Benjamin McLin, Richard McLin.
                          Signed: William Crookshanks

THOMAS NELSON   March 7, 1835
To son, Robert - 83 acres including barn, part of my dwelling stillhouse,
still and tubs if he pays Matthew Stephenson the price of the large still,
not to include orchard and spring on land I bought of John Simpson, adjoining Lewis Richards, Matthew Stephenson. The little orchard and
spring is to go to my grandson, William C. Nelson, son of my second son
Andrew. To son, George M. Nelson - the remaining part of plantation.
To daughters Lucinda Shields and Juliana - each ten hundred dollars.
To dau. Margaret Jane - $200. To grandson, John, son of John - $100
when he is of age. Juliana and Mary Jane to have old part of house with
liberty of firewood on any part of plantation as long as they live. The
3/8 of Robert McLins estate to be divided - to Robert one part, George
one part and grandson William D. one part. Executor: Robert B. Nelson,
my son. Wit.: Matthew Stephenson, Jonas McPheron, Emaline Charlton,
John B. (X) McCracken.   Signed: Thomas Nelson

WILLIAM KING   January 23, 1832
To daughter Martha A. King - 4 negroes, horses and cattle. To son Thomas
King - land in Sumner County near Drakes Creek. To son George B. King -
land I live on with negroes. Son Thomas - $138. Executors: Sons Thomas
and George G. King. Wit.: Richard Carr, Alfred Carr, James M. Carr.
                          Signed: William King

JOHN TIPTON   October 3, 1831
Three children: Samuel P., Elizabeth S. and Edny M. Tipton. Other
children: Abraham, Tipton, Mary Ann, Margaret V., Emaline, Marian P.
and Lucinda M. Wit.: A. McClellan, Christian Carriger.
                          Signed: John Tipton

HENRY BOTTLES   August 29, 1825
Wife, Mary E. Bottles. Four sons: Jacob, William, John and Joseph.
____ Wright have a horse and saddle and bridle. Children of my daus.
Elizabeth Kiker and Sarah Byble have all movable property to death of
my wife. Executors: Sons John and Joseph Bottles. Wit.: Asa,
William R. and Reuben Bayles.   Signed: Henry Bottles

CHRISTIAN GROVES   February, 1837
Children, Thomas, Catharine, Susan and wife, Jane, to live together.
Children to be schooled. There will be 600 - 700 lb. bacon, stove and
pipe in my shop and a shotgun I want sold to pay my debts. My house
and lot. Executors: James Brown, Wilton Atkinson. Wit.: James Brown,
Wilton Atkinson, John A. Wilds.

DANIEL BOWMAN   September 9, 1833
Wife, Rebecca. To son, Jacob, 268 Acre Love Tract. To daughter,
Catharine Guston, the Rose Tract of 300 Acres I bought of Nathan Shipley.
To son, Samuel, the 168 Acre Hunt Tract. To daughter, Susannah widow of

Solomon Crouse - 100 Acres I purchased of Joseph Malven. To son, Daniel, the grist and saw mill, dam and water power to Ellens corner. To son, John, land and to allow my wife Rebecca to live with him. Executors: Jacob and Samuel Bowman, my sons. Wit.: John Blair, John P. Chester, William P. Chester Jr.   Signed: Daniel Bowman

JONATHAN WADDLE
To son, Samuel, the George horse and a saddle. To son, Thomas, the Mike horse, saddle and cloak. To wife, Hannah, 4 horses. Son, Jonathan, to have a colt. Two little daughters. Probated 1836.
                              No Signature

JACOB KEEBLER   October 21, 1828
Wife, Mary. Children: Sarah Kincheloe, John and Jacob Keebler, Elizabeth Bacon, Caroline and Mary Ann Ingersoll and Lindy Haws. To son, Samuel Keebler, my plantation - he to care for his mother, daughter Mary to live with them. An equal share to Catharine Ingersol's two daughters. Executors: Sons Samuel and John Keebler. Wit.: Nathan Shipley, William Whitlock, George Jackson.
                        Signed: Jacob Keebler

HENRY SLAGAL   June 21, 1830
Wife, Eleanor. Daughter, Sarah. Other children. Executrix: Wife Eleanor. Wit.: James Robinson, John Howard, Samuel Hunt.
                        Signed: Henry Slagal

JACOB BROWN   May 13, 1831
Wife, Elizabeth. Daughter, Ruth. Son, William - Polly Hunter, Rebecca Templin, Jacob Davis and Jacob K. Brown to be charged with his extra schooling and board. Other names: Malinda, Harriet, Patrick - children or slaves. Executor: Son Bird Brown.
                        Signed: Jacob Brown

HENRY SLYGER   March 26, 1834
Wife, Elizabeth. Executors to sell 50 acres called the Winkle Tract, and her part of William Ingle Tract for her use. Executors: Sons Adam and William Slyger. Wit.: Joseph Kyker, James B. Cloyd, Enos Campbell.
                        Signed: Henry (X) Sligar

HENRY BANNER   January 26, 1829
Wife, Judy, to have all plantation as far as Dry Gut next to what I rented to Benjamin P. Hopkins - after Hopkin's time I give it to my son Lewis for his schooling. Children: Lewis, Catharine, Elizabeth, Ann, Mahaly, Mary Hopkins. Brother, Ephraim Banner, is to make his home with my family if he wants to. Executors: Wife Judy, Phillip Banner, John Edwards. Wit.: Joseph Longmire, Hannah Longmire, Benjamin P. Hopkins. Recorded September Term, 1841.   Signed: Henry Banner

JOHN NELSON   September 8, 1833
To daughter Nancy Mathes - my whole estate, real and personal. To grandson Alexander Nelson - 10 acres of land in a separate deed and which lies mostly in his uncles field. He is to have $3000 when he becomes of age. Executor: Son-in-law Ebenezer C. Mathes. Wit.: Ewing McClure, G.W. Telford.   Signed: John Nelson

GEORGE I. HAIL   June 8, 1835
Wife, Elenor. All my children. Wit.: William T. Ensor Sr., James T. Shipley.   Signed: George Hail

34

HENRY BOTTEL   August 29, 1835
Wife, Mary E. Bottels. Four sons: Jacob, William, John and Joseph.
Bound boy, James Wright, to have saddle and bridle, falling ax, scythe
and cradle. Children of my daughters Wlizabeth Kiker and Sarah Byble.
Executors: Sons John and Joseph Bottels. Wit.: Asa, William A. and
Reuben Bayles.   Signed: Henry Bottels

JONATHAN BRADLY   September 6, 1839
Wife, Elizabeth. Wit.: Thomas H. Crouch, Joseph Osborn.
                          Signed: Jonathan (X) Bradly

JACKSON HALE   April 30, 1839
Wife, Elizabeth. Daughter, Harriet. Son, Elijah. Wife to live with my
father, if she remarries my executor is to take and raise children.
Executor: Henry Neale. Wit.: Allison Neale, Thomas Galoway, Joseph
Crouch.   Signed: Jackson Hale

WILLIAM KINCHELOE   August 6, 1840
Wife, Minerva. Daughters: Sarah and Mary - $500 each. Three sons:
Archibald, George and John - $500 each. Executors: John Kincheloe.
Wit.: Valentine Sevier, Smith Irwin, James Kincheloe. Probated
September Term, 1840.   Signed: William (X) Kincheloe

JANE A. DOAK   March 31, 1838
To mother, Jane Doak, my saddle and trunk. Daughters: Elizabeth and
Mary. Two brothers: Alexander W. and James A. Doak. Get what is due
me from Calvin Mathes and Daniel Graham. Executors: 2 Bros. Alexander
W. and James Doak. Wit.: Daniel Graham, Jesse Payne, Joshua Green.
                          Signed: Jane A. Doak

WILLIAM MEAD   No date
Wife, Rebecca. Five children: Elenor, Elizabeth, John, Benjamin, Polly
Ann Mead, when they become 21. Executors: Benjamin L. Yokley of
Sullivan County and John Bowman Jr. (of John). Wit.: James Hodge,
Isaac Boring.   Signed: William Mead

JACOB HAMMER   September 27, 1836
Wife, Catharine. Children: Ann Range, Deborah Young, Samuel Hammer,
Catharine, Jonathan and Isaac Hammer, share and share alike after my
wife's decease. Executors: James White, Jacob Range. Wit.: Asa
Shipley, John White. Probated March Term, 1841.
                          Signed: Jacob Hammer

CHRISTIAN ZETTY SENR.   February 10, 1841
Wife, Barbara. Daughters: Mary Crompeeker?, Christiana Barger, Hannah
Wattenbarger, Elizabeth Hinkle. Hannah Wattenbarger - $62. Elizabeth
Hinkle - $100. Son, Christian Zetty, has his part. Executor: son-in-
law George Hinkle. Wit.: Isaac McPherson, Jonathan Bancroft, Zachariah
M. Botles. Probated April Sessions, 1841.
                          Signed: Christian Zetty

WILLIAM GREENWAY   March 13, 1839
To son William - land I bought of James Graham round to Richard Greenways
line. To sons, John H. and Jesse H. - the remainder of my land including
the family burying ground. Daughter, Martha, comfortable support during
her celibacy. Daughter Mary Ann McNeese, Anna Loony, heirs of Polly Ann
Johnson, Hannah Waddell, Richard Greenway, Susan Green, Elizabeth Payne,
Dorcas Jordan, Patsy, George. Executors: son Jesse H. and John H.
Greenway. Wit.: William Patton, G.W. Telford. Probated _____, 1839.
                          Signed: William Greenway

35

HENRY MOLER   October 28, 1837
Wife, Margaret. To son Samuel - $10. Executors: Wife Margaret and
Jacob Douglas. Wit.: W.T. Ensor Sr., John Mead. Probated _____.
                            Signed: Henry Mohler

THOMAS EMMERSON   April 11, 1837
Wife Catharine - everything I own to her and her heirs forever. Son,
Thomas B. - to have my volumes of <u>Tennessee Farmer</u>, have the first 12
volumes bound and continue the publication to and of the third year if
he should think proper to do so and can procure a competent person to
superentend its publication. The contract with Mason R. Lyon to last
till the end of the year. If my Executors does not see fit to sell my
printing press he is authorized to lease it. My prentice boy's board,
clothing and washing bills are to be paid to my wife out of my estate.
Executor: John G. Eason of Jonesborough, if Mr. Eason cannot serve, I
appoint my brother Arthur Emmerson of Portsmouth, Virginia and my son
Thomas B. Emmerson. Wit.: S.J.W. Lucky, M.R. Lyon.
                            Signed: Thomas Emmerson

SARAH GLASSCOCK   May 28, 1840
Sister Jane Hays. I bequeath to Sarah Baxter. I give to Sarah Doggan
the whole part of her mother's part of my estate. To Thomas Caldwell,
my book case and large family Bible over and above his part. To
Elizabeth Miller, my white bedcover and quilt that is not quilted.
Executors: Terry White, Valentine Sevier. Wit.: James Mitchell,
Smith Irwin. Probated July Term, 1840.
                            Signed: Sarah Glasscock

WILLIAM SMITH   July 16, 1834
102 acres on Cassi Creek in Washington County on wouthside of Nolachucky
River adjoining Godfrey Mock and the Big Survey - to my two sons John and
David Smith, also my still and tubs, clothing and bedding. Executor:
Michael Cox. Wit.: William Wilson, Benjamin Cox. Probated January
Sessions, 1835.   Signed: William (X) Smith

JACOB ROBINSON   July 11, 1838
To sister Catharine Helton $9. Three sisters: Mary, Susannah and
Elizabeth. Brothers to have my clothes. Executor: Brother William.
Wit.: Charles Hilton, John P. Hulse. Probated 183 words.
                            Signed: Jacob (X) Robinson

HENRY HARTMAN   March 24, 1838
To wife Polly - a forty dollar note on John Blair, land, furniture and
a comfortable living forever. Two oldest sons: Jonathan and Henry
Nelson Hartman - land adjoining John Hartman, George Hale to have rents
till Henry Hartman arrives at age 21. Two youngest sons: Jesse Paine
Hartman and John Blair Hartman - where I now live. Six daughters:
Matilda, Senith, (other 4 not named). Executors: Jonathan Hartman,
John Martin. Land to William Kellace?. Wit.: Smith Hunt, Jesse Hunt.
Probated April Sessions, 1838.   Signed: Henry Hartman

JANE ALLISON   July 5, 1818
Two daughters: Polly Ann Conly and Hannah E. Thompson - money in hands
of Duncan and Blair and John F. Deaderick. Three grandchildren: Amanda
Jane Russell, Harriet and Robert A. Russell. My daughters: Nancy and
Rachel Russell. Executors: Two sons: Robert A. Thompson and Jonah
Conley. Wit.: John Stephenson, Thomas C. McAdams, Allison Long.
Probated _____.   Signed: Jane Allison

JOHN ROCK   July 28, 1838
Wife, Nancy. Grandson, George Washington Combs. Katy Conkins children.
Jane Dickerson to live with my wife Nancy. Wit.: Anson Haile, Senr.,

Robert G. Hale. Probated _____. Signed: John (X) Rock

LAWRENCE EARNEST   August 25, 1837
Wife, Hannah. Sons: Jacob B. Earnest, Lawrence W. Earnest, Jonah W.
Earnest. Children: Wesley, Elizabeth Coon, Syntha, Axley, Marilla
Broyles, Antamond? Payne, Rebecca Payne, Lavinia Barnett, William S.,
Jonah W., Jacob B. and Lawrence W. Earnest. Executors: Brother-in-law
Nathan Barnes, E.L. Mathes. Wit.: William, William G. and Jesse R.
Payne. Probated May Sessions, 1838.

WILLIAM JACKSON   July 26, 1838
To son Willie Jackson - 120 acres I purchased of Dodson. To son Smith
Jackson - 82 acres. To daughter Barbara Jackson - 146 acres I bought of
Lite O. Gott. Slaves to be set free when 30 years old. All my Children:
Jacob, Peter and George Jackson, Deborah Fulkerson, Samuel, Willie, Smith
and Barbara Jackson. Executors: 2 sons George and Peter Jackson. Wit.:
John Kennedy, Charles Bacon, Daniel Barron.
                              Signed: William (X) Jackson

MATTHEW STEPHENSON   February 12, 1838
To American Bible Society - $500. To Board of Foreing Missions -
Presbyterian Church - $500. To friends James Cowan and Mary Russell -
$300. To wife Mary A. - the mill and plantation, 20 barrels flour for
the store. Five thousand dollars. Slave, Fanny, to be sent to Ohio.
Black boy, Alfred, to be sent to Liberia if he desires. Brother, John
Stephenson. Sister, Elizabeth McEwen. Land purchased from John McGinnis,
McCardle and George Cunningham in Greene County and lots in Leesburg - a
life estate for my wife. I'm in partnership with Isaac McPherson in
store at Leesburg for 5 years. 10 shares in Charleston and Cincinnatti
Railroad. To Matthew McPherson - $200 for work in store. Executors:
Bro. John Stephenson. Wit.: Seth J.W. Lucky, Harvy Buchanan, James
Patton.   Signed: Matthew Stephenson

JAMES BALLENGER   March 25, 1837
Executors: Wife Polly, son Bluford Ballenger. Wit.: John Blair, Mark
L. (X) Fields.   Signed: James Ballenger

JOHN COWAN
Wife, Sarah. Children: Sarah P. Cowan, John F., Paul M., William and
Joseph Cowan. Executors: Wife Sarah, Matthew Stephenson. Wit.: Mary
A. Stephenson, Samuel B. Cunningham. Proven November Term, 1839.
                              Signed: John Cowan

WILLIAM THACKER   January 7, 1834
Wife, Mary. My children by my first wife get nothing since they neglected
me in my old age. Wit.: William K. Blair, I. Howard. Acknowledged 25
December 1835. Probated _____. Signed: William (X) Thacker

JAMES BROYLES SENR.   July 17, 1837
Wife Ellender to make my daughters Malinda and Ellender equal to my
other daughters Polly Mauk and others. Land adjoining Adam Painter,
John Broyles and others granted to me by State of Tennessee 30 September
1835 to be sold if not needed. Polly Mauk, my daughter, to have 18 acres
at the head of Maple Swamp on the southside of Chucky River. Sons John
and Mathias have their part which is $1500. Son Lewis has received
$850 and is to receive $200 more provided the note on James Allen Esq.
can be secured. Son James has received $1000. Sons: Jacob and Ephraim,
246 acres. Son Simeon, 50 acres more. Samuel Mauk has land in his own
right. Executrix: Wife Ellender, sons Jacob and Ephraim to assist her.
Wit.: Joseph West, Jacob F. Broyles. Angus Grahal Probated November
Sessions, 1839.   Signed: James (X) Broyles

HUGH CAMPBELL   February 21, 1835
Wife Suzy Campbell. Daughters: Polly, Sally and Fidella Campbell.
Sons: Andrew, James. Daughters: Margaret Carson, Nancy Howe. Son
Brook Campbell - 160 acres I bought of Samuel Biddle. $100 in hands of
Amos Holliday. Executors: Brooken Campbell, my son and John M.
Crawford. Wit.: James I. Sehorn, John M. Crawford, William R. Sehorn.
                              Signed: Hugh Campbell

JACOB BROWN   February 19, 1841
Wife, Mary. Children: John, George, Mary. Daughter Nancy Ball's
children. Jacob and Wyley Brown's children not included. To son
Richard - my rifle that J. Graham let him have. To step daughter Mary
Cloyd. Executor: E.L. Mathes if he cant use Henry Taylor. Wit.: John
and Harrison Mitchell.   Signed: Jacob (X) Brown

KINCHEN KELLY   April 9, 1835
Wife, Elizabeth. Son, Kinchen. Grandson, Joseph Houston. Children:
Jonathan, Margaret wife of Jacob Miller, Barbara wife of George Little,
Mary wife of John Miller, Fathee wife of Jonathan Range. Daughter
Elizabeth's sons, Joshua, William, John. Executor: Son Jonathan Kelly.
Wit.: Nathan Shipley, Richard Carson, Alfred Carr. Probated April
Sessions, 1840.   Signed: Kinchen Kelly

ENOCK COULSON   June 5, 1839
Wife, Hannah, 201 acres during her natural life. Executor: Wife Hannah.
Wit.: John Blakely, Bluford Ballenger, Matthew Blakely. Probated
September Sessions, 1840.   Signed: Enock (X) Coulson

HENRY BOYD   December 7, 1839
I have no real estate but do have notes for $330. I give to my children:
Daniel, Rosannah Salts, Jacob, Margaret Mitchell, Mary, Elizabeth, Susan,
Hannah, Nancy, William and Henry. Granddaughter Betsy Boyd. Executors:
Daniel Dewald, David Boyd. Wit.: W.W. Barell, William Patton.
                              Signed: Henry (X) Boyd

MARY GIBSON   August 22, 1840
Property coming to me from my father's estate. Children: William,
Jemima $20 each, Sarah $10, Elizabeth $10, Rachel $10, Mary $10.
Executor: Thomas Fulkerson. Wit.: J.W. Fulkerson, Jess Headrick,
Charles Cox. Probated _____. Signed: Mary (X) Gibson

JACOB ROBINSON   February 7, 1840
Wife and Bosom friend, Elizabeth Robinson - 1 small and 1 large patent
plough, 2 shovel ploughs with tongue, windmill, 2 clevices after
Elizabeth and Sarah gets their part. Six pigs bought of John Robinson.
Daughters: Mary wife of John Robinson, Sarah, Elizabeth. Son Fielding
F.B. Robinson. Executor: Son Samuel Robinson. Wit.: Thomas Fulkerson,
George W. Gibson.   Signed: Jacob Robinson

GEORGE E. KINCHELOE   June 27, 1840
Children: John, William, James, Nancy McPherson, Mary wife of James
Owen decd., Sarah, Elizabeth wife of John Whitlock, Clary wife of Chase
Hale, Margaret wife of John W. Brown. My watch to my grandson, George
Kinchelo, son of my son John. Executors: Sons: John, William and
James Kincheloe. Wit.: Thomas Fulkerson, George J. Jackson, Elijah
Ellis.   Signed: George Kincheloe

ESTHER YOUNG   June 28, 1853
Nephew, Thompson Crockett. To Joseph L. Burtt. To stepdaughter
Elizabeth Burtts, Mary Esther Burtts, John Crockett Burts, James H.
Burtts, Emeline T. Burtts, Cordelia L. Burtts, Belvadora Burtts,

Margaret Burtts. Executor: Joseph L. Burtts. Wit.: E.L. Miller, Samuel W. Hoss.

MARY KEEBLER   August 8, 1839
Wife of Jacob Keebler, deceased. Daughter, Mary. Son, Samuel.
Executor: Son Samuel. Wit.: Brookins Campbell, Emanuel Arnold.
                              Signed: Mary Keebler

KATHARINE RUBLE   April 4, 1837
Son, Henry. Daughters: Katharine Bitner, Eve Roberts. I have a legacy
left by my brother Jacob decd., late of the state of Pennsylvania.
Daughters: Elizabeth Koplinger, Barbara Copelenty?. Executor: My son
Henry Ruble. Wit.: John C. Harris, Nelson Scott, Jacob Hartsell.
                              Signed: Katherine (X) Ruble

JACOB COPP   October 29, 1842
Wife, Mary, to have 1/3 part for her support. Children: George, Peter,
Andrew and Clerissa Capp, Elizabeth Winkle, Margaret, John, Catharine
Capp. John Winkle Jr. Michael Copp. To son, Andrew, the place where
Joshua Greene now lives on road leading from John Walters. George —
$845.56 to pay on his Harmon Place. Executors: George Copp and Henry
Ruble. Wit.: John Walters, Peter Copp.
                              Signed: Jacob (X) Copp

SARAH KINCHELOE   June 9, 1842
All my property I bequeath to grandsons Washington and William Slaughter.
$1 each to Abraham, Isaac, Jacob and John Slaughter, my four sons. Sary
Carswell, $1. Executor: Abraham Slaughter. Wit.: John and George
Jackson.   Signed: Sary (X) Kincheloe

CHARLES DENHAM   September 21, 1836
Wife, Mary. When Thomas Dunham and Peter Light come to 21 years they are
to have colts they claim. To son, Thomas, land on road leading to
Jonesborough. Peter Light, grandson of my wife Mary, land if he stays
with his grandmother until he is 21. Executrix: Wife Mary. Wit.: John
Kincheloe, Thomas Cade.   Signed: Charles Denham

SAMUEL MAYS   March 9, 1842
Children: John, Casmere, Eliza, George, Mary Anon, James G., William,
land I got from my father-in-law, John Million. Executors: Wife Mary
and 2 oldest sons John and Casmere. Wit.: William Slemmons, Madison
Boothe, Harrison Mitchell.   Signed: Samuel (X) Mays

SAMUEL WRIGHT   March 1, 1842
To wife Sarah — my debts and all species of property and to make a deed
in fee simple to Philip Swonger for 50 acres land I sold him. Exec.:
Wife Sarah. Wit.: Thomas T. Young, John Howard.
                              Signed: Samuel Wright

JOHN STEPHENSON   December 29, 1841
Wife, Elizabeth. I have 350 acres including an entry of 80 acres. To
son-in-law, Thomas C. McAdams, land, Miller Tract and Isaiah Conley
tract. To son David — all my interest in the Washington Iron Manufac-
turing Company including dividends. My deceased brother, Matthew. I
am entitled to ½ the Charlton Place at the death of his wife Ann.
Grandson, Milton S. Strain, to go to Washington College. Slaves to be
hired out and if that is not satisfactory, send them to a free state.
Executor: Son David Stephenson. Wit.: Joseph Duncan Senr., Charles
Deakins, David Cunningham.   Signed: John Stephenson

RICHARD CARR   October 17, 1843
Wife, Martha Carr. Children: Susan, Elizabeth, Alfred, James M., Aley,
Levina, Richard Y. Executors: Alfred and James M. Carr. Wit.: Abraham
Saylor, Jonathan Kelly.   Signed: Richard Carr

JOHN C. HARRIS   July 2, 1842
Wife, Sarah and one dependent daughter Sarah Ann H. Harris - all landed
estate on the Cherokee. Drag and Phoebe?, slaves?. Oldest son Michael.
To son Crampton Harris - ¼ acre in town of Jonesborough on which there
was a business shop. $50 to William Dugan. Daughter Mary E. Casson,
sons William H., James, Caleb W. C. Harris - all land from Jonesborough
to Cob Hartsell's. Daughter Miranda Hunter. Son Alexander N. Harris.
Son John E.T. Harris. Joseph Hunter, my son-in-law, cleared the swamp
land. $384 for son Edward's education (John E.T. = Edward). My Library
- medical books. Amputation instruments to go to son Alexander N. if he
practices medecine, if not to go to John E. Cosson and put in his case,
in his shop. Son Alexander N. has been traveling as a minister of the
Methodist Church and may continue, I want him provided for and not be
dependent on the Society. No land cleared next to Jefferson Range and
Mr. Joseph Hunter. Father Ragans grave to be finished and my father and
mothers grave on the old place to be walled as I have directed at the
expense of my estate. The furniture and medicine of the Medicine Shop
to go to C.W.C. Harris, he may use it in practice. Executors: Son
Crampton, son-in-law Joseph Hunter. Wit.: Edward Armstrong, John Blair,
John P. Whistler. Long Codicil - James A. Harris decd. etc. Wit.:
Edmund Armstrong, John Blair, John P. Chester. Probated November Term,
1842.   Signed: J.C. Harris

BENJAMIN DRAIN   October 9, 1840
Wife Rachael. Daughter Jane Boren. Great grandson Henry A. Wilds - my
shot gun. Executors: Wife Rachael, John A. Wilds. Wit.: J.C. Harris,
John Blair, W.K. Blair.   Signed: Benjamin Drain

ANDREW HANNAH   April 30, 1838
Wife Jane. Daughter Esther D. Hannah - bureau I purchased of A.G. Hannah.
Daughter Lucinda F. Hannah. Grandson James Patton. Daughter-in-law Ann
Hannah. Children: Miriam Anderson, Margaret Barkley, Esther D. Hannah,
John D., Lucinda T. Hannah and Amanda D. Telford. Executors: Wife Jane,
Joshua Green, G.W. Telford. Wit.: Jno. Collins, E.L. Mathes. Probated
May Term, 1843.   Signed: Andrew Hannah

JOHN MILLION   February 2, 1842
Wife Sarah. Children: Polly May, my son Edward Million's heirs, son
John Million, dau. Sarah Million - to have land adjoining Joseph Kiker
and Reuben Bayles, Yates and others, 120 acres more or less. Daughter-
in-law Elizabeth Million - $5. Grandson Jacob Million - $5. Executors:
Wife Sarah, son John. Wit.: Adam Sligar, Allen Kyker, Robert Million.
Probated April Term, 1842.   Signed: John (X) Million

JOHN BOWMAN   October 2, 1840
John and Madison to take care of my wife Eve. Katherine Klepper has her
part. To Sarah Zimmerman - $1000 after Jacob gets $400. Mary Highsinger,
Joseph and Isaac Bowman have their part. Rebecca Meads and Daniel Bowman
have their part, so has Benjamin and Samuel Bowman. Executors: Sons
Joseph and John Bowman. Wit.: William D.S. _____, Johnson, Joseph
Bowman. Probated July Term, 1843. Signed: John Bowman

CHANA (CHANCE?) BOREN   April 8, 1834
Wife Jane. Youngest daughter Loretta P. Boren to be educated. To wife,
one secretary, 6 Windsor chairs, large falling leaf table. Daughter
Cyrena C. Wilds, wife of John A. Wilds - ½ tract of land in Washington
County on Brush Creek adjoining Elijah Boren. Daughter Casandra Lyle,
wife of Samuel A. Lyle - land on Sinking Creek with Mill and water.

Daughter Sabrina A. Young, wife of Thomas T. Young - land on Sinking
Creek and another tract where Benjamin Drain lives on Brush Creek.
Daughter Lucinda P. Lyle, wife of John Lyle. Daughter Lauretta P. Boren.
$600 to John Dorsey Boren, grandson of Nicholas Boren. Executors: John
A. Wilds, Abraham Hoss. Wit.: Nicholas Prescutt, Henry Hoss, Abraham
Hoss, Benjamin Drane. Signed: Chance? Boren

ABRAHAM FINE   August 23, 1843
Wife Ann and two little sons. Son David Fine. To 4 daughters, an equal
divide. John and Vinet to have saddle. Executors: David Fine, Wilson
Whitlock. Wit.: Robert H. Parks, Abraham Andes. Proven December Term,
1843. Signed: Abraham Fine

JOHN GOTT
Wife Mary Gott. Executors: Wife Mary and nephew John Gott. Wit.:
Allen Fulkerson, John Madden. Probated May Term, 1843.

JOHN OVERFELT   October 3, 1842
Wife, Susannah, executrix of this will. Wit.: Jacob Douglas, Mary Hats,
Jacob Bacon. Probated February Term, 1843.
Signed: John (X) Overfelt

JOHN WHITLOCK   October 4, 1837
Wife Sarah - note I hold on Gerity West. Children: Elizabeth Robinson,
Polly Cox $40 each, Sallah Cox children $50, Grandson John Cade. Grand-
daughter Nancy Hammonds. Charles Whitlock's daughter, Hannah. Daughter
Katharine's heirs. To son Charles - note on Samuel Cade. To William
Irvin - property I have given him. Executor: Son George Whitlock.
Wit.: Laurence B. Wells, Francis Irwin. Probated August Term, 1843.
Signed: John (X) Whitlock

JOSEPH HALE   July 17, 1843
Son Benjamin - 150 acres adjoining John Kincheloe and Dunham. Daughters
Lucy and Susanna - remainder of land divided. Wife Isabella. Daughter
Louisa, wife of Landon Hale - to live with wife and take care of her.
Daughters: Martha Jackson, Nancy Guess, Mary Billingsley, Ann Hale,
Sarah Billingsly, Susanna Cade. To daughter Marth - 8 acres in Tenn.,
Perry County on southern branch of Coles Creek. Executors: Son Benjamin
Hale and Landon Hale. Wit.: Joseph Crouch, Samuel Sherfy. Probated
March Term, 1844. Codicil - Paid $24 in Western District.
Signed: Joseph (X) Hale

WILLIAM STEVENSON   January 23, 1839
To Jesse Hales Crouch, who married my relation Jemima McGuire - all my
plantation on Fall Branch containing 300 acres. His son, William
Stevenson Crouch, shall have 100 acres of same when he is 21, adjoining
Alexander Whitlock. To Amy Crouch, daughter of Jesse and Jemima -
furniture. Executors: Jesse Hale Crouch, George Crouch. Wit.: John
Blakely, Anson Given, J.K. Crouch. Probated July Term, 1845.
Signed: William Stevenson

JAMES RUSSELL   April 10, 1845
Wife Margaret, To daughter Harriet - my Bible and Hymn Book. To Robert
and John J. Russell - the balance of my books that they may learn to
read and be wise, also to each an ax, maul and wedge that they might go
to work. To daughter Louisa and my 3 youngest children. Executors:
G.W. Nelson and Samuel Conley. Wit.: G.W. Nelson, Henry McCracken,
Jacob Whisler. Probated September Term, 1845.
Signed: James Russell

SINGLETON PRICHETT   October 4, 1845
Sons: John, William Hiter, James. Daughters: Caroline Crouch,
Elizabeth Keys. Two sons Mark M. and Samuel H. Prichett, and Shepherd.
Two daughters Nancy and Emily to have all brick buildings jointly.
Executors: Son Mark, dau. Nancy Prichett. Wit.: Laurence Bowers,
John Crouch, Thomas H. Crouch. Probated November Term, 1845.
                         Signed: Singleton Prichett

ROSANNAH WELCHANCE   July 23, 1843
Son William Welchance - to have everything and be Executor of this my
last will. Wit.: Jacob Hyder, Linville Hunter. Probated November
Term, 1845.   Signed: Rosannah (X) Welchance

JOHN SHERFY   March 31, 1843
Wife Magdalena. My children. Executor: John W. Hoss. Wit.: Joshua
Sherfy, John W. Hoss. Probated January Term, 1846.
                         Signed: John (X) Sherfy

SAMUEL BOWMAN   November 30, 1845
Wife Ann. My part of Grist Mill to be sold. My mother to be and remain
in her room unmolested and supported in a comfortable manner. Executors:
John A. Bowman and Ann Bowman. Wit.: George and James Crouch. Probated
January Term, 1846.   Signed: Samuel Bowman

ADAM HARMON   April 13, 1833
Sons Conrad and Phillip Harmon. Wife Barbara - ¼ of everything. Three
daughters, Susannah, Sally and Elizabeth - to be made equal to daughters
already married. Daughter Margaret Mcheal, 3 sons Jacob, Ira and John -
have received their part. Executrix: Wife Barbara. Wit.: Augustus
Graht, Ira Harmon. Probated June Term, 1844.   his
                         Signed: Adam ᘓ Harmon
                                       mark

JOHN GREEN   June 3, 1844
Sell the place where George T. Hale lives, my farm lying between Olivers
and Montgomery Irvines, my land near Jonesborough rented to John Blair
toward Embreeville, to pay my debts, if that is not sufficient sell land
next to Daniel Kenney where Thomas Leonard now lives. My slaves and
land I purchased of John Kennedy not to be sold. Wife Elizabeth - to
get the Mill Place where we live. Children: Eliza C. Emmerson, George,
Charles, Tolbert, Allen, Mary, Evaline, Thomas and John Green. Minor
children to be supported and educated. Eliza T. Emmersons part to be
given her free and apart from the influence of her husband Thomas B.
Emmerson. If it is legal, she is to take a life estate for her and her
children only. If son Allen is not of a good character, he is to
receive only $25.00. Executors: Wife Elizabeth, George and Charles
Green and Thomas B. Emmerson - they are also guardians of my minor
children. Wit.: Thomas A.R. Nelson, John Keys, Daniel Kenney, Levi
Bowers. Probated July Sessions, 1844.
                         Signed: John Green

GEORGE COCHRAN   June 5, 1844
Wife Rebecca. Children: Nancy Jane King, John, Sarah, Daniel, Franklin,
Samuel, Jacob and Angeline Cochran. Executors: Wife Rebecca, Ebenezer
Barkley. Wit.: Isaac McPherson, James W. Duncan, William McRoberts.
Probated August Term, 1844.   Signed: George Cochran

EZEKIEL LYON   January 1, 1845
Wife Polly Lyon. Children: Samuel E., Wilson, Amanda and Franklin Lyon
are still at home. My youngest sons Wilson and Franklin to receive the
greater portion of my plantation, if their conduct and behavier is good.
Executors: Wife Polly, son Wilson. Wit.: Mark Hale, Samuel E. Lyon.
Probated February Term, 1845.   Signed: Ezekiel (X) Lyon

SARAH BARKLEY   February 7, 1846
Rebecca Cochran to have a note I hold on George Cochran. To Sarah
Cochran, my furniture at Ebenezer Barkley's decd. One other to Delila
Tennessee Barkley. To Sarah Jane Barkley and Emaline Barkley, daughters
of John Barkley. Pay Daniel Barkley a $30 debt I owe him. Pay Jacob C.
Cochran $100 between John, Daniel, Franklin D., Samuel C. Cochran and
Sarah Jane King daughter of Edward King. Sarah Ann Patton, Mary Cameron,
Sarah Jane Bright, Evelina Gammon, Susannah Barkley daughter of Elizabeth
Barkley Kentucky and Sarah Martin daughter of E.S. and Mary Martin.
Executors: Ebenezer Barkley. Wit.: Daniel Barkley, John B. Cochran,
John Barkley. Probated March Term, 1846.
                              Signed: Sarah (X) Barkley

JOHN FORD   April 11, 1838
Wife Susanna. Children: Thomas, Grant, Jonathan, James and John
Washington Ford. Susan Ford - land I purchased from James T. Shipley,
McCracken Tract, David Kitzmiller Tract and William Proffitt Tract.
Single daughters: Elizabeth, Rhoda, Sarah, Franky and Barbara. Grand-
daughter Mary Elender. Married daughters: Mary Ford, Benjamin Ford and
Nancy Brit and James Brit her husband. Executor: Son John Washington
Ford. Teste: David Kitzmiller, James Jackson.
                              Signed: John (X) Ford

WILLIAM WALKER   August 9, 1841
To sife Susannah - $5. To my eldest daughter, Mary Rector, second
daughter Jane Hartman, 3 daughters Nancy Jones, Ann Deakens, Margaret
Hunt - $10. To my youngest daughter Susannah Walker - $75. To Grand-
sons William Rector son of Mary, William Hartman son of Jane, Sam
Deakins son of Ann - I give $10 each. $10 also to William Hunt son of
Margaret. My daughters-in-law Treacy Walker, Mary and Sarah Walker. My
stock of bees. William Walker son of my youngest son Andrew - $10. Wife
Susannah to live with son Andrew Walker. Executors: All my heirs.
Wit.: Caleb Martin, Levi Nelson. Signed: William Walker

JACOB HOLT   February 28, 1846
Wife Elizabeth. Eldest daughter Usley. Son William B. Holt has his
part. Other children. Executors: Equilla Moore, John Hunt. Wit.:
B.F. Swingle, Jacob W. Constable. Proven August Sessions, 1846.
                                     his
                    Signed: Jacob 𝒪 Holt
                                    mark

WILLIAM TEMPLIN
My youngest, Isaac Templin, Executor. Teste: George Reed, William B.
Templin. Probated August Term, 1846.
                              Signed: William (X) Templin

HENRY MARSH   September 20, 1845
Two daughters Elizabeth and Hannah. Son Henry - land I bought of William
Miller. Henry's 3 sons Gravener, William and John. Note on Samuel
Stonecypher - to my grandson Henry Stonecypher. $50 to Elizabeth Stone-
cypher, my daughter Jane Stonecypher. To Samuel Stevens, that now lives
with me - $200. Land facing John Good. My son Jonas, his oldest
children Henry, George and Betsy Ann Marsh, my grandchildren. My sons
Henry, James, Abel, Erasmus, daughter Rebecca Richard, grandson Henry
Richard, daughter Hannah Jones. Executors: 3 sons-in-law: John
Richard, Samuel Stonecypher and Henry Jones. Wit.: Aaron Hammer, Enos
Pickering, Jacob Ellis, Isaac M. Pierce, Jesse Wright. Probated August
Term, 1846.   Signed: Henry Marsh

MARTHA BOWSER   August 7, 1846
Father and mother John and Elizabeth Bowser. Harrison Jones son of
Zachariah and Rhoda Jones. Zachariah and Rhoda Jones to move into house
and take care of father and mother. ½ land to Harrison Bowser, my

brother. Executor: Zachariah Jones. Wit.: Robert G. Hale, Jacob Hale, Vina Carberry. Probated September Term, 1846.

Signed: Martha (X) Bowser

JOHN HALE   July 21, 184_
Wife Elizabeth to have all – at her death it is to go to heirs of John Hale. Wit.: Samuel M. Hunt, Thomas Hale.

Signed: John (X) Hale

ISAAC HENLEY   December 4, 1840
Wife Elizabeth to be equal with my children. Children: Luther R., Jonathan S., Thomas R. Henley, Louisa Brown, Mary Henley, Isaac B. Henley. My mother lives on land adjoining Joshua Henley and Jacob F. Broyles. Executors: Sons Jonathan S. and Thomas R. Henley. See pp 384 and 385 for explanation.

JAMES FORD   January 18, 1845
Two daughters of Grant Ford, namely Elizabeth and Cassy. To Rebecca Ford – 2 tracts of land (130 acres). Wit.: William B. Proffitt, Daniel B. Proffitt. Probated December Term, 1846.

Signed: James ⁓ Ford
his mark

JANE DOAK   September 1, 1840
Sons Archibald A. and James A. Doak – land I bought of William Bonell. Daughters Elizabeth and Mary – $100 each and they are to pay Washington College $25 in current bank notes for the term of 5 years. Executors: 2 sons Archibald A. and James A. Doak. Wit.: William Istran, Joshua Green, Nancy M. Earnest. Probated September Term, 1849.

Signed: Jane Doak

CATHARINE MILLER   November 9, 1842
Beloved son-in-law and daughter Sell shall have my property. Executor: James White. Wit.: John Longmire, George Crouch, Massy Sell. Probated November Term, 1848.   Signed: Catharine (X) Miller

BENJAMIN McLIN   April 13, 1843
To my brother, Richard McLin, all my real and personal estate and be my Executor. Wit.: Jonathan Rush, William B. Rush, George N. Rush. Probated February Term, 1849.   Signed: Benjamin McLin

ELIZABETH AIKEN   June 15, 1843
Granddaughter Evalina Brackett. Adelaide Gammon formerly Adelaide Aiken. To my sister Margaret Deaderick. Executor: My nephew John F. Deaderick. Wit.: James W. Deaderick, Rebecca Deaderick. Probated February Term, 1848.   Signed: Elizabeth Aiken

JAMES SEVIER   November 18, 1843
Elbert – to have my clock. Elbridge – desk and large glasses. Elizabeth Johnston – the large drawers. Minerva – the two tables. Mary – small falling leaf table. Louisa – the soup ladle. Mary E. Jones – a set of tea spoons. Rowena Sevier – teaspoons. Clariss, Louisa and Mary – 2 large spoons each. Ann E. Jones – a bedstead. Jane Stuart – a bedstead. Catharine Ann Jarvis – bedstead. Sarah Lewis Sr. – bedstead. Ann Stuart – bureau her grandmother gave her. Sarah Meek – small bedstead. Sarah Hale – bed curtains. Nothing in the house is to be sold but parceled out to girls by Elbert and Mr. A.H. Jones. Elbert and James H. Jones will sell property. Pay $100 debt to Alexander M. Nelson and O.H. Jones note. September 7, 1844. Probated February Term, 1847.

Signed: Jas. Sevier

THOMAS EDWARDS   March 21, 1844
Wife Elizabeth. Two daughters Mary and Matilda - saddle and bridle each.
Executors: My esteemed son-in-law M.T. Erwin Esq. and son John Edwards.
Wit.: George Tilson, Samuel W. Bogart. Probated July Term, 1849.
                          Signed: Thomas (X) Edwards

JONATHAN BARCROFT   July 6, 1844
Wife Jane. Children: Jane, Ambrose, Elizabeth and Martha Barcroft.
Grandson Ambrose Bell, son of John and Aily Bell - $300. Daughter Mary
Cowan - ½ land in Greene County. Executors: Daus. Jane and Martha
Barcroft. Wit.: Isaac McPherson, James W. Duncan, Samuel D. Powell.
Probated August Term, 1849.   Signed: Jonathan Barcroft

THOMAS R. KENNEDY   July 5, 1847
Wife Harriet - to have 1/3 during her life. Other 2/3 to be divided
equally between my 2 children Margaret and Charles A. when they come of
age. Executors: John Ryland, William K. Blair. Wit.: Thomas R.
Chester, Daniel Kenney. Proven August Sessions, 1847.
                          Signed: T.R. Kennedy

ROLAND HODGES   September 1, 1845
Wife Hannah. Son James, dau. Susannah Allison, dau. Elinor Allison decd.
daughters Elinor, Polly and Susannah have received $700 each. Executor:
Son James. Wit.: John Bowman, Madison M. Bowman.
                          Signed: Roland (X) Hodges

LEWIS JORDAN   January 31, 1845
Sons: Archibald A., Lewis W., Lewis. Daughter Sera, son Samuel A.,
dau. Mary Stephenson, dau. Malinda Patton, granddaughter Mary Jane Patton.
Archibald A. Jordans 3 daughters: Mary, Adelaide and Eliza. Son Samuel
A.'s oldest dau. Mary. Stepson James Trimble. Sold land in West Tenn.
to my son John. All heirs to receive slaves. Executor: E.L. Mathes.
Wit.: Josiah W. Earnest, Henry McCracken. Probated September Term, 1847.
                          Signed: Lewis Jordan

MICHAEL GARBER   May 18, 1846
Children: Samuel, Catharine, Jacob, Grandchildren Catharine and Michael
Sellers children of David and Nancy Sellers, Elizabeth wife of John Neal,
Solomon Garber, Easter Hilbert wife of Jacob Hilbert, Abram Garber.
Executors: Jacob Hilbert, Jacob Garber. Wit.: Daniel Frances, Young
Bayles. Probated May Term, 1847.   Signed: Michael Garber

MAGDALENAH SHERFEY   November 26, 1846
Stepson Joshua Sherfey. To Aley and Nancy Sherfey, infant daughters of
Joshua. Note of John Crowe for $10. I give my cloak to Sarah, wife of
Joshua. Executor: John Hoss. Wit.: Eliza Ann Taylor, Levi Wilson,
Sarah Wilson. Probated April Term, 1847.
                          Signed: Magdalenah (X) Sherfey

DARLING JONES   June 13, 1846
Five last sons by my last wife, Nancy Jones: Darling, Lewis, William,
Henry, Isaac and Alfred. Land adjoining Joseph Birch. Children to be
educated. Executors: D.R. Kinnick, Abraham Hoss. Wit.: D.R. Kinnick,
James Harrington, Alfred Carr. Probated February Term, 1849. (Henry
by first wife? - G.F.B.)   Signed: Darling (X) Jones

ELIZABETH BOWMAN   August 2, 1846
I bequeath to: David, Elias, George & John Bowman, Mary Calvert, Barbary
McConnel & Elizabeth Simpson - each $1. To Maria Smith - all personal
property and my real estate. Executor: John T. Smith. Wit.: Wiley
Tucker, James Smith. Probated June Term, 1847.
                          Signed: Elizabeth (X) Smith

ABRAHAM MAUK   September 28, 1846
To 3 sons Montgomery, Jacob & Embree Mauk - my interest in mill and forge
where James M. Mauk now lives, bought from Julius Broyles. Executors:
James M. Mauk, W.H. Smith. Wit.: Thomas M. McAdams, Samuel K. Bitner,
George Copp. Probated July Term, 1847.
                                     Signed: Abraham Mauk

THOMAS BELL   September 11, 1846
Wife Elizabeth - all my land, stock, farming utinsils, household and
kitchen furniture, all crops in ground, grain in bins, cash, notes and
accounts. My niece Mary Emily Ferguson, whom I have raised from child-
hood, is to support and care for my wife Elizabeth - at Elizabeth's
death to receive everything. Executor: Robert F. Ferguson. Wit.:
William Smith, John H. Carr. Probated February Term, 1848.

WILLIAM T. ENSOR   December 4, 1847
Wife Martha - to have use of everything and at her death her wearing
clothes to go to her daughters. To Sara Honeycut - a horse beast. To
Martha Cunningham - $50 in good trade. William B. Ensor Jr. and Thomas
P. Ensor - 212 acres on Stage Road - Jonesborough to Blountville. Land
adjoining William Hale and Edmond Hodges. George W. Ensor, my grandson,
to have an equal share with William Beedles children, I have raised him
from 6 weeks old. William Beedles to have a bedstead painted red,
gunstock made by Mr. Gross, gunsmith of Sullivan County. Executor:
Thomas P. Ensor, my son. Wit.: Hiram D. Hale Esq., William Hale.
Probated April Term, 1847.   Signed: William T. Ensor Senr.

IRA GREEN   December 21, 1847
Wife Mary and single daughters: Amanda E. and Malinda J.H. Green. Sell
75 acres land in Greene County, south of Chucky River on which I gave a
Deed of Trust to Peter Earnest and sons to pay this debt and other debts.
Land adjoins Lawrence Glaze and Jacob Reser. Sell several entries in
Greene and Washington Counties to pay debts. Children: Rosannah
McRoberts, J.N. and R.B. Green, Susannah Zimmerman, Adam B., Amanda &
Malinda J.H. Green. At the death of Adam Broyles Senior, if my Executor
thinks it to the interest of my estate, check an agreement between him
and the heirs of Reuben Broyles and if proper, prosecute a suit and pay
for prosecution from my estate. Executor: Son-in-law William McRoberts.
Wit.: Jacob Neff, G.W. Telford. Codicil - I received parts of well.
Probated June Term, 1847.   Signed: Ira Green

JOHN M. BRABSON   September 11, 1847
Wife Mary S. Brabson, Brothers: Alexander W. & Alfred Brabson - to
convey to Alfred 700 acres, jointly owned adjoining William Haws, Joseph
Royston, John Biddle, William Lunly and others. Wife to sell and buy
near a school where my children can be educated. My 3 children: Samuel
Powell Brabson, Alexander Crutchfield Brabson and Oscar? Brabson and an
unborn infant. Executrix: Wife Mary. Wit.: Brookins Campbell,
William Pierce. Probated May Term, 1848.
                                     Signed: John M. Brabson

CHRISTIAN ZETTY   July 1, 1847
Wife Jane - a childs part. Children: Daniel Kenney Zetty, Sarah Zetty.
To Daniel - a mare in possession of Christian Boyles. Youngest daughter
Catharine. Sell land and pay Wyland Barger $600, $150 to John B. Blair
to be collected and paid on my debts. Executors: Wyland Barger, Daniel
Brubaker. Wit.: Brokins Campbell, Jesse Hunt, John Neal. Proven
August Sessions, 1847.   Signed: Christian Zetty

JESSE MULKEY   November 16, 1847
$10 to Baptist Foreign Missionary Society. Put rest of money on interest
for my daughter Sarah Elizabeth Mulkey. My other cash and interest in my
father's estate - daughter Sarah Elizabeth. My mother to get my bed and

46

bedding. My fur hat and debts coming to me - to my father. My saddle -
to brother Hiram Mulkey. My overcoat to Howard Mulkey. Two brothers
Philip and Robert Mulkey. Executors: Isaac Mulkey, Jesse Riggs. Wit.:
R.J. Furgason, Henry Keephaver, John Keephaver. Probated February Term,
1848.   Signed: Jesse Mulkey

FREDERICK DEVAULT   July 23, 1847
Son Henry $2500 - $1000 has been paid 3 Sept. 1832, also the same to
Peter Davault. Daughter Mary Anne wife of James W. Duncan. Daughter
Catharine wife of A.H. Crawford. Sons: David - $1800, Samuel - $3000,
and dau. Louisa - $1600 cash. Son John. To wife Peggy - $15.00 in cash
which is due me in Pennsylvania for her spending money. Executors: Son
John Davault, William McRoberts. Wit.: Samuel Y. Wyley, Josiah Stuart,
Walter J. Chase. Probated September Term, 1847.
                                   Signed: Frederick Davault

JAMES S. JOHNSTON   December 31, 1847
Wife Elizabeth C. Johnston - to be Executrix and emancipate our colored
people at her decease. Wit.: William R. Sevier, John Hunt. Probated
February Term, 1848.   Signed: James S. Johnston

JANE HANNAH   January 7, 1845
Two daughters Esther and Lucinda - what was left me by my husband, Andrew
Hannah decd. Grandsons William Hannah, Andrew Hannah. Daughter-in-law
Ann Hannah. Daughter Margaret Barkley. Executor: G.W. Telford. Wit.:
Joshua Green, Willie W. Green. Probated May Term, 1847.
                                   Signed: Jane (X) Hannah

ABRAHAM MILLER   February 12, 1847
To William Elija Miller and my dau. Sarah Jane Miller - $20 each for
their use by their guardian. Eight children: Elizabeth, Martha, Peggy
Ann, James A., Daniel Y., Polly, Sarah Jane and William Elija Miller.
Executor: Son Daniel Y. Miller. Wit.: William P. Reeves, Alfred Carr,
Peter M. Reeves. Probated April Term, 1847.
                                   Signed: Abraham Miller

CANDAY HALE   June 21, 1848
Children: Richard, Elizabeth, D. Malindy, Sarah, Hannah Jordan Elbert,
Jane and the heirs of my daughter Darcus (Samuel, Franklin, Darcus &
Hobart). Executor: My son Jordan Elbert Hale. Wit.: Hiram D. Hale,
Benjamin Shipley. Proven July Term, 1849.   her
                                   Signed: Canday (X) Hale
                                                     mark

JANE BOREN   July 31, 1847
My mother. John H. Wilds to be paid for services of his black boy.
James Edmunds my grandson. My daughters: Carolina, Cassandra, Sabrina
and Lucinda - $1 each. Daughter Loretta - horses, sheep, hogs and grain.
Executors: John E. Cosson, John A. Wild. Wit.: John E. Cosson, J.C.T.
Harris. Probated September Term, 1847.
                                   Signed: Jane (X) Boren

ELIJAH FINE   April 21, 1848
Wife Barbara. Executors: Wife Barbara, Elisha Fine. Wit.: W.H. Smith,
G.W. Willet, Daniel Kenny. Probated September Term, 1848.
                                   Signed: Elijah Fine

THOMAS FERGUSON   January 19, 1848
Sons: Henry, Robert S. Ferguson - if one owes the other, balance it.
Daughter Elizabeth Bell. My slaves divided among my children and set
free when they are 28 years old. Granddaughter Mary Emily Ferguson -

$200. Executors: 2 sons Henry and Robert Ferguson. Wit.: Michael Dashor, James F.D. Sherfey, Jesse Wilcoxen. Probated February Term, 1848.   Signed: Thomas Ferguson

DAVID STEPHENSON   January 19, 1849
My Executors to make sale of all my fathers real estate which I was authorized to sell. I'm in a mercantile business in Jonesborough styled Stephenson, Dosser and Wilds. Wilds is slightly involved and about to retire. I want the business then to be Stephenson & Dosser until 1 Sept. 1849 - give James H. Dosser full power and authority to carry on should I die before that date. On Sep. 1, 1849 the business is to be closed and a division made. I am in a business in Leesburg in partners with James H. Dosser and Walter J. Chase - it is to cease May 1, 1849. If my Executors think best, continue the operation. To nephew William J. Strain - a gun I got of my father. All my estate to go to my four sisters: Martha A. Strain, Cynthia McAdams, Mary A. Wyly, Emily H. Mitchell. Brother-in-law Jonathan C. Mitchell. Executors: Jonathan C. Mitchell, Thomas C. McAdams. Wit.: Seth J.W. Lucky, D.F. Wilds. Probated February Term, 1849.   Signed: David Stephenson

RICHARD GREENWAY   March 7, 1849
Wife Sally. Son Pleasant. Hire slaves out and use money for my wife and to school my children. Six daughters: Eliza Jordan, Lettice E. Greenway, Sally Ann McCracken, Mary E. Greenway, Susan M. Greenway & Matilda E. Greenway. To my son Pleasant W.C. Greenway - a farm known as the Charley Graham place with a few acres I purchased from William Middleton. Executors: Wife Sally, son Pleasant, brother Jesse H. Greenway. Probate August Term, 1849.   Signed: Richard Greenway

JOHN WHITLOCK   July 13, 1849
Wife Rebecca - 15 acres including house where Jesse Jobe now lives adjoining Jefferson Ingle and William Crouch. To son Thomas - young mare, saddle and bridle worth $25. To daughter Unicy Whitlock - bed and furniture, a calf, 4 sheep and $25. All my children: George, William, Elizabeth, Johnson, John, Nancy, James, Thomas & Unicy. Executor: Son George Whitlock. Wit.: E.W. Headrick, James Wright, Thomas Porter. Probated December Term, 1849.   Signed: John Whitlock

HENRY SLAGLE   September 10, 1849
Wife Elizabeth. Three children, not named. Executor: Dr. Thomas T. Young. Wit.: John Howard, Thomas Leonard. Probated November and December Terms, 1849.   Signed: Henry (X) Slagle

DAVID MAINS   November 19, 1849
Wife Mary. My heirs (not named). Executors: Hiram Mains, J.M. Grimsley Wit.: Jacob B. Bacon, Henry Hale, William White, John Crouch. Probated December Term, 1849.   Signed: David (X) Mains

JOHN W. BROWN   December 1, 1849
Wife Margaret - 200 acres including buildings and spring, up Snapp's Ferry Road. Nine daughters: Mandy, Mary Ann, Elizabeth, Sary, Martha White, Nervy Jane, Clarissa, Liza, Elvira. To son William - 100 acres adjoining Leneas B. Brown on Snapps Ferry to Jonesborough Road. To son George - 100 acres when he is 21. Executor: Joseph Crouch. Wit.: Archibald G. Register, James Barding. Probated (date not given). Signed: John W. Brown

SUSANNAH CAMPBELL
Daughter Fidelia Campbell - $500 in 3 years after my decease. Daughter Sarah and John Carson her husband - $500 in 3 years after my decease, to their Mary Susan $50 when she is 15 years old. Daughter Mary and her husband Joseph Carson - $500, their Hugh Campbell Carson when he is 21.

Daughter Margaret and her husband Edward R. Carson - $400, their son
Andrew Carson - $100, and their dau. Susannah - $50. To grandson John
Smith Haws son of Nancy - $100. To my son James Campbell - land I
inherited from my husband Hugh Campbell. To son Brookins - $300. To
my children - my interest in the landed estate of my father James
McWhorter at the decease of his wife Elizabeth, which I may lawfully
inherit. Executor: Son James Campbell. Wit.: Francis Robertson,
William R. Sehorn?. Probated _____ Term, 1850.
                          Signed: Susanna Campbell

JOHN HUNTER   February 24, 1850
Sell slaves to pay debts. Wife Mary. Two eldest sons: Montgomery C.
and William B. Hunter, Elizabeth Ann McLin, Amanda R. Lady, T.E.R.
Hunter, Jane P. Hunter, Dorcas G. Hunter, Margaret M. and Henry H.
Hunter. If either or both of my sons, Thomas and Henry, wish a
Collegiate Education, my Executors and 2 oldest sons to provide for it
and take expense out of their part of my estate. Executors: Wife Mary
Hunter, son Montgomery Hunter. Wit.: Henry E. Ruble, G.W. Telford.
Probated May Term,' 1850.   Signed: John (X) Hunter

JOHN KELSAY   April 21, 1849
Three sons: Samuel, Robert & David - have all my real estate and pay my
2 daughters Nancy? Odell and Marget Rink - $100 each. Sara Ann Bayles -
$2. John Kelsey - $10 and William Kelsey - $2. Executors: Samuel
Kelsay & Henry McCracken. Wit.: Charles Sullenbarger, Solomon Garber.
Probated March Term, 1850.   Signed: John Kelsey

JOHN KORTY   April 24, 1850
To daughter Emaline Slaten - all real estate, lots in Leesburg. To
heirs of my son Martin Korty decd. - $1. Executor: Edmund Ellis.
Wit.: Samuel Conley, Samuel Y. Wyly. Probated May Term, 1850.
                          Signed: John Kortz

ELIZA ANN HALL   August 13, 1850
Margaret Hall - 1 bed & bedding, drawer, 2 chairs, cow & calf. Elizabeth,
a black girl - 1 bed & bedding. Thomas Hall's dau. Eliza - one saddle &
a calf. My brother James Hall - to have all other property & pay all
debts. Executor: _____. Wit.: Hiram D. Hale Esq., John Gamble.
Probated September Term, 1850.   Signed: Eliza Ann (X) Hale

JOSEPH BOWMAN   August 18, 1850
Wife Christena. Two youngest sons, David & Joseph - to support wife and
when she dies, bury her decently where I was buried. My oldest daughter
Susannah Crouch - land where she lives, her husband James Crouch. Oldest
son John H. - to have no more as I have given to him. To Elizabeth wife
of Henry Basher - no more. Third daughter Mary Ghant - $450. Second
son Daniel - no more. Fourth daughter Catharine Lear and husband John
Lear - $450. I paid a debt of $600 for David Lear father of John. My
fifth and youngest daughter Sarah Bowman - $500 in cash and personal
property. Brother Jacob Bowman - to have food and raiment. Settlements
to be made with Henry Bashor, Henry Ghant, John Lear. Executors: John
H. Bowman, John Lear. Wit.: Christian Wine, Peter M. Reeves, Abraham
Ross. Probated September Term, 1850.
                          Signed: Joseph Bowman

EDWARD WEST   April 2, 1842
Children: Thomas, Richard, Samuel, West decd. heirs, Edmund Humphreys,
Ann Clark, Mark, Elizabeth Looney, Jentsey and Joseph West. All real
and personal estate to be divided among the above named. I have hereto-
fore emancipated several slaves. Now my colored man, Airy, is to get:
1 horse, $50 cash, plow, hoe, straw beds in kitchen, 5 acre entry on the
ridge adjoining Joseph West and James Jones. Purchase land for freed
slaves in state of Ohio. Executors: Edward West, John Humphreys.

Wit.: William Slemons, Robert McKee, A.E. Jackson.
Signed: Edward West

HENRY HALE   October 1, 1850
Wife Harriet. Children: Martha, Sarah & Harriet Hale my granddaughter.
Smith H. Hale, Joseph L. and Finley Hale, my 3 younger sons, who may
assist their mother in managing the estate and affairs of the farm. Six
remaining children above. Sons William K. & Franklin D. Hale are already
provided for. All seven children & Harriet my grandchild to share alike.
Son-in-law Jackson Hale to be charged for my keeping Harriet, my grand-
child. Daughter Mary Beard - provided for. I gave son Franklin $500
when he went West. Executors: William K. Hale, Joseph Hale & wife
Harriett. Wit.: Samuel B. Cunningham, Mark Hale, Henry Hale, Archibald
Hale. Probated November Term, 1850.
Signed: Henry Hale

MICHAEL KROUSE   February 22, 1851
Wife Catharine. Son Michael - 100 acres adjoining Young grandson
William T. Krouse. Daughter Susanna Larmon - to be made even with
other heirs. Executor: Son Daniel Krouse. Wit.: George Crouch,
Austin Hyller, Henry Swadly, Michael Krouse. Probated March Term, 1851.
Signed: Michael Krause

JOHN WHITLOCK   May 19, 1851
Five sons: Edmund, James M., William K., Paten B. & Elven Whitlock - to
have all land equally. Daughters: Mary Comwell, Sarah Humphrey, Nancy
Proffitt, Margaret Proffitt & Louisa Wolf - to have all money from sale
of personal property including my black boy, Lee. Executors: Edmun &
Paten B. Whitlock. Wit.: Jesse Riggs, James Kincheloe. Probated
December Term, 1851.
Signed: John Whitlock

NICHOLAS CHINOWTH   January 6, 1850
Wife _____. Sons Nicholas H. & Richard - to have land adjoining William
Ellis and Widow Hale. The H. Milhorn tract of land to be sold and the
money divided between my daughters: Elizabeth Chinowth, Agnes Gray &
Ruth Gray. Ruthaw Henry Preston and John Addison Chinowth, heirs of
John Chenowth - $50 each. Archibald Chenowth living in Kentucky - $150.
Two sons Joseph & Henry have $10 each. Executor: Nicholas H. Chinowth.
Wit.: Jacob Douglas, Ezekiel R. Chinowth, George W. Gray.
Signed: Nicholas (X) Chinowth

ELBERT L. EMBREE   March 18, 1851
To Elihu, Mary Elizabeth & Susan Marie Embree, minor children of my
cousin Charles Embree decd. - $100 each for their schooling. I give
Thomas J. Wilson - all left over, he has cared for me. Executor:
Thomas J. Wilson. Wit.: John Keys, A.N. Harris. Probated April Term,
1851.
Signed: Elbert S. Embree

GEORGE JACKSON   January 25, 1850
To my son George Jackson - all land and tenements by his paying other
heirs $75 each. Elizabeth Jackson, my daughter - half the household
belongings and $25. All my children: Rachel Bacon, Dorcas Bacon, Lear
Bacon, Jemima Bacon, Hannah Conken, Elizabeth Jackson, William, Laban &
George Jackson - my 4 sons. Executor: George Jackson. Wit.: Young
Douglass, Chase Hale, William B.C. Jackson. Probated August Term, 1851.
Signed: George (X) Jackson

THOMAS A.R. WALDRON   May 2, 1851
Wife Margaret A.B. Waldren. Son Milton A. Waldron. My sister Caroline
and child of my brother Franklin. If anything left after death of my
wife and sons, use it for tombstones and Misshonary cause of Methodist
and Baptist Church. Executors: Wife Margaret & William Read. Wit.:

William Read, Hiram Glass. Probated August Term, 1851.
Signed: Thomas A.R. Waldren

JAMES McALISTER   April 18, 1850
Wife Susan. Son Samuel R. - horse and plantation where I now live, after
his mother's death. $1 to daughters Frances Murray and Eliza R. Harper.
To daughter Louisa Crockett - my negro Polly and her son Alex. Money for
education of James McAlister. Daughters Eleanor R. King, Margaret C.
McAlister. Notes of Miller or Millard of Sullivan County. Note on A.A.
Broyles. Executors: George W. Telford, E.L. Mathes. Wit.: Pleasant
W.C. Greenway, Samuel G. McCracken. Probated December Term 1851.
Signed: James McAlister

MARY WILCOX   February 27, 1851
To four children of my brother, Abram Bayles decd.: William E., Eleanor
Valentine, Mary Louisiana & Susan Baylis. Executor: Samuel B. Cuming.
Wit.: A.E. Jackson, James E. Murphey.
Signed: Mary (X) Wilcox

   Codicil. 3 gold rings, 2 breast pins, $2.50 gold piece, pocketbook,
2 silk shawls, silk dress, ribbon and beads, 2 gingham dresses, cashmere
shawl and a gingham apron to be kept by my Executor and later given to
my heirs mentioned above. My calico dresses, skirts and capes to Sabray
Smith, my friend. Wit.: Robert Blair, Hosea Hishaw. Probated April
Term, 1851.
Signed: Mary (X) Wilcox

SAMUEL HUNT   June 21, 1848
Wife Sarah. Sons: Franklin, James, William, John B. Hunt. Grandsons:
Samuel son of William, John son of Joseph decd. Executrix: Wife Sarah.
Wit.: Peter M. Reeves, James W. Deaderick. Probated _____.
Signed: Samuel Hunt

SARAH HUNT   August 3, 1852
Sons: Samuel - $400, James S. - ½ note given me by my husband Samuel
Hunt decd. on William H. Crouch. To sons: Franklin, James S. & Samuel
Hunt. Executor: Son Samuel Hunt. Wit.: W.H. Smith, Peter Miller.
Probated _____.
Signed: Sarah (X) Hunt

THOMAS GIBSON   March 29, 1852
Wife Sarah. Son William - land on Baire Hill. Son Boswell - land near
Pearce Spring. Daughter Permicy - land adjoining Boswell. Daughter
Minervy - land adjoining William. To daughter Elizabeth Gibson - the
remainder of land including buildings. Two sons Pleasant & Caswell -
land on Brush Creek adjoining Henry King and Henry Bashore. Executor:
Vincent Boring?. Wit.: James M. Sellars, Boswell Gibson.
Signed: Thomas Gibson

JONAH KEENE   December 28, 1846
Youngest son Robert A. Keene, Joseph Keene - 50 acres adjoining John W.
Coxe. Son R.A. Keene - to live with and provide for me and by my Exec.
Wit.: Thomas Fulkerson, William H. Wood.
Signed: Jonah Keene

MOSES W. CARSON   No date
Wife Margaret. Children: Jane Barger - $50, Synthy Crawford - $50, 3
youngest daughters Elizabeth D., Martha Margaret & Visian Carson - the
Wyly Barger farm which I purchased from him and Daniel Brubaker as
Executors of Christian Zetty decd. Two oldest daughters Jane & Sinthy.
Son Alexander - the plantation where I now live. Note on John P. Lane
& Company - $500. To John R. Carson - $100 in Railroad Stock. My still
and utencils. Note on William Clack. Executors: John P. Carson and
Alexander H. Carson. Wit.: James Campbell, Allen H. Gillespie. No
date or probate.
Signed: M.W. Carson

51

EPHRAIM FRANCES   April 10, 1852
Wife Ann. Six last children: Franklin, Thomas, Myrantha, Mariah, son
Manooth?, Daniel. Executors: Thomas Francis, Ann Francis. Wit.:
William Cassidy, Daniel Francis.   Signed: Ephraim (X) Francis

JOHN CANNON   July 30, 1852
Wife Elizabeth Cannon. Two sons: Elbert S. & William Cannon. Son
George. Daughters: Martha J. Cannon, Mary A. Cannon, Matilda Broyles.
Executor: George Cannon. Wit.: John C. Burgner, John Good.
                              Signed: John (X) Cannon

SAMUEL MAXWELL   September 13, 1852
Daughter Rebecca A.E. Drinnell - 1/3 my estate. Son William Henry
Maxwell - to have remaining 2/3 of my estate. Samuel G. Maxwell.
Negroes to be emancipated. Grandchildren: Albert, Hester, Grayson
& Catharine Allen, children of Samuel - hogs, cattle etc. for their
support. Daughter Jane is excluded. Grandson Samuel Allen does not
need it. Executor: Son William. Wit.: William R. Sevier, John
Dunlap.   Signed: Samuel Maxwell

PETER JACKSON   September 20, 1852
Two sons: John W. & George W. Jackson. Two daughters: Sarah & Icy?
Jackson. Executor: John W. Jackson. Wit.: Samuel W. Barnes, Jonathan
Bacon, John Cox.   Signed: Peter (X) Jackson

POLLY ANN CONLY   January 19, 1842
Sell my 500 acre farm on waters of Limestone adjoining Thomas McAdams,
R.A. Thompson, John Martin - husband, Josiah Conly, to use proceeds from
interest on minor heirs part to provide for them. All children to share
equal. Executors: My husband & son Robert A. Conly. Wit.: David
Stuart, R.A. Russell, Amanda Davault, Samuel Conly.
                              Signed: Polly (X) Ann Conly

SUSANNA McNUT   February 3, 1853
Sister Elizabeth, who is insane - all my portion of my Father's estate,
put in hands of R.S. Ferguson who has taken care of father, mother,
brother and sister and myself for 14 or 15 years. R.S. Ferguson is my
cousin. To Sarah Ferguson, daughter of Benjamin - my red silk dress.
To Cynthia Jane Ferguson - my green silk dress and delph dish. Father's
Bible to go to Thomas P. Ferguson, son of R.S. Ferguson. Take care of
my sister. Executor: R.S. Ferguson. Wit.: Mattie Osbourn, W.R.
Sevier.   her
                    Signed: Susannah ⌐ McNut
                                         mark

SAMUEL TEMPLIN   December 21, 1852
Two sons: Benjamin & Jimmy. Two others. Executors: James Mauk and
Benjamin F. Templin. Wit.: George Reed, Jacob G. Brown.
                              Signed: Sam Templin

JOHN KINCHELOE   December 21, 1852
Wife Sarah - my yellow girl Harriet. Oldest daughter Mary Hunt and her
bodily heirs - 61 acres I bought of Benjamin Hale. Mary's husband Uriah
Hunt may for a wright to land. Youngest daughter Clary Jones - the
Nicholas Hale tract. Youngest son James Kincheloe - 100 acres of the
homeplace. Son Enos - 100 acres adjoining tract he got of George
Kincheloe. Daughter Elizabeth Keese - to have an equal part. To John
Hale, if he stays with his grandmother - a horse, saddle and $18.
Minerva Hale - cow and calf. Railroad stock to be divided among my
heirs. Executors: Enos & James Kincheloe. Wit.: R.L. Stanford, B.
Ballenger.   Signed: John Kincheloe

JOSHUA GREENE   April 28, 1853
Wife Susan. Son William W. Green - to have 15 acres where he lives, he
has done my blacksmith work for twelve years without pay. Executor: son
James R. Green. Teste: E.L. Mathes, William Payne.
                         Signed: Joshua Green

HENRY DIEL   February 9, 1853
Wife Margaret. My Executor to sell my estate not given my wife and pay
debt I owe Dew Deaderick + a $30. Pay all my debts. Buy a lot of land
to enable my wife to raise and school my 2 children. Executor: G.W.
Nelson. Wit.: John Fillups, Jane Beddel.
                         Signed: Henry Diel

POLLY CORNWELL   July 30, 1853
To my sons Milton, John & Paten Cornwell - $10 each. Money from my
fathers estate to my 3 youngest children: Elizabeth, Martin Van Buren
and Sarah Cornwell. Executors: My brother Edmund Whitlock & James
Kincheloe. Teste: Chase Hale, James Kincheloe.
                         Signed: Polly (X) Cornwell

PHEBE MATHES   February 7, 1854
Children: E.E. Mathes & Susan Mathes. Granddaughter Phebe Mathes (of
Susan) - a feather bed. To granddaughter Phoebe Wilson - a feather bed.
Executor: E.E. Mathes. Teste: E.E. Mathes, Alex M. Wilson.
                         Signed: Phoebe (X) Mathes

JOHN STUART   September 3, 1853
Wife Ann Stuart - 1 slave. Children: David - ½ share, Robert - 1 share,
Mary Russell - 1 share, John - 1 share, Josiah - 1 share, James - 1 share.
To Emily Stuart, daughter of my son William - 1 share. Executors: John
T. Smith, Josiah Conley. Teste: J.D. Gibson, M.B. Stuart, John T.
Smith, Josiah Conly.   Signed: John Stuart

DANIEL BARKLEY   January 20, 1854
Wife Margaret - to be cared for by son Jacob Barkley. Land adjoins
Blair, William S. Barkley, Maxwell. Wife to receive 50 lb. coffee, 100
lbs. sugar. Sons Andrew H. & Jacob E. Barkley. Son John decd. - $600
and I sent $20 to Missouri when he died to pay on land, he had one child.
To son Ebenezer M. Barkley - $450. To daughter Susan Bright - $640, her
husband William Bright. Daughter Sarah Patton - $800, her husband
James Patton. Son Daniel - $700. To daughter Jane and her husband
Elisha B. Meade -. $600. To son Andrew H. - my black girl "Fanny".
Daughter Margaret and her husband James H. Blair - $700. Executors: My
3 sons Daniel B., Andrew H. & Jacob C. Barkley. Teste: Samuel B.
Cunningham, D.J. Gibson, Ebenezer Barkley.
                         Signed: Daniel Barkley

JOHN HOWARD   March 2, 1832
Wife Elizabeth. Son Adam M. - 28 acres adjoining Mordecai Price. Son
William W. Howard, dau. Permela Adalade Howard, son Ira Howard. Rest of
our children got their part. Executor: Dr. Thomas J. Young. Teste:
Young Bayles, Joseph D. Price.
                         Signed: John Howard

     Codicil - To daughter Nancy Susanner - 2 stands bees. Daughter
Elizabeth - 2 stands bees, her dau. Martha - fine table cloth. To my
son Abner - 1 clay bank mare. To daughter Permelia Swanson - 2 stands
bees, book Living Oracles. To son William Howard - 1 bay mare and
Guiness Medical Book. My grindstone and augers to be left on my farm in
Illinois - to be sold by Elkanah Howard. The next draw due me of my
pension money. Teste: J.D. Price, M. Price.

NANCY CONLY   May 29, 1851
Son Samuel Conly - fifty dollar note with interest executed to Josiah
Conly and signed over to me. To son Josiah. Black woman "Harriet" to
be set free in 15 years. Black boy "Frank" to be free in 2 years.
Joseph Conly son of Samuel Conly. Executors: Samuel & Josiah Conley.
Test: John F. Smith, John Stuart. Signed: Nancy (X) Conly

HIRAM GLASS   Non Cupative
Wife Sarah - to receive remainder after debts are paid. Wit.: W. Read,
John McCracken.

VALENTINE BOLTON   March 28, 1854
To wife Magdalena & son John Bolton - the plantation I purchased of my
son Henry Bolton. John to pay my sons Henry & Daniel Bolton - $300 each.
To son Valentine - land where he lives. Executor: Son Daniel Bolton.
Test: E.L. Mathes, John Pence. Proven June Sessions, 1854.
                        Signed: Valentine Bolton

PHILIP PARKS   March 22, 1834
Children: Philip, Elizabeth wife of John Booth, Nelly Nelson, Nancy
Tinker, Robert Parks, William Parks, Sarah White, Katharine Andes,
Rebecca - $50 each. Tilda Jane Freeman is supposed to be daughter of
my son John Parks, decd. - $100. My son Philip Parks - $50 and the
value of a mule retained by Samuel Erwin's wife Mary Irwin, my dau.
Executor: Son Philip. Test: George Reel, Joseph Howell. Probated
June Term, 1854.   Signed: Philip (X) Parks

NICHOLAS KEEFHAVER   March 3, 1831
Wife Catharine. Daughter Elizabeth - $640. Heirs of Henry Keefhaver,
decd., where he lived adjoining James Duncan and James Keebler. To son
Nicholas - land adjoining Hampton and Bacon, at my wife's death.
Elizabeth Orrick?. Executor: Son Nicholas Keefhaver. Test: ?
Probated July Term, 1854.   Signed: Nicholas Keefhaver

NANCY ROCK   July 9, 1841
Jane Dickson - pots, pans. Nancy Combs. Nancy Jane Combs. Margaritha
Dickson - a coverlid. Catharine Combs - quilt. Emaline Combs - cover-
lid. Caty Combs - little wheel. Nancy White. James, Margaret, John
and Sarah Conkin - $1 each. Executors: Samuel Douglas, Chase Hale.
Test: George J. Jackson, Samuel Cox, John Guin.
                        Signed: Nancy (X) Rock

HENRY P. BARKLEY   Non Cupative
Henry P. Barkley died July 1854. He gave his horse, saddle and bridle
to his brother, John K. Barkley. Property to be sold and money divided
between mother, brothers & sisters. Executor: His uncle, Ebenezer
Barkley. Wit.: Rebecca Cochran, Sarah Jane Barkley. Proven November
Term, 1854.   Signed: Henry Hoss

WILLIAM MITCHELL   August 27, 1854
Wife Malie - farm, household furnishings, all stock, and at her death to
go to daughter, Rebecca. 25 acres is to go to the children of daughter,
Serephina. $20 to my son Albert. Daughters: Eliza & Elizabeth - $20
each. Executors: G.W. Telford, Samuel Y. Wyly. Test: Ez Birchfield,
David Bell. Proven November Sessions, 1854.
                        Signed: William (X) Mitchell

ELIZABETH MAWHORTER   November 10, 1853
To Burton Knight - where he now lives in District 17 Washington County,
which was willed to me by my husband James Mawhorter. If the said
Knight will take me and care for me and my horse and cow and pay me

$1000. Executor: Dr. Alexander A.B. Brabson. Attest: G.W. Telford, A.B. Brabson. Probated November Term, 1854.

Signed: Elizabeth (X) Mawhorter

MARY ODELL   March 21, 1854
To Nancy Odell during her widowhood - if married she is debared any recourse on the land. To my grandchild of Nancy Odell - the entire farm, horses, wagon and cattel. To grandsons David & James Odell - a bed & bedding. To my daughter Rebecca Keener - one set of drawers. Executor: John McCracken. Test: John McMasters, James R. Green. Probated January Term, 1855.   Signed: Mary (X) Odell

ARCHIBALD HALE   March 24, 1854
Wife Mary Hale. Daughter Minerva Slaven - no more. To daughter Ruth Allison - $200. Daughter Martha Hunt - no more. Daughter Emeline Hale - $100. Daughter Mary Brown has her portion. Daughter Amanda Jane Prichett has her portion. Daughter Telema Duncan has enough. To grandson John Hale son of Allison Hale - land running from Hugh A. Crawfords to the Bugaboo Springs, to John Keyes line including house and spring where Jeremiah Boyd now lives. Lucinda, widow of David Hale - to live on farm, raise and educate her son John Hale. To grandson John Hale - all remaining of the Bugaboo Farm. To my son Abednego Hale - 3 negro boys. To my son William Hale - the farm where I now live, purchased from John and Robert Allison. Executors: 2 sons, Abednego & William Hale. Test: William Lyon, James H. Allison, Franklin Lyon. Probated January Term, 1855.   Signed: Archibald Hale

DAVID WHITE   January 25, 1855
Wife Sythe. Daughter Anne - to be maintained as long as she is single. To daughter Sarah and the heirs of my daughter Elizabeth and Mary Ann and Rebecca - $10 each after the death of their mother. To the heirs of my son Isaac - 25 acres adjoining Duncan. To heirs of daughter Nancy - land. Executor: William I. White, Test: Jerry White, James H. English, James Crabtree. Probated February Term, 1855.

Signed: David White

JAMES SIMPSON   January 25, 1855
Daughter Serephina Palmer - $500 to be put on interest and give her $20 every six months for her support. This is in addition to the farm I have given her. To daughter Margaret Lane - $500. To daughter Eliza Shannon - $200. To son Joseph R. Simpson - $10 and what I have already given him. To son George W. Simpson - $150. To 2 sons James & S.C. Simpson - $100 to be equally divided. To daughter Nancy Odell thru her husband Samuel Odell - $300 for her part. To heirs of my 2 sons G.W. & F.H. Simpson - $4. To son John W. Simpson - $150 for my coffin and box. To grandson John B. Simpson - $50. Executor: George W. Willett or John B. Deadrick. Wit.: D.J. Gibson, Elijah Hashbarger. Probated March Term, 1855.   Signed: James Simpson

JOSIAH PARKER   March 25, 1844
Wife Jane. Youngest daughter Sarah Parker. Grandson James Arter Parker - he to have 2 shares of my estate. Rest to be divided among my heirs. Executors: Wife Jane, John Hoss. Test: D.R. Kinnick. Probated May Term, 1855.   Signed: Josiah Parker
                                                Jane Parker
                                                John Hise

WILLIAM T. M. OUTLAW
Learn of what little I have from my friend Rev. William Cate at Jonesborough, friends and relatives at Raleigh, N.C. Wait 4 to 5 years on notes on Mary and Thomas H. Hartman, also note on E.D. Rader. I owe $831. I have $330 in my purse. I want Mary's boarding paid. Executors: My friend Brother Ree Wilkins, A. Williams Esq. and Sarah A. Williams.

Test: _____. Probated May Term, 1855 - Henry Hoss.
                                Signed: W.T.M. Outlaw

ELIJAH SHANNON   April 5, 1855
Wife Elizabeth Shannon. When the children are all of age, divide your-
selves. Executors: My 2 sons, John S. & James F. Shannon. Wit.: John
Stout, Francis W. Polser. Probated June Term, 1855.
                                Signed: E. Shannon

ELIZABETH ROBINSON   May 2, 1855
Elizabeth Robinson, wife of Jacob Robinson, decd. Children: F.F.B.
Robinson, Mary Elizabeth Robinson, John Robinson. Grandson Jacob Henry
Robinson, son of F.F.B. To Franklin Robinson. William, Samuel & F.G.
Robinson. Executor: F.F.B. Robinson. Wit.: Thomas Fulkerson, Silas
Ratcliff. Probated June Term, 1855.
                                Signed: Elizabeth (X) Robinson

THOMAS MILLER   April 16, 1855
Wife Sarah - to live on place during her widowhood. My first 6 children
which I had by Mary Miller - to have $1 each in five years after the
youngest child, Joseph, becomes of age. Son Elcany - $1. Son James -
the plantation where I live. Daughter Susannah Norrice - $1. Son
Joseph - $400, a horse and bridle. Son James to pay all above legacies
and have the property. Attest: Daniel Fox, William S. Paw. Proven
August Sessions, 1855.

THOMAS GUINN   April 23, 1855
Wife Lise - to have all property she had when I married her and she is
to live with my children. Children: Matthew, David, Polly, Margaret &
my 2 daughters. Andrew, James, William, Thomas, John, Josiah - $100
apiece. Two grandchildren: Thomas & James Humphres - $5 each. Sons
William, Isaac Newton - $500 at 21 years of age. Executor: Joseph
Crouch. Wit.: Matthew S. and David S. Guinn. Probated August Term,
1855.   Signed: Henry Guinn

JOHN SAYLOR   November 3, 1854
The Grist Mill Tract and Plantation on Sinking Creek now occupied by my
son Isaac Saylor, containing 159 acres - to be sold. Children: Godfrey
& Sarah - land etc. worth $1200. Ruble Place containing 134 acres I
bought of William Smith - to be sold. To Patsy, widow of my son John
and her children - $400. To daughter Elizabeth, wife of John Howard -
$600. Sons-in-law: George Gilley, Lemuel Bogart & William Odle, their
heirs: Nancy Gilley, Hannah Bogart, Margaret Odle. Sons William - $600,
Henry Saylor - $600, Isaac, Abraham - $600 each. To grandchildren
Godfrey & Sophrona Saylor, children of my decd. son Joseph - $300 each.
To daughter Sarah Saylor - horse, cow, furniture etc. To Sophrona Smith,
wife of William Smith, Sarah & Catharine Gilley, all children of my dau.
Polly Gilley - $600, $200 apiece. Executors: Sons Henry & Abraham
Saylor. Wit.: A.W. Taylor, Henry Johnson, T. McInturff.
                        Signed: *John Saylor in German*
                                 John Saylor in German

ISAAC MULKEY   August 25, 1849
Wife Rachel to raise my children who are underage. Executors: My sons
Philip & Robert H. Mulkey. Test: R.S. Ferguson, John Murray. Probated
October Term, 1855.   Signed: Isaac Mulkey

WILLIAM HALE   September 28, 1855
Four heirs namely: Hannah Liza, Mary, John B. & William C. Hale - 4
shares of my father's, George C. Hale, estate. Executor: Hiram Hale.

Test: William C. Hale, Howell Jenkens. Proven November Sessions, 1855.
                    Signed: William (X) Hale

HAM FOLLY   May 3, 1855
To sister Polly Carmichael - 1 acre during her lifetime and then to her
grandson, Billy Bayless, a little boy who has waited on me. To Any
Carmichael - my mill 2 acres. Contract between R.S. Ferguson, James M.
Osburn and myself. My son Samuel - 3 acres. Daughter Winney - 1 acre.
Daughter Harriet - 1 acre including the house where I now live. I
direct R.S. Ferguson and James M. Osborn to lay it off in lots. I
contracted to Ferguson & Osborn concerning mines and minerals on my land.
If the mines prove profitable, I'm to share in the profits. My free
children. My granddaughter Hannah Eliza, that is bound to Henry
Ferguson, be counted as one of my children in her mother's stead.
Executors: R.S. Ferguson, James M. Osborn. Wit.: John Beals, Elijah
Archer. Probated November Term, 1855.
                    Signed: Ham (X) Folly

JAMES MOORE
Wife Lain - 1/3 of land etc. Four heirs: Sophia, E.M.P. Moore, Sarah &
Amanda Moore. Executors: Stephen D. Stuart & my son E.M.P. Moore.
Test: E.L. Mathes, Daniel Moore. Proven December Sessions, 1855.
                    Signed: James Moore

MARTHA HALE
To Franklin D. Hale & Joseph S. Hale - my undivided interest of land
left to me by my father where Harriet Hale now lives, 1/7 part. My
undivided interest in the slaves of Henry Hale decd. - to my 3 brothers
William H., Smith H. & Finley D. Hale. Executors: Bros. William K. &
Joseph H. Hale. Wit.: H.K. Chase, Harriet Hale. Probated January .
Term, 1856.   Signed: Martha E. Hale

JAMES BELL   November, 1855
Wife Sarah - everything during her widowhood, if she marries she gets a
child's part. Executors: Wife Sarah, son Frederick Bell. Wit.: Henry
Hoss, Abram Cassady. Probated February Term, 1856.
                    Signed: James Bell

THOMAS KING   August 28, 1853
Children: Ruth King - 50 acres, Billy F. King, Albert King, Jonas L.,
Henry, Albert, Fraim King and the heirs of John King decd. (viz.) Thomas
L. King & Jno. King. To grandson John King - a cherry bureau. Sell my
stock in East Tennessee & Virginia Railroad since it cannot be divided.
Executor: Son Albert King. Wit.: Vincent Boring, Landon C. Hoss.
Codicil - 25 January 1856. Probated March Term, 1856.
                    Signed: Thomas King

JOHN BIDDLE   June 31, 1856
Son Samuel D. Biddle. Son Thomas - land. Son John - one clay bank mare
and 125 acres at $10 per acre. To granddaughter Mary A. Hale - bed and
bedding, side saddle and a cow. Furniture to 3 daughters: Elizabeth
Hall, Margaret Temple, Mary A. Klepper. Executors: J.L. Biddle, Thomas
Biddel. Wit.: G.W. Nelson, Thomas Biddel. Probated March Term, 1856.
                    Signed: John Biddel

G.W. WILLETT   June 21, 1855
Executor, John F. Deaderick, to manage my estate the best he can for my
family. Probated July Term, 1856.

ROBERT MILLION   March 8, 1856
To be buried at Cherokee graveyard with a suitable head and foot stone

at my grave. To Jane H. Bacon and Sarah Million - furniture equally divided. Deceased wife, Mary Million's bed I give to Robert Shelton Bacon and my wife's bed to Mary Nancy Bacon. To sister Nancy Hartsell - $10. To sister Sarah Brown - $50. To Mary Nancy Bacon, Robert Shelton Bacon, Jeremiah & Mary Million his dau. - I give land, horses, cattle, etc. Divide between the 4 last named. Executors: Mark Bacon, Jeremiah Million. Wit.: John H. Crawford, Thomas E. Dosser. Probated 16 Sept., 1856.   Signed: Robert Million

SARAH WRIGHT   May 31, 1855
To neices: Adelaide & Sarah Cordelia, daughters of Mary Newel, formerly Mary Price - $2000 each. To Thomas Wright, son of William Wright decd. - $100. To nephew Madison Price - to be paid by Mordecai Price. Executor: Mordecai Price. Wit.: Thomas F. Young, Thomas Harvey. Probated October Term, 1856.   Signed: Sarah Wright

NATHAN PAGE   October 18, 1856
Wife Elizabeth - 27 acres adjoining William Keen. To James Crabtree. Remainder of my land for $65 divided to Reuben Scalf, Susan Charlton, Jane Monteeth, Moses Page, John Pages heirs, Andrew Page, Branden Page, 8 heirs. Executor: David T. Hall. Wit.: Terry White, Samuel H. English. Probated November Term, 1856.
                                        Signed: Nathan (X) Page

JOHN JONES   January 19, 1850
Wife Jane. Three sons: John W. Jones, Thomas E. Jones - piece of a saddle, James H. Jones - $55 horse. Vina Cooters heirs - $5 in trade. Daughter Elizabeth Cooter - $10 and a cow. To daughter Eliza Britain - $1. Daughter Nancy Jones - horse and $20. Daughter Mary Shipley - $55 horse. Executor: John W. Jones. Test: Samuel & Young Douglass, Elisha Smith. Probated November Term, 1856.
                                        Signed: John Jones

HENRY TAYLOR
Wife Delilah - where I now live and gave to my son Skelton Taylor and conveyed at his request to John Ryland and Abraham Taylor - I give her a life estate. Children: Abraham, Skelton, Polly Barkley, Hannah Miller. Executors: Abraham Taylor, Ebenezer Barkley. Wit.: J. Blair, William K. Blair, R.L. Blair. Probated November Term, 1856.
                                        Signed: Henry Taylor

WILLIAM ANDES   December 29, 1856
To Levina Andes. Lawful heirs: Mary Parks, Barbary Walter, Allen Andes, Rebecca Davis, John J. Andes, Abraham Andes, Catharine Leach, William D. Andes & Ruth Parks. Executors: William Walter, David Fine. Wit.: J.M. Peoples, D.W.F. Peoples, Henry Andes. Proven January Term, 1857.
                                        Signed: William Andes

DAVID CARMICHAEL   August 4, 1856
To Isabella Spears, formerly Carmichael and Archibald Carmichael - ½ land - the other ½ belongs to R.S. Ferguson later sold by John & George Carmichael. To wife Lavina Carmichael - stock and personal property her lifetime then to Isabella Spears and Archibald Carmichael if they separate the old woman. Executor: Jeremiah K. Sherfey. Wit.: F.W. Dove, H. Ferguson, Daniel Carmichael. Probated January Term, 1857.
                                        Signed: Daniel Carmichael

EMILY PRICE   November 3, 1856
To husband Gardner L. Price - 100 acres land on Sinking Creek adjoining Thomas Harvey and Elizabeth Howard. Wit.: Daniel Frazier, Abner D. Howard. Probated March Term, 1857.
                                        Signed: Emily (X) Price

JAMES POINDEXTER   January 31, 1857
Son William - land near Brownsborough adjoining Samuel D. Mitchell,
Abram Snapp and others. William B. Hunter has my deeds. Daughter Martha
E. Poindexter. Elbert I. Poindexter, Houston & William M. Poindexter.
Sons: Thomas, John & Gar Poindexter. Daughter Sarian Crockett. Wit.:
W.H. Humphries, William B. Hunter, W.M. Mitchell. Probated April Term,
1857.   Signed: James Poindexter

NATHAN PEOPLES   February 16, 1857
Youngest son Pleasant J.C. Peoples - my 160 acre farm for $1500 and he
is to care for me. Ruth is to stay with one of the children - she chose
Jonah S. Keplinter - he is to have her for 1 cent and not let her be
bought or sold. Ruth shall have all little articles she has bought and
paid for herself. (Ruth - slave?). Oldest son James H. Peoples - to
have 2 years learning before he is of age. Third son Nathan A. Peoples,
second son Azariah Peoples - the Parker Farm. Second daughters, Basmith
& Joannah - the cupboard and Rachel - my larg chest. Heirs to wit:
James H., Azariah, Nathan A., D.W.F., & Joseph M.P. Peoples, Rachel T.
Rowe, Bethmoth Bayles, Joannah L. Keplinger. Pleasant and Pinckney to
pay me 1/3 of all grain - busheled out. Executor: D.W.F. Peoples.
Attest: Jacob Fine, Elisha Fine. Probated May Term, 1857.
                              Signed: Nathan Peoples

MONTGOMERY IRWIN   April 21, 1857   Non Cupative
Montgomery Irwin died _____. John Rhea should move his family to
Irwin's house and take charge of his property. Rhea to keep the children
at home and educate them as much as possible. Suit with W.H. Crouch to
be settled or prosecuted by Rhea. Test: M.P. Brewer, Elizabeth Hunley.
Probated June Term, 1857.   Signed: W.R. Rhea
                                        E.R. Buckannin

JOHN BACON   September 19, 1851
Son Jesse - to have plantation and support my wife Elizabeth good and
comfortable during her lifetime. To son Mark Bacon - the lower planta-
tion known as the Kyker Place with Grist and Saw Mill. Four daughters:
Malinda Kyker, Dalooney Sliger, Sileta Bayles & Polly Ann Chase.
Executor: Son Mark Bacon. Test: John W. Crawford, James H. Dosser,
W.H. Smith. Probated October Term, 1857.
                              Signed: John Bacon

JANE BANCROFT (BARCROFT?)   February 7, 1852
Daughter Mary Ann _____. Grandson Ambrose Bell. Home Mission Society
of Presbyterian Chirch. Three daughters: Jane Bancroft, Martha
Bancroft & Elizabeth Bancroft - to be my Executors. Wit.: E.L. Mathes,
L.E. Lynn. Probated October Term, _____.
                              Signed: Jane (X) Baracroft

MICHAEL STAR   January 10, 1855
Children: Polly Galloway, Martha Star - beds and drapes. George
Galloway - $1. Catharine Combs, Emaline Harrison. Wit.: William W.
Deakins, James Deakins. Probated _____, 1857.
                              Signed: Michael (X) Starr

JOHN BACON   February 14, 1858
Wife _____. Sons Joseph L., Elijah. Sister June Kiser. Executor:
John W. Hunt. Wit.: Jeremiah Nelson, J.P. Hartman. Probated March
Term, 1858.   Signed: John Bacon

MARY E.G. JORDAN   February 20, 1858   Non Cupative
Mary E.G. Jordan died at Malinda Pattons where she had been confined 10
days. To her sisters, Melinda & Jane Jordan - her child and negro girl

59

Emaline. Proven May & July Sessions, 1858.
Signed: Mary J. Cowan
Jacob Nead

SILAS RATCLIFF   August 4, 1858
Children: Robert, Jane, Tabitha wife of James Price, Nancy Ratcliff,
Phoebe wife of John Smith, Mary wife of Charles Bond, Silas, Eli, Reuben,
& James Ratcliff. The heirs of Alexander and Mary Gobble. Wife _____.
As long as we both may live. Executor: Son Ely Ratcliff. Wit.: Thomas
Fulkerson, Charles Cox. Probated November Term, 1858.
Signed: Silas Ratcliff

JOHN ENGLISH   March 20, 1857
Children: Samuel H., Margaret Hayes wife of John H. Hayes, heirs of
daughter Anna (Margaret, Nancy, Jane & Malinda McCoy). Heirs of Margaret
Patterson have received $80 of their mother's part. Two sons: Nathan J.
English & John W. English - tracts of land. Executors: William T. White.
Wit.: James A. Wells, James Crabtree. Proven December Sessions, 1858.
Signed: John English

JACOB MILLER SENIOR   February 10, 1857
Bury me at Mt. Bethel Meeting House in Greene County. To granddaughter
who now lives with me, Mary Davault - my quilted quilt, pattern known as
Rose of Sharon. To son John - slave Daniel to be treated with kindness.
$300 in East Tennessee & Virginia Railroad Stock to Mt. Bethel Church in
Greene County, Tennessee to use ½ the dividends for the minister as the
elders think proper. The other ½ to the American Bible Society inst? in
the City of New York 1816. Ten children: Mary Davault, Peter R. Miller,
Abraham E. Miller, Catharine Zimmerman, Elizabeth Bowman, Eliza Bowman,
Jacob Miller, Matilda Campbell, John Miller, Chelnesse Reese. My wife
Hannah has been living separate from me for about a year and took with
her more than she brought at our marriage - she is not to interfere with
this will. Executors: 2 sons Jacob & John Miller. Wit.: James W.
Deaderick, John B. Klepper. Proven December Sessions, 1858.
Signed: Jacob Miller

JAMES W. CLOYD   January 16, 1861
Children: Jenny, John, William, James. My widow _____. Executors:
Son John P. and Samuel Cloyde. Att.: Samuel G. Bayles, Barton B.
Cloyde. Probated March Term, 1861.
Signed: James Cloyde

60

CATHARINE EMMERSON   September 22, 1858
Of Jonesborough, Tennessee. Granddaughter Adaline B. Emmerson - house
and lot where I live with best furniture, piano, wardrob etc. Well and
well house are on lot. Rent house for its upkeep and to support the
pastor of the Presbyterian Church in Jonesborough. Rent or sell house
and lot for benefit of Cause for Missions & The American Tract Society.
Lot I sold Masonic Lodge in Jonesboro. I want a plain iron railing
around our graves. Granddaughter Adaline B. Emmerson - all left after
debts are paid. Executor: _____. Wit.: A.G. Graham, W.P. Brewer.
                                  Signed: Catharine Emmerson

Codicil - To Miss Catharine Murrell - my gold ring. To my namesake
Catharine E. Reese? - $50. To Miss Elizabeth Smith - $10. Wit.: James
H. Dosser, H.G. Graham. Probated January Term, 1859.

JAMES HODGE   October 27, 1858
To wife Mary - the farm and all thats on it to raise and educate my
children, when youngest son William is 21, there is to be a division.
Daughter Elizabeth. The boys. Executors: Jesse Allison, William R.
Rhea. Test: Henry H. Hyder, William R. Rhea. Probated January Term,
1859.   Signed: James Hodge

JOSEPH HOWARD   January 7, 1859
Wife Rachel. Son George has his horse. Minor heirs. Executors: My
sons Enock & David Howard. Test: J.F. Trewitt, M.T. Workman. Probated
February Term, 1859.   Signed: Joseph (X) Howard

WILLIAM E. ASHER   January 26, 1859
Wife Agnes Asher. Two children I raised, Eliza Jane Laws now married to
Calvin Vines and the boy named Hamilton Bunton - to have my property at
my wife's death. Executrix: Wife Agnes. Wit.: Alpheus Dore, J.M.
Carr. Probated February Term, 1859.
                                  Signed: William (X) E. Asher

NICHOLAS PRING   September 4, 1858
I am in my 85th year of age. Daughter Susanna Batts - to have all ready
money and notes on hand. Eldest granddaughter Taritia Salts. Daughter
Elizabeth Brown. Daughter Susan Salts wife of John Salts - to take care
of me and have my U.S. Pension ($8.00 per month) on roll of Jonesboro
Agency. Wit.: A.C. Collins, J.P. Cloyd. Proven _____, 1859.
                                  Signed: Nicholas Pring

MICHAEL CLINE   March 8, 1859
Sarah & Margaret McLin to have my black girl. To wife Harriet - a childs
part. Daughter Mary - $250 more than other heirs because she has no one
to provide for her. My daughters to have their parts free of their
husbands and in no way to pay their husband's debts. Executor: Peter
Miller. Wit.: Thomas C. Cooper, James Brown. Probated July Term, 1859.
                                  Signed: Michael Cline

WILLIAM CANNON SR.   May 20, 1855
Wife Sarah. Son George C. to care for his mother and children until
they come of age, also his brother John. Six daughters. Executors:
Son George C. Cannon, my wife Sarah. Wit.: William Cannon Jr., John
C. Burgnor. Probated April Term, 1859.
                                  Signed: William (X) Cannon

JACOB HORNBARGER   March 24, 1859
Children: Sarah Ann Robertson, James W. Hornbarger, Maranda E. Hornbarger,

Ruth A. & Mary E. Hornbarger. Wife Ann – to have ample support and live
in room of her choice. Daughter Emily C. Hunt's children. My son
William M. Hornbarger. To my daughter Thurza Maria Payne's children.
Executor: J.J. Yeager. Test: E.L. Mathes, John S. Collar. Probated
May Term, 1859.   Signed: Jacob Hornbarger

ROBERT McKEE   June 16, 1855
To sons Thompson W. & William M. McKee – my plantation (340 acres)
adjoining William Tyler, E. West, John Smith's heirs and others, they are
to pay daughters Eveline P. Brown & Margaret M. Alexander each a horse
beast worth $75. Son Robert M. McKee. Granddaughters: Mary Jordan,
Adalaide Jordan, Eliza Jordan. Other children: Ewen Y. McKee, James P.
& John C. McKee, Euphrasia A. Mathes, Rebecca J. Baker. Executors:
Ebenezer L. Mathes, E.L. Mathes. Test: Edward H. West Jr., David P.
West. Proven January Term, 1859. Signed: Robert McKee

ENOCH JOB   August 3, 1850
Daughters: Patience & Sarah. Sons: James, Moses. Grandson William
Marian Job. Executors: Sons Moses & James. Wit.: George C. Beard,
John Barnes, C. Longmire. Probated _____.
                            Signed: Enoch Job

WILLIAM HOUSTON   April 27, 1859
Of Washington County. Wife Jane – all lands on North side of Bush Creek
adjoining Madison M. Barnes & John M. Basher. Children: Stephen Houston
& Emaline his wife, Eliza Buck – land on southside of Brush Creek adjoin-
ing Liza Shope, James Range, John L. Murry, also knob land. To daughter
Delia Ford, Andy J. Ford?. At wife's death divide between the 3 children.
Executors: Stephenson Houston, Andy Ford. Wit.: Andrew D. Taylor,
Vincent Boreeng. Probated August Term, 1859.
                            Signed: William Houston

JOHN C. SHIELDS   June 14, 1852
Wife Nancy. Sell my lots in Dandridge – Jefferson County, Tennessee,
shop tools and guns – put the money on interest and use only the interest
for raising family. Wit.: William Shields, David Ellis.
                            Signed: Jno. C. Shields

JOHN McCRACKEN   November 19, 1856
I am advanced in age and my wife Ann is suffering under a severe afflic-
tion. Children: Elizabeth D. McCracken – $1500, William K., Mary A.
Shields, Susan B. May, Catharine K. Hundley wife of Matthew C. Hundley –
$1000 to County Trustee for her and her children. Grandsons John
McCracken Greenway, John M. McCracken son of William McCracken, William
G. Greenway of my daughter Margaret, William L. Hundley, William & John
J. Shields. Land was soal to Eams. Executor: William Shields. Test:
William K. Blair, R.L. Blair Jr. Probated September Term, 1859.
                            Signed: John McCracken

JAMES KEEBLER   February 16, 1856
Wife Sarah. Daughters Malinda English & Mary Hous – to have farm I
bought for them from Jane & Elizabeth English Haws, adjoining James
English. Heirs of my son James (Joseph, Mary & Elbert) – $210. I
provided for son James in his lifetime with land and money. To sons
Valentine & John A. Keebler – nothing. Two sons Joseph & Benjamin –
land, slave and 3 shares of East Tennessee & Virginia Railroad Stock,
wagons and thrashing machines, and pay daughters Catharine, Narcissus
& Seraphine – $1000, a horse, saddle and bridle each. Executors: My
brother Samuel Keebler. Wit.: R.S. Ferguson, Charles Bacon. Proven
December Term, 1859.   Signed: James Keebler

REV. WILLIAM CATES   December 29, 1859
Wife Mary. After Mary's death my library is to be divided between:
Baptist Church in Jonesboro and to the Holston Baptist Female Institute.
$500, piano and other books. Executor: Wilson Bayles. Wit.: W.W.
Mullendore.   Signed: William Cate

JONATHAN BACON   December 20, 1859
Wife Deborah. Minor children to have their schooling. Sons John &
Joseph Bacon - land adjoining John Muncey. Children: John, Joseph
Bacon, Ellendlind Brown, Dicey Douglas, Lyddian Keefauver, Nancy
Galloway, Martha, Catharine, Elizabeth, Sarah & Deborah Bacon.
Executor: Son John Bacon. Wit.: Nathan Shipley, Joseph Crouch.
                    Signed: Jonathan Bacon

EDWARD W. CLARK   January 28, 1860
Wife Susah Penelope - slave I bought of John Presnell. Three children:
Mary A. Clark, Susan F. Clark, George C. Clark. John Presnell is to pay
$3000 to Stephen D. Stuart and myself for land adjoining R. Chase. My
Executors to settle with Stuart and get title on land where I live.
Executors: R.M. Chase & my wife S.P. Clark. Wit.: E.L. Mathes, Perry
Hunter & Mock H. Clarke. Proven February Term, 1860.
                    Signed: Edward (X) W. Clark

PETER HARRINGTON   February 2, 1860
Sons: James, Henry,Richardson & Peter Harrington. Daughters: Ann &
Mary - land adjoining John Little, Alfred Carr and Montgomery Hoss.
Polly and Richardson to act as Peter's guardian. Executors: Son
Richardson & daughter Mary. Test: A. Carr, E.F. Yeager. Probated
June Term, 1860.   Signed: Peter (X) Harrington

JAMES MELVIN   January 28, 1860
Wife Stacey. Children: James R., Susan & Mahala - 80 acres including
spring and orchard. Wit.: Azariah Peoples, William C. Melvin. Exec.:
James R. Melvin. Probated July Term, 1860.
                    Signed: James Melvin

JOSEPH DUNCAN SENR.   March 31, 1856
Son Robert A. Duncan - the money he paid to Frederick Davault. Sons:
Samuel C. Duncan, Nelson Duncan. Our children: Rachel, Robert, Ann
McAdams, Joseph, James W., John B., Allen, Nancy T. Lyon & Samuel P.
Duncan. Executor: James W. Duncan. Wit.: Jacob Hartman, David Guin.
                    Signed: Joseph Duncan
                            Polly (X) Duncan

Polly Duncan had gotten land from her father, Robert Allison, deceased
and never included her husband in deed. Joseph Duncan's Codicil names
S.P. McAdams as husband of Ann and changes amount of money to son. Son
Robert Duncan dropped a law suit against his father's estate. Slaves
were conse?. Executor of Codicil: Son James W. Duncan - 7 Dec. 1858.
Will and Codicil proven August Term, 1860.

PHOEBE NELSON   January 10, 1858
Son Thomas A.R. Nelson. Lydia Eliza Nelson - house and lot on Elizabeth-
ton, Tennessee. My husband David Nelson's Will. No Executor. Wit.:
John Blair, David Kenny, Sarah B. Cunningham.
                    Signed: Phebe Nelson

Codicil - A change of inheritance between Thomas A.R. and Lydia Eliza
Nelson - A negro slave had died. Lydia Eliza is now the wife of Alfred
H. Mathes. I sold house and lot to Tilburn Berry. This deal is strictly
between Lydia Eliza and me. - 8 June 1855. Wit.: Daniel Kenny, Thomas
E. Dosser, W.P. Brewer. Proven September Term, ____.

HERVEY BUCHANAN   December 12, 1860
Wife Mary A. - 1/3 of farm to educate my children and support my mother.
Five children: Sarah J., Martha A., Frances T., Laura L. and John C.D.
Buchanan. Commissioners to divide land: Thomas C. McAdams & Josiah
Conly. Executor: W.G. Strain. Test: Thomas C. & Matthew J. McAdams.
Proven January Term, 1861.

JAMES B. CLOYDE   January 16, 1861
Daughter Jenny. Sons: John, James, William. My widow _____. Executors:
Sons John P. & Samuel Cloyde. Test: Samuel G. Bayles, Barton B. Cloyde.
Probated March Term, 1861.   Signed: James Cloyde

MARY CHESTER   March 1, 1859
Lot sold to Jackson Ross in town of Jonesborough - redeemed by William R.
Sevier, sale of Laura, a girl of color - in all about $400 is now in the
hands of my son-in-law William H. Crouch. My youngest daughter Catharine
is to have all my money after funeral expenses are paid. Granddaughters:
Susan Rebecca and Mary Chester Crouch. Executor: _____. Wit.: T.H.
Crouch, James W. Cox. Proven February Term, 1861.
                                   Signed: Mary Chester

LOUISA E. RUSSELL   December 18, 1860
Two children William Harvey & Rebecca Jane Russell. Executor, Robert F.
Russell, to be their guardian. Test: D.B. Barkley, William Archer.
Probated April Term, 1861.   Signed: Louisa E. Russell

ROBERT ALLISON
Wife Mary & her 4 children Archibald Chester, John, George & Alphia - my
old farm near Jonesborough called State Hill and the tract of 200 acres
which I exchanged with Mark Hale for the John Bowman tract. Daughter
Mary Hale - $300 with what interest to secure a note due from G.W.
Allison. Daughters Martha Maxwell, Deborah Hughes. Executors: Wife
Mary, Henry Hughes. Test: George H. Range, T.J. Galloway. Probated
April Term, 1861.   Signed: Robert Allison

ROBERT ALLISON RUSSELL   January 26, 1861
A native of Washington County, Tennessee and now confined to a bed of
sickness in Marion County, Florida. Have a plain marble slab at the
head and foot of my grave. Property I hold in ownership with Samuel B.
McAdams to be sold by my Executor and pay my portion of the debt of the
firm McAdams & Russell. To my half sister Margaret Amanda Russell -
$500. To nephew Allison Russell Duncan - $300. Half brothers: John
Irvin & James Madison Russell. Half sister Louisa Melvina Russell.
Executor: Robert Allison Thompson. Wit.: George B. Hunter, C.H.
Phinny, R.C. Simpson. Sworn to in Marion County, Florida 5 April 1861 -
In Oceola.   Signed: Robert A. Russell

GODFREY SAYLOR   May 24, 1861
Wife Susannah - one pair fire dogs, shovel and pot ramble. Children:
David, John, Henry, William, Mary Ann & Godfrey S. Saylor. Executor:
Abraham Saylor. Test: Vincent Boring, Joseph Woolf, George Little.
Probated June Term, 1861.   Signed: Godfrey (X) Saylor

MARTIN KITZMILLER SENR.   March 10, 1859
Sons David, John & Martin have their part. Daughter Elizabeth is to pay
son Henry's heirs $500 in one year - sooner if she can. Daughter Mary
Hodges has her part. Executors: Son John Kitzmiller & grandson
Valentine Davault. Wit.: Canada Hodges, Martin Hodges, Abraham Gregg.
Probated _____.   Signed: Martin Kitzmiller

ANN S. McADAMS   April 18, 1861
Wife of Samuel B. McAdams and formerly Ann S. Duncan. My father &
mother, Joseph & Polly Duncan's will dated 31 March 1856. My share to
my husband and at his death what is left to go to my son Joseph D.
McAdams, if he is not living my husbands child Samuel B. McAdams.
Executor: My husband Samuel B. McAdams. Wit.: R.A. Thompson, Josiah
Conly. Probated August Term, 1861.
                              Signed: Ann (X) S. McAdams

MANERVA G. KINNEY   June 26, 1861
To my husband Dr. Kinney - $1000 in County Bonds, $350 in East Tennessee
& Virginia Railroad, $450 on John Ryland's estate. Sister Mary Stuart,
her daughter Mary Minerva - 10 parlor chairs and my rocking chair. To
Daniel Kinney Meek, son of Charles & Sarah Meek - 16 acres on Ball
Mountain Road south of Jonesborough. The lot I own in Jonesborough
being a part of the Judge Emmerson property to Henry Hoss & George Hoss?.
Money to Methodist Publishing House. My house, part of Judge Emmerson
Estate - to Methodist Church for a parsonage. To my nephew Alexander
Nelson - $1000. Executors: Henry Hoss, James H. Dosser. Test: John
H. Crawford, A.G. Masan.   Signed: Minerva G. Kinney

Codicil - Nephew George Jones - my silver teaspoons, other things.

ELIZABETH JOHNSON   September 20, 1861
Slaves to be free or taken to a free state at my estate's expense.
Niece Eliza Jane Carter - land on Nolachucky River adjoining Dr. Isaac
Taylor and others. Three sisters: Sarah H. Hale, Louisa M. Jones,
Mary M. Stuart and Ann M. Hoss my cousin, wife of Henry Hoss. Nephew
Lemuel J. Hale. Executors: Henry Hoss, John F. Deaderick. Test: Seth
J.W. Lucky, Stephen C. Mosely. Probated November Term, 1861.
                              Signed: E.C. Johnson

JOHN WINKLE   February 11, 1861
Four heirs of Jacob Winkle. Daughter Mary - all bed clothing and close
she has made. Daughter Elizabeth Wilson. Sons John, Henry, Joseph
Winkle - $100 each. Daughter Sally Johnson - $100. Son Philip - to have
farm and farming utencils including gears for 4 horses, swingle tree,
dung shovel etc., to care for Mary her lifetime. Son Abraham. Executor:
Henry E. Ruble. Wit.: Andrew Copp, Thomas Bitner.
                              Signed: John (X) Winkle

JOHN MURRAY   August 13, 1850
Wife Elizabeth - land adjoining Jeremiah Bacon and Hiram Hampton, also
land on Sinking Creek adjoining Daniel Sherfy, Shadrach Murray decd.,
Jonathan Brown. Son Mattesson to take care of Elizabeth. Son Harlin.
Executor: Jesse Murray. Attest: Joseph Crouch, Valentine Shipley.
                              Signed: John Murray

WILLIAM R. RHEA   November 28, 1861
Minor children. Executors: Wife Mary A.M. Rhea, son William R. Rhea,
friend John Anderson. Wit.: L.F. Stepp, Jas. D. Rhea. Probated 5
March 1862.   Signed: Wm. R. Rhea

JACOB KLEPPER   January 18, 1862
Wife Catharine. Son Henry - 200 acres. To daughter Eliza Hagy - 140
acres where she lives adjoining William Mathes, Jacob Bowman and others.
Sons & Daughters: Joseph, John B. & Henry Klepper, Sarah Carr, Susannah
and Catharine Range. To Eliza - a note on A.J. Hagee. Other children
not named. Executors: Son John B. Klepper, son-in-law John N. Range.
Test: William J. Strain, G.W. Telford. Proven April Term, 1862.
                              Signed: Jacob Klepper

JOHN FERGUSON   January 26, 1848
Land to 4 sons: Robert M., George W., Alexander F., Henry A. Ferguson.
Daughter Elizabeth Gibson and her daughters Amanda & Susannah Alexander?.
Executors: Sons George W. & Henry A. Ferguson. Grandson George W.
Gibson - 1 colt. Test: Joseph Duncan, Francis Gibson, Philip Mulky.
Probated May Term, 1862.

TURNER SMITH   October 13, 1860
Wife Mary. Granddaughter Martha Ellen Humphreys. Grandson Roswell
Smith. At my wife's death sell property for cash. Children: David,
Delila, Louisa Tragdon, Rachel Brown, Mary Ann, John, Margaret Head.
Executors: Son John Smith, son-in-law Alfred Brown. Wit.: G.W.
Telford, Alexander Miller. Probated June Term, 1862.
                              Signed: Turner (X) Smith

CASANDER M. BROWN   April 30, 1862
Children: Lucinda wife of Montgomery C. Hunter, Julia C. Piper,
Elizabeth C. Chester, Sons Cyrus W. Lyle, Charles J. Lyle, Matthew H.
Lyle, Samuel A.L. Brown son by my last marriage. Grandchildren:
Catharine, Casander Rebecca, William P. Chester - minor children of
William Chester deceased. To daughter Julia C. Piper - 30 acres on
Sinking Creek adjoining Doct. Thomas Young & Samuel Miller, which I got
from my father. My first husband Samuel Lyle. Executor: Wilson Bayles.
Wit.: A. Taylor, Wilson Bayles. Probated August Term, 1862.
                              Signed: Cassandra M. Brown

CATHARINE NOEL   July 30, 1861
I will my slaves to this County - for a just division. Daughters Mary
S. Brabson, Adelaide B. Carden & Malvina Evans (her daus. Marth Adelaid
& Mary Malvina Evans). Executor: Mary S. Brabson. Wit.: A.B. Brabson,
Francis Robertson. Probated August Term, 1862.
                              Signed: Catharine Noel

JOHN WALTER   November 22, 1860
Wife Margaret. George & Sarah, minor children still living with me.
Other children have their part. Executors: Sons John P. & Isaac Walter.
Wit.: A.F. Broyles, E.S. Painter, Alfred Painter. Probated September
Term, 1862.

JOHN RHEA   August 23, 1862
Administrators: James R. Rhea, Robert P. Rhea of Sullivan County. Wit.:
James S. Rhea, W.R. Sevier. Probated September Term, 1862.
                              Signed: John Rhea

ABRAHAM HOSS   May 20, 1856
Daughter Mary wife of Peter Davault now living in Missouri - a negro I
took out there to her in 1835, money and other articles. Daughter Salina
Yeager. Daughter Margaret Ann wife of Jesse Collett - 3 shares RR stock
and negroes. Son Henry A. Sons Franklin, Montgomery - land adjoining
Abram Jobe. Daughter Caroline wife of Ephraim Link. Son Nathaniel K.
Executors: Sons Franklin & Montgomery Hoss, Landon C. Haynes. Wit.:
James H. Dosser, James H. Beuts. Probated March Term, 1862.
                              Signed: Abraham Hoss

ELIZABETH HUNDLY   April 24, 1863
Divide all my property between my sister's children at Knoxville,
Emaline Henderson, Matilda Harper, David & James Felts. My house and
lot in Jonesboro now occupied by William Reese as a shoe maker shop to
be sold and money divided between the heirs above. Executor: W.W.
Crouch. Wit.: W.H. Bates, William C. Slemons. Probated July Term,
1863.   Signed: Elizabeth (X) Hundly

DANIEL WIGHTSMAN   May 23, 1862
Wife Catharine. Daughters Amy & Martha. Sons John & Peter. If the
girls marry, I will their part to them and their heirs. Son Daniel to
have his support from the farm and be cared for by John & Peter. Eldest
daughters Mary, Elizabeth & Rebecca. Son Samuel. Executors: John &
Peter my sons. Wit.: J.K. Armentrout, Joseph Sherfy. Probated July
Term, 1862.   Signed: Daniel Wrightsman

PHOEBE STUART of Jonesboro   January 12, 1859
To Mary Stuart Slemons - china tea set with pot, sugar bowl, 11 cups,
12 saucers. To Alice G. Slemons - ½ dozen silver spoons. To James H.
Dosser's dau. - ½ dozen silver dessert spoons. To Thomas E. Dosser's
dau. Cally - my silver creamer spoon. To Alice Nelson - my secretary.
To Ann Nelson - silver table spoons. To Mr. William C. Slemons, Rev.
R.P. Wells - $100. To my bound boy Ed - my bed. To my bound girl
Minerva - my sleeping bed. Sell my house and lot, pay expenses and get
a tombstone, enclose it. $600 to Odd Fellows Female High School of
Jonesboro to repair and complete their present buildings, school for
poor girls. Executors: A.G. Graham, James W. Dosser. Wit.: John
Keyes, William P. Brewer. Probated July Term, 1863.
                               Signed: Phoebe Stuart

ELIZABETH EUTZLER   February 13, 1863
5 acres on waters of Cherokee and adjoining J.E.T. Harris, R.S. Young &
others - to children of my son Noah Eutzler (Catharine, John, Elizabeth
& Frances Edna & others maybe yet unborn). Personal property to be sold
and proceeds to go to Dunkard Church. My riding mare - to Thomas
Burleson. Executor: Robert S. Young. Wit.: W.R. Sevier, L. Burleson.
                               Signed: Elizabeth (X) Eutzler

Codicil - My son Noah is away, his wife Mary Jane to remain on farm.
Wit.: W.R. Sevier, L. Burleson. Probated March Term, 1863.

PETER MILLER   October 3, 1856
Son William to pay son Samuel $100. To son Elbert - a negro woman and
boy. I paid on his education to be a Doctor. Son James. Son-in-law
Alexander McNeil husband of my dau. Elizabeth. Daughters: Sarah Powder,
Nancy Easley, Mary Thompson, Emma - $100 per year until she marries or is
21. My shares in RR stock to American Bible Society organized 1816.
Executors: Sons Samuel H. & Elbert S. Miller. Proven 4 May 1863.
                               Signed: Peter Miller

JOHN STROUD   April 11, 1863
All real and personal estate to my mother. Sister Mary - $50 after my
mother's death. At mother's death divide between my 3 sisters: Mary
Higgins, Dicey Carter, Sarah Moor. Executor: Ellis Higgins. Wit.:
William Lawing, Ellis Higgins. Probated July Term, 1863.
                               Signed: John (X) Stroud

JAMES BROWN of Jonesboro   January 26, 1863
Wife Margaret & her children - all my property in Jonesboro. I used
part of house as a saddler's shop - remove petition before sale to pay
debts & William R. Sevier for purchase of house. My children be put
apprenticed to learn some good trade or profession. Executrix: Wife
Margaret. Test: John A. Wilds, Jos. H. Logan. Probated March Term,
1863.   Signed: James Brown

MARGARET BEARD   January 21, 1862
Sell 6 acres and pay my debt to Daniel Barkley for tract I now live on.
Granddaughter Evalina Morley - 1 acre. Rest of land to grandson
Cornelius Eugene Beard. To Laura Leonard - 1 falling leaf table. To
granddaughter Adaline Anderson, my son Robert Emmerson Beard - all the
rest. Executor: Robert E. Beard. Wit.: Thomas E.R. Nelson, S.C.
Morley. Probated 1 June 1863.   Signed: Margaret (X) Beard

ELIZA COX   August 1, 1862
Everything to son Ephrain D. Cox. My brother Barton Bayless to be his guardian. Executor: Bro. Barton Bayless. Test: E.L. Mathes, A.A. Broyles.

THOMAS BARRON   October 8, 1859
To my children, oldest on down: Lear Epperson & Nancy Epperson, Daniel Barron, Jacob Barron, Sarah Bacon, Deborah Bacon, John Barron, Thomas Barron, Lyddian Bacon & Phoebe Cox. These is my heirs. Executor: Nathan Shipley. Test: Thomas Epperson, John W. Bowers, Nathan Shipley. Probated February 1863 2nd day.   Signed: Thomas Barron

ADAM BROYLES   March 24, 1862
Wife Nancy - interest on $1000 and her wearing clothes - levity and justice be extended to her. To daughter Mary Green wife of Ira Green who brought a lawsuit against me in Chancery Court - ½ share. To daughter Elizabeth Bacon formerly Elizabeth Collet whose husband A. Collett who was connected with lawsuit with Ira Green above - ½ share. To Rosannah Prater & her heirs - 1 share. To children of Lean Vaught - 1 share. To Malinda Tral? - 1 share. To John Bowman & his children - 1 share. To Isaac Broyles - 1 share. Executors: Son Isaac Broyles & William J. Strain. Test: E.L. Mathes, Daniel Moore, John H. Greenway. Proven December Term, 1863.   Signed: Adam Broyles

JOHN DEAKINS   October 12, 1854
To my son John Deakins children. 2 tracts land I bought of John Denton Oct. 3, 1803, land where Mary Deakins, widow of John now lives. They use it until 1 January 1863 and no longer. It is to be sold and the proceeds equally divided between my heirs. Daughters: Priscilla & Louisa. Executors: Jonathan H. Collum, Peter Miller. Test: Thomas J. Wilson, Jonah Lillicon?. Probated 4 January 1863.
                        Signed: John Deakins

MARGARET HANKAL   January 8, 1861
To be buried at Buffalo Ridge Church Yard as near mother & father as possible. My sons J.C.M. Hinkle, Hezekiah Hinkle have had 2 lawsuits about my property and have been heavily taxed - refund their part to them. Find son Jephtha in 3 years, if not divide between 5 heirs. Hezekiah, Margaret Collins, Elizabeth & Nancy to have personal property, Elizabeth to divide & Nancy take her choice. Executor: R.F. Ferguson. Wit.: Henry Haire, Samuel C. Haire. Probated _____.
                        Signed: Margaret (X) Hankle

FREDERICK ARMENTROUT   May 22, 1857
Wife Catharine - to be supported by son Philip Armentrout. Daughter Layamora to live with her mother if she wants to. Executors: Hiram & Philip Armentrout, my sons. Test: J.R. Armentrout, Michael Armentrout. Probated February Term, 1865.
                        Signed: Frederick Armentrout

JOHN BROWN   January 25, 1864
To the children of my son John L. Brown - 140 acres on the waters of Kendrick's Creek adjoining George Jackson, Hannah Kincheloe & others - to John L. and his wife their natural life. My heirs: Sarah wife of Andrew Walker - $15; Mary wife of William Walker - $15; Zachariah - $100; Abigail wife of George W. Ferguson - cupboard, clock, bureau and 2 small spinning wheels & loom; Aseneth wife of Henry A. Ferguson; Margaret wife of Shadrach Chase; Matilda wife of Henry Martin; Rachel wife of Isaac Garber; Martha Ann wife of James M. Chinoth. Executors: G.W. Ferguson, Josiah Conley. Wit.: Josiah Conley, R.A. Conley. Probated January Term, 1865.   Signed: John (X) Brown

JOHN E. COSSEN (Doctor)   August 18, 1858
Wife Mary E. Cosson & children - where I live and ¼ of the lot I bought
of Samuel G. Chester, rents and profits from my Limestone Farms now
deeded to my son Orfella E. Cosson plus proceeds of my Panther Spring
Farm. At my wife's death, house and lot goes to Clovinda D. Cosson.
Other children: Angeline E. Mason, Orphella E. Cosson, Mary B. Cosson,
John L. Cosson & Sidney H. Cosson. Angelina Mason's son J.W.E.C.
Ryland. Edison W. Cosson. To John & Sidney - all my Panther Springs
lands in Jefferson & Grainger Counties in Tennessee. If one of my sons
should read medicine for a livelihood, he is to have my medical shop
tools etc. Proceeds of Railroad Stock - $200 to be divided yearly.
Executors: Alexander N. Harris, John A. Wilds. Test: A.G. Mason,
William M. Fleming. Probated 20 January 1865.
                        Signed: John C. Cossen

ALEXANDER MATHES   December 7, 1863
My latter wife Isabella - by agreement she was to have $1000 at my death
to dispose of as she pleased, which amount she has given to Washington
College & other institutions - I have already paid the College. Heirs
of Thomas Riddle - $200. To my wife Polly. Sons: Alexander Mathes &
E. Smith Mathes. Lucinda D. McNees, Jane Barrit - J.D. Barrit's note
to be taken off Jane's part. Executors: Sons Alexander & E. Smith
Mathes. Wit.: A.H. Mathes, Lydia E. Mathes, Nancy A. Eads. Probated
March Term, 1865.
                        Signed: Alexander Mathes

ISABELLA MATHES   August 3, 1860
Wife of Alexander Mathes Sr. $1000 to be divided in 3 parts - 1 to
Washington College to be solely under control of Old School Presbyterian
Church, 1 to Presbyterian Church, United States of America. Executor:
Alexander L. Mathes Esq. - if he is not living George W. Telford.
Attest: E. Smith Mathes, A.H. Mathes. Probated March Term, 1865.
                        Signed: Isabella Mathes

                        March 8, 1857
Marriage Contract of Alexander Mathes and his wife Isabella. She was
formerly Isabella McChesney. Isabella had money of her own which
Alexander was and did put on interest, to use only the interest for
their support but still the property of Isabella. At the time of their
near $1000 was loaned to George Jones and Samuel W. Doak. The part
loaned to George Jones has been paid amounting to $680 with interest.
Doak's part has not been paid and still in Doak's hand. Alexander
agrees that if Isabella should die first, he binds himself out of his
estate to pay the $1000 to whoever his wife may wish. If the note on
Rev. S.W. Doak is not paid at the time of their deaths, it is to be
included and estimated as part of the same. Test: Samuel Greer, S.W.
Telford, E.L. Mathes. Probated March Term, 1865.

CHRISTIAN SLIGAR   July 18, 1865
To Margaret L. Sligar for waiting on me - $30. My last wife Rachel's
legal heirs to have - chest, cloak, cupboard, feather tick, straw tick,
etc. Money in hands of Adam Slygar Jr. be collected and divided equally
among the heyres. Executor: Montgomery P. Boring. Wit.: Jesse
Crosswhite, Isaac W. Hartsell. Probated 18 July 1865.
                        Signed: Christian (X) Slyger

STEPHEN MOORE   July 9, 1862
Wife Sarah. Children: Elizabeth McNeese, Jane, Catharine, Russell,
Alex, Crawford, Amanda, Stephen, McNeal, Emily Antwil. Sons to have
$30 when they come of age. Executor: My brother Moses Moore. Test:
E.S. Mathes, Nancy A. Mathes, Daniel Moore.
                        Signed: Stephen Moore

Codicil - Money to my girls and their heirs.

CHRISTLEY BASHORE   April 28, 1865
Son John - to have the farm where I live if he returns from the war. If
he does not return the farm is to go to son-in-law F.W. Dove and he is
to pay the other heirs $100 per annum beginning with daughters Anna,
Margaret, son Isaac's children and so on until $500 each is paid. The
Meeting House I built on the place - to the German Baptist or Dunkard
Church with land sufficient for roads to the church. The dishes I bought
for the Meeting House are to remain. My Railroad Stock to be divided.
Son Isaac's widow to be cared for. Executors: John Walters & F.W. Dove
my son-in-law. Wit.: James H. Dosser, Daniel Kenney. Proven August
Term, 1865.   Signed: Christley Bashore

PETER MILLER   September 1863
Children: Solomon, Marh Ann Eakin, Delila Umphreys. Wife Mary.
Executor: Son Solomon. Test: Samuel Keebler, A.B. Barkley.
                               Signed: Peter (X) Miller

EDITH BEARD   July 11, 1865
Sons David, Samuel, Matilda Gray - the windmill and gearing and farming
utensils, Matilda & Emeline are my only surviving daughters. To William
Hyter Humphreys, my deceased daughters husband - $1. To heirs of my son
William, deceased - 1 full share. Executors: David & Samuel Beard my
sons. Wit.: J.F. Deaderick, James H. Deakins. Probated November Term,
1865.   Signed: Edith (X) Beard

JAMES BARDING   February 17, 1860
Wife Loutisha - to have all lands, negroes and stock. Heirs: James D.
Barding, William Chester B., Desa A., Louisa H., Louisiana G., Stephen
P. Barding. Son John M. has his part - I give him $1. Executor: Robert
A. Thompson. Attest: Everett Mahoney, William Mitchell. Probated
November Term, 1865.   Signed: James Barding

WILLIAM L. HUMPHREYS   July 30, 1865
I have portioned all my children except the last 4: Margaret, Thomas G.,
James C., _____. Sons: William H., Moses A. & John R. Humphreys.
Sons Lemuel N. & James C. bound themselves in a $10,000 bond for the
complete and ample support of myself and my beloved wife Sally during
our natural lives. Son Isaac. Executors: Sons James C. & Lemuel
Humphreys. Proven October Term, 1865.

REESE BAYLES   February 18, 1864
Eight years after date I promis to pay Rees Bayles $1000 in notes for
value received - to be paid to his 5 daughters: Anna Bayles, Isabel
Hartsell, Eliza Broyles, Cynthia Hartsell & Martin McAmish - 24 February
1863.   Signed: John Bayles

Due to the fact that I have been of far greater trouble to my son John
Bayles than I anticipated and will be more trouble to him - I forever
release and acquit him from the payment of the within note. Attest:
Jno. W. Simpson, Catharine E. Bashor, Henry V. Nave.
                               Signed: Thos. Bayless

JAMES FITZGERALD   September 6, 1854
In the sum of $10,000 I bind my Executors to make a good lawful title to
the lands adjoining John F. Gresham, Joseph & Henry Hale, John Ford,
Jonathan Ford & Joseph Martin containing 400 acres unto: James H.,
Alfred J., Mary Elizabeth, John W. and Henry N. Milburn to have and to
hold forever. Wit.: Nathan Shipley, James R. Shipley, John Goforth.
                               Signed: James Fitzgerald

I James Fitzgerald give to my black people Sal, Jack, Ham, Sal, Fan, Joe,
Clary, Milly, James & Madison - 100 acres adjoining Joseph Walker old
tract, to hold unto them forever. Proven January Term, 1866. Nathan
Shipley, Administrator.   Signed: James Fitzgerald

JAMES WHITE   December 6, 1865
To the church at Union - $300 as long as it remains Baptist. My children.
Daughter Jane McFarland to have a reasonable compensation for caring for
me. Executor: John White. Test: Joseph Bowman, Y.H. Range. Proven
January Term, 1866.   Signed: James White

JAMES HUMPHREYS   Non Cupative
He said he wanted Newton N. Humphreys to have his bay hoss. John and
Tennessee, Newton's children - to have bed and bedding he then lay on.
Other property to be sold, debts paid and divided equally between his
brothers and sisters. Probated March Term, 1866.
                         Signed: Thomas Weams
                                   Marget (X) Thompson

JACOB WHISTLER   August 13, 1859
Wife Mary - to stay on place, sell what she dont need, put money on
interest to pay taxes. If she and Mary Ann Guinn stay on together.
At my wife's death all real and personal property to be sold and
divided among my heirs except Elizabeth Biddle - $200 and Susannah
Sligart - $100. Executor: Son-in-law William Guinn. Test: E.L.
Mathes, Jacob L. Propst. Probated April Term, 1866.
                         Signed: Jacob Whistler

ABRAHAM SHERFEY   December 22, 1865
Wife Magdalena - everything as long as she lives, then to be divided
between: Dau. Mary Ann Sherfey & her heirs - ½ of estate, Dau. Rebecka
Emeline Sherfey & her heirs - the other half. Executors: Magdalena
Sherfey, Vincent Boring. Test: Samuel S. Sherfey, Vincent Boring.
Probated April Term, 1866.   Signed: Abraham Sherfey

EWING McCLURE   November 28, 1865
Wife R. Antoinette - farm etc. as long as she lives and give support my
daughter Mary McClure and my niece Mary McClure while they remain single.
At my wife's death: dau. Mary - ½, son Ewing G. - ¼, G.W. Telford &
James H. Dosser - ¼ for the use of my son John F. McClure who is being
sued and I am unwilling to pay his debt. It is to be for his use. If
Mary gets married she is to get 1/3 as well Ewing & John. I am security
for my son John in trying to collect debts due the estate of Samuel
Sherfey. Executors: G.W. Telford, Jas. H. Dosser. Wit.: Wilson
Bayless, Jesse Bacon. Probated April Term, 1866.
                         Signed: Ewing McClure

SAMUEL KEPLINGER   September 19, 1862
To son Samuel W. - 140 acres where I live I bought of my father Joseph
Keplinger 8 Sept. 1810, adjoining land I sold Samuel B. Keplinger 18
March 1856. To my son Samuel B. Keplinger - 44 acres on side of the
mountain, corner cupboard, rifle gun etc. if he pays my son Adam
Keplinger $300 without interest in bank notes. Executor: Son Samuel
B. Keplinger. Test: Thos. J. Wilson, C.W.C. Harris. Probated March
Term, 1866.   Signed: Samuel (X) Keplinger

GOERGE CROUCH   March 22, 1866
Wife Susannah - my farm her lifetime - at her death everything to be
sold. Four daughters: Elizabeth Hunter, Julia Allison, Susan P. Clark,
Sarah Galloway - proceeds of sale, equally. Four grandchildren to also
share equally with above: George P. Crouch, George C. Bowman, Martha J.
Deal & James K.O. Bowman. To son William - all I intended for him to
have. I give ½ acre for a family burying ground including the present
site at the back of my orchard to be free of access at all times.
Executor: Perry Hunter. Test: Jas. C.M. Hankal, G.W. Range. Probated
May Term, 1866.   Signed: George (X) Crouch

ESTHER HANNAH   August 7, 1864
To sister Lucinda J. Hannah - all my estate. Executor G.W. Telford to
carry out and perfect contract I am part of with John H. Payne and when
sale is completly and collected, my part goes to Lucinda. Wit.: J.L.
Biddle, William Reed. Probated June Term, 1866.
                                  Signed: Esther (X) Hannah

JOHN DRAIN   May 12, 1866
Children Eliza, Mary & John Drain share and share alike - all to have a
guardian. John's guardian to take care of his morals, education and
training. If any of my children wish to return to Decature to live -
their expenses are to be paid by my Executor. Executor to take charge
of property I have in Alabama. Daughter Mary disposed of some of my
property in Decature, Alabama without my consent, that value is to be
taken from her share. Executor: A.C. Collins. Wit.: Edward Armstrong,
Daniel Kenny. Probated May Term, 1866.
                                  Signed: John (X) Drain

JOSEPH ARCHER   June 16, 1854
Wife Mary Ann - all property she brought with her when we were married.
If she chooses to stay in house with my son Elijah - he is to supply her
support, she being his step-mother. I have given full shares to my
children: Silas, William, Joseph, Jonathan & daughter Nancy. Three
daughters: Susannah Merritt, Looamy Smith & Elizabeth Archer. Two sons
Jurial D. & Thomas Archer. My oldest son Benjamin has not been heard of
by me for many years - if he returns in 2 years is to receive $10 from
son Elijah. I'm in partnership with Joseph A. Conley in mining business.
Mining rights do not go to Elijah but to my heirs. Executors: R.S.
Ferguson & son Elijah. Test: John Nelson, Joseph Balser. Probated
July Term, 1866.   Signed: Joseph (X) Archer

ALEXANDER ADAMS   May 5, 1864
Wife Lydia M. Two daughters Mary J. & Sarah F. Adams to live with their
mother while they are single then to have a good bed and bed cover and a
side saddle. My heirs: Polly Ann Ford decd. or her heirs, Elizabeth
Isenberger, Catharine Hawk, Emeline Brown, Susannah Hodges, Alvin Adams,
Christina Hawk, Martin K. Adams, Mary Jane & Sarah F. Adams. My 90 acre
farm. Executor: John F. Gresham. Test: William Mohler, John F.
Gresham. Probated August Term, 1866.
                                  Signed: Alexander Adams

WILLIAM HUMPHREYS   July 16, 1866
To son David A. - my farm and he is to furnish my widow Delila a decent
support. My 2 youngest daughters Jan & Eliza to live with family while
single. Wit.: John F. Smith, Smith Armentrout. Probated August Term,
1866.   Signed: William (X) Humphreys

JULIUS BROYLES   January 31, 1866
Sons: Philip, Alexander & Ephraim have their part. Daughter Louise
wife of George Miller has her part. Five daughters: Lucinda wife of
Jackie Broyles, Mary Ann wife of David Good, Amanda wife of Elbert Fox,
Nerza wife of Joseph Snapp, Sarah wife of James Henley. Executor:
Harvey Richardson. Test: Alexander Broyles, Henderson Presnell.
Probated December Term, 1866.   Signed: Julius Broyles

ACHY McINTURFF   March 6, 1855
Daughter Serephina wife of Robert Allen - an amount equal to my other
children's amount received from their father Gabriel McInturff decd.
Executor: Calvin Hoss. Test: Henry Hoss, William Patterson. Probated
December Term, 1866.   Signed: Achy (X) McInturff

JAMES TINKER   May 1, 1866
Wife Nancy. Two sons: Philip P. & Jesse P. Tinker - to have farm and
pay 1/3 proceeds to my wife Nancy and minor children. Executors: Sons
Philip & Jesse P. Tinker. Wit.: William Parks, J.B. Erwin. Probated
October Term, 1866.   Signed: James Tinker

PETER RANGE   March 25, 1859
Wife Matilday - to be provided for by sons James & William. Three
daughters: Susanna, Louisa & Elizabeth - $100 each. Daughters: Mary,
Elendor, Martha - $200, horse, bridle & saddle. Executors: Sons James
& William Range. Test: Hiram Hale, John H. Bowman. Probated January
Term, 1867.   Signed: Peter (X) Range

CATHARINE KLEPPER   February 1867
Daughter Eliza Smith. Son John B. Klepper. Executor: Son-in-law
William Smith. Test: J.S. Biddle, W.J. Strain. Probated March Term,
1867.   Signed: Catharine (X) Klepper

MARTHA STARE   January 19, 1867
To Edmund Bacon - all money and all property for caring for me.
Executor: Nathan Shipley. Test: William P. Barron, A.D. Sharp.
Probated June Term, 1867.   Signed: Martha (X) Stare

DANIEL L. BAYLESS   February 4, 1867
Daughter Elizabeth Duncan has received her part. To each of her heirs -
$5. To William Duncan - $5. To Eliza Bayles - my clock and to my son
William M. Bayless - all household furniture. Executors: Sons William
M., Alfred G. & Bird D. Bayless. Test: Joseph West, Thomas J. Wilson.
Probated May Term, 1867.   Signed: Daniel L. Bayless

THOMAS KING   December 18, 1855
Son James F. King, Wife Elizabeth made will. Daughter Carolina Crumley -
40 acres. Son Thomas - $1, he needs a guardian. Daughter Martha King -
land. Children: Jane, Jackson & Landon. Executors: Son Jackson King
& E.W. King. Wit.: Hugh P. Young, Richard Northington. Probated
August Term, 1867.   Signed: Thomas (X) King

GEORGE W. BROOKS   January 23, 1866   Non Cupative
Brother William E. Brooks to have my discharge papers & other papers.
Wit.: George Hale, Samuel T. Rogers. Probated September Term, 1867.

WILLIAM R. SEHORN   August 18, 1867
Son William A. Seehorn to provide and care for my wife Anna and daughter
Susannah A. Seehorn. I sold my farm in Greene County to Harvey & William
Allen for $4500. I bought a farm in Washington County from George W.
Ferguson - 144 acres at $23.50 per acre - son William is to have this
farm at wife Anna's death by dividing $1000 to: sons John W. Sehorn,
James G. Sehorn & 2 daus. Margaret C. McLin & Susannah A. Seehorn.
Executor: Son John W. Seehorn. Wit.: S.E. Lyon, David Stuart.
Probated September Term, 1867.   Signed: W.R. Seehorn

GEORGE HEISKEL   June 17, 1867
Wife Rebecca to have the lot where I now reside during her life & then
to go to Julia Heiskel, alias Madison or her heirs. Executor: John
Reubush. Wit.: Alexander Mathes, E.E. Mathes.
                Signed: George (X) Heiskel

SAMUEL B. CUNNINGHAM   July 10, 1856
Wife Anna A.D. Cunningham to retain possession of dwelling and lots where
we now live on Main Street bounded by Genl. Jackson on the east and by

William H. Maxwell on the west, adjoining lot bounded by Genl. Jackson, Chestnut Street south & by William Flemming. Sarah J. Foster & Jane Davis - slaves. Daughter Sophia Mody Cunningham to be educated. Cornelius Eugene to have a liberal education at Washington College - if not the money to be given to him when he comes of age. Slave boys Barney & Manson to be liberated or go to Liberia. Property of my wife to be conveyed to her children. Dock Sevier to have all my medical books and instruments in the shop. Son Samuel. Daughter Sarah Pane Cunningham. Youngest child Sophia Moody, Sarah Jane. Executors: Wife Ann, Robert L. Blair, A.R. Nelson. Probated October Term, 1867.

ROBERT A. THOMPSON   July 29, 1867
Agreement with my first wife Hannah E. Thompson and having made a sort of joint will with her in regards to lands inherited from her father Robert Allison Jr. and lands I had purchased adjoining this land she owned, between my son Josiah C. Thompson and myself 22 January 1851 - I wish strictly carried out. Lands I bought to be divided between my present wife Louisa G. and my son Josiah W. Thompson, he to have the Mill seat. This land in District 14. To son Josiah - my silver watch, button bureau, a $500 note on Samuel McAdams dated Oct. 27, 1860 and a $652 note on Joseph Duncan Jr. - all in U.S. gold. To sister Mary Jane Twindley? - 2 feather beds. Executors: Samuel B. Ellis, William T. Range. Test: S.E. Lyon, David Stuart. Probated October Term, 1867.
                                 Signed: R.A. Thompson

SAMUEL G. BAYLESS   February 25, 1867
Son Hiram to live with and care for my wife and his mother on land toward Barton Bayles. A.J. Kiker & Thomas Bayles to continue tending fields. At my wife's death - land to be laid off equally, Thomas' part adjoining him and Julia's part adjoining her. Executors: Sons Thomas & Hiram Bayless. Wit.: F.S. Bayles, Cassamer E. May, George W. May. Probated November Term, 1867.   Signed: Samuel G. Bayless

Agreement between Josiah C. & Louisa G. Thompson 29 November 1867 heirs at law of Robert A. Thompson and sole heir of Hannah Eliza Allison Thompson. Josiah is also distributor in estate of Robert A. Thompson Jr. by will dated 18 July 1812. This land was to Hannah Eliza in fee simple and afterward divided between Robert A. Thompson, Polly Ann Conley & Josiah Conley. Hannah Eliza deeded to Robert A. Thompson 348 acres and the Mill Tract owned by Robert A. Thompson in his own right, if he would make Josiah C. Thompson a deed for ½ of land because of the fee simple - the deed was not legal. Robert owned 579 3/4 acres bought from Ezra Pearce 1841 and 27 3/4 acres from William Harris 1857. Josiah C. is dissatisfied and they make an agreement as to what she gets and at her death it goes to Josiah. Test: William H. Maxwell, W.J. Range. Probated December Term, 1867.   Signed: Josiah C. Thompson
                                         Louisa G. Thompson

JOSEPH CROUCH SENR.   November 26, 1867
Wife Elizabeth. Children: Elbert, Martin, Agnes Range decd. heirs, Catharine Range, Martha Ross, July Keebler, Elizabeth Sherfey, Mary Kitzmiller & Joseph Crouch Junior. Executor: Nicholas Keefauver. Test: Nathan Shipley, W.A. Sherfy. Probated Fabruary Term, 1868.
                                 Signed: Joseph Crouch

MARTHA JANE CRUMLEY   January 14, 1868
Husband John H. Crumley. Sister Caroline Crumley. Pay Doctor Seehorn for his services. My part of my father's estate due me from Aunt Martha Hyslers estate be sold to pay debts. To Mary E. Crumley - my first class bed. My nieces: Martha Ann & Sarah Catharine Crumley - all personal property. Executor: James Crumley. Wit.: Delia A. Rose, Malinda J. Rose. Probated March Term, 1868.
                                 Signed: Martha Jane Crumley

E. L. MATHES   November 3, 1867
To Elders & Deacons of Salem Church - 5 county bonds of $500 each, making $150 yearly interest to aid and support the Old Union Doctren, Also $150 yearly to pay a teacher of the Parochal School at said place. $50 to Home Missionary Society. I sold my wife's land for $860 in cash. I bequeath to her only nephew Alexander Nelson of Alabama 2/3 of said amount provided we make a deed to George Gillespie for nob and 5 acres between Jonesborough and Ball Mountain Roads - part of old Nelson plantation. Laurence Sparks and his wife to have house and lot where they live. Whatever of my property that remains is to be divided in 2 parts. One to G.W. Telford, E.E. Mathes, Nancy Earnest, E.S. Mathes, Nancy Gerald & Lavinia Earnest. The other half to Salem Church to assist in teaching the poor of all denominations at Washington College. Executors: G.W. Telford, E.E. Mathes. I have written every word and letter of above will. Probated 8 January 1868.
                              Signed: E.L. Mathes

PETER SMITH   December 9, 1867
My am an equal partner in Hoss & Lampson & Co. with J.M. Hoss & J.L. Lampson - my part is to go to my sife Lucinda Smith, plus a town lot in Knoxville on which we are building a house. My Sewer? farm on Sewer? Creek in Meigs County on Tennessee River - be sold and all the money given my wife except $500. My sister Penelope Smith - land in Rhea County adjoining Gear tract. Bryant Smith to sell Sewer? Farm. The other $500 to go to Peter Smith son of James Smith and my nephew - money to be placed in hands of W.B. Reynolds at Cleveland, Tennessee as a trust for educating my said nephew. I also leave Peter Smith my Gear Farm in Rhea County on northside Tennessee River. James W. Gillespie & Dana Waterhouse to mark off Gear Farm. My nephew James Smith father of Peter is to live on place and care for it until Peter is of age. Executors: J.M. Hoss, Joseph Lyle. Wit.: William M. Gresham, John A. Wilds. Probated February Term, 1868.
                              Signed: Peter Smith

SAMUEL M. HUNT   February 21, 1868
Executor to sell land adjoining Ruth Fulkerson, Henry A. Martin. Wife Elizabeth. Two sons Robert E. & Jesse J. Hunt to have land adjoining Ruth Fulkerson, John Maden, H.A. Martin Walker at mouth of Pritchett's Lane adjoining Lemuel Keebler, toward J.F. Grisham. My daughter Elizabeth Con. Son Jesse to support dau. Lutitia. Daughter Lucinda Hale wife of William C. Hale. Son Jesse is young. Executor: John F. Grisham. Wit.: John Meaden, Nicholas Keefhaver.
                              Signed: Samuel M. Hunt

Agreement - William B. Proffitt vs Chinowth Hale & wives - 29 May 1867
        William B. Proffitt and wife Emily Proffitt and Barbary Ellender Chenoth of one part and Katharine Hodges of the other part, agree that to maintain and keep Katharine Hodges as well as they live themselves. She may live at either the Proffitts or Chenoths. Mrs. Hodges daus. are Emily Proffitt and Barbary Ellen Chinoth. W.B. Proffitt is to manage Katharine Hodges dower - she owes $600. Wit.: Jacob Douglass, Joseph Good. Probated March Term, 1868.
                              Signed: By all 5 above

JOSEPH BEALS   June 6, 1856
Wife Mary. Son Solomon's heir. My son Isaac. Son Joseph and daus. Mary Ann Archer, Rebecca Pitcock, Hannah Ellis. To John Beals and daughter Susannah Beals - to have my farm adjoining Hannah McGinnes & Michael Bashor to care for my wife Mary, at Mary's death it is to be divided and be theirs. Executor: Son John. Wit.: R.S. Ferguson, Elijah Archer.   Signed: Joseph Beals

THOMAS P. EDWARDS   February 20, 1868
Joseph Tucker Esq. to be the guardian of my children and he is to be my

Executor. Wit.: Samuel A. Edwards, W.T. Erwen. Probated June Term, 1868. Signed: Thomas P. Edwards

JACOB BOWMAN   No date
Wife _____. Daughters: Margaret Hagy, Sarah Bowman - to receive property and pay son James $1000. Executors: Madison Miller & David Hagy. Wit.: Maj. G. Mahoney, M.S. Mahoney. Proven July Term, 1868. Signed: Jacob Bowman

MARY A. TREADWAY   November 17, 1868
My children to be put out to homes by my Executors. Three youngest children. Executors: Casamore E. May, George W. May, Wit.: Joseph West, Thomas J. Wilson. Probated December Term, 1868. Signed: Mary (X) Treadway

WILLIAM S. BARKLEY   October 2, 1868
Wife Mary Louisa - all my estate real and personal her lifetime - 160 acre Old Barkley Homestead - household items, a library. Three children James M. Barkley, Margaret Carolina Payne & Blanche Jane Barkley. Blanch to have homestead. Other heirs. Probated December Term, 1868. Signed: William S. Barkley

JAMES A. WELLS   July 21, 1868
Wife Jane S. Wells & James A. Wells to have farm with dwelling house on Bulls Gap or Shipley's Ferry Road - 100 acres I bought of Nathan English & T.J. Murrell that once belonged to the estate of Samuel English decd., land I bought of Jesse J. James & Enoch Whitlock. To son Wilberforce Wells - 259 acres my McCall or Stanford farm on Blakeley Creek. To son John Emory Wells - my farm on Horse Creek in Sullivan County called Goad Farm adjoining John B. Hunt, G. Vincent & others - 259 acres. To son John Emory Wells, when of age - $1500. To son Thomas Monroe Wells - my farm on Walkers Fork of Horse Creek in Sullivan County - 204 acres. To daughter Sarah L. Wells - $3500 when of age. To sons - brick store house, tanyard & house, large stable & other buildings across road from my house. 52 shares of railroad stock. Children to have a good Collegiate Education. Executors: Wife Jane L. Wells & son Wilberforce Wells. Test: William McClellan, Thos. J. Murrell, George M. Murrell. Probated January Term, 1869. Signed: James A. Wells

HENRY KING   May 9, 1867
My wife Elizabeth D. King. Sell these tracts: Sherfey tract where Stephen Butterworth formerly lived adjoining Jno. L. Murrey Esq., Daniel McInturff, A.D. Taylor decd. on Lick Creek adjoining J.W. Baird and others in Carter County. One tract owned by myself and Joseph S. Rhea adjoining Crockett Carr, F. Williams & Gibson heirs, A tract adjoining George Stephens, Henry Swadley, Mike Kenny & Jacob Adler. To son John J. King - ½ home tract adjoining Jno. Hughes, David Feathers - to him also the saw mill and water power. To wife Elizabeth - other ½ of homestead, 11 shares railroad stock - at her death to my daughter Ann E. King & her heirs. Executors: Son John L. Kine & Samuel A. Cunningham. Test: Francis Williams, G.W. St.John. Proven February Term, 1869. Signed: Henry King

JOHN INGLE   November 19, 1868
To wife Jane Ingle - all my estate, sell land to pay debts - at her death divide equally. Executor: William M. McKee. Test: Robert (X) McRen, William Slemons, C.E. May. Probated February Term, 1869. Signed: John (X) Ingle

JESSE RIGGS   June 11, 1866
Wife Hannah - 167½ acres farm where we live adjoining John Whitlock decd. heirs, Charles Bacon, Endymion Yoakley & Uriah Hunt. Son William - land.

Granddaughter Elizabeth Combs. Daughter Elizabeth Murray decd. and
husband Jesse Murray sold their interest in my estate during her lifetime. Executor: Henry Lady. Test: Nathan Shipley, Elbert S. Shipley.
Probated April Term, 1869.   Signed: Jesse Riggs

ELIZABETH ALEXANDER   April 20, 1867
Of the township of Pulaski in the County of Laurence, State of Pennsyl-
vania. My real & personal property. Brother Josiah Alexander - ½ of my
share of the undivided land of my father John Alexander in Washington
County, East Tennessee. To brother Samuel - the other half. I also
give my brothers my share of the money of my mother Martha and sister
Suzan Alexander. Executor: Bro. Samuel Alexander. Wit.: James Hill,
West Middleton, Mercer Co., Pa.; William Mayers, West Middleton, Mercer
Co., Pa.; Samuel Alexander, Lawrence Co., Pa. Probated April Term, 1869
Lawrence County, Pennsylvania - copy sent to Washington County, Tenn.
                              Signed: Elizabeth Alexander

ANDREW WALKER   May 8, 1869
Wife Sarah. Son Henry - the old timepiece. Oldest son John B., Second
son William, 3rd son Zachariah, oldest dau. Nancy Ann Keys, 2nd dau.
Susannah Jones. Executor: _____. Test: J.W. Hartman, Payne Squibb.
Probated June Term, 1869.   Signed: Andrew (X) Walker

MARY A. STEPHENS
To nephew James C. Cowan - land, lots in Leesburg. Railroad Stock to
J.C. Con. Neice Mary Jane Cowan widow of James M. Cowan. J.C. Cowan
to pay his half sister Bertie $200. Executor: William H. Cowan.
Wit.: S.E. Lyon, Amanda Lyon. Probated June Term, 1869.
                              Signed: Mary A. Stephens

JOHN GRAHAM   February 17, 1869
Wife Mary. Three sons: James R., Samuel E. & Adam B. Graham. Daus.:
Susannah Coplinger, Sarah Armstrong decd. heirs, Elizabeth Loyd, Ann H.
Tinker, Minerva D.F. Ryker & Mary E. Walter. Executors: Son James R.
Graham, son-in-law Enoch Kyker. Test: William R. Bayless, G.W. Brown,
Arty M. Treadway.   Signed: John Graham

MICHAEL BASHOR   July 8, 1860
Wife Sarah to have everything, sell any of my lands or personal property
to pay my debts and raise my children. Executrix: Wife Sarah Bashor.
Test: R.S. Ferguson, John Fulner, James Fletcher. Probated July Term,
1869.   Signed: Michael Bashor

JOHN R. FAIN of Blountville, Sullivan County   February 17, 1866
Daughter Ruth E. Anderson wife of George Anderson - land called the
Waterford Farm, to her & her heirs. Daughter Nancy decd. wife of Henry
Anderson decd. - to her heirs. Executors: My sons Hugh E., John H. &
Thomas Fain. Test: H.J. Cox, George Anderson. Probated July Term,
1869.

JOHN TEMPLIN   May 7, 1869
Sons: Elbert, James A. & Samuel Templin. Daughters: Martha McNeese,
Eliza Estes, Emaline Lovelace, Malinda Wyan, Amanda Loyd & Elizabeth
Templin. Executor: Son Elbert Templin. Wit.: Ebenezer Booll, E.
Armstrong. Probated July Term, 1869.
                              Signed: John Templen

S. J. W. LUCKY   May 12, 1864
Wife Mary all my estate real & personal. Three unmarried daughters.
Wit.: Henry Hoss, J.F. Gresham, S.T. Logan. Probated August Term, 1869.
                              Signed: Seth J.W. Lucky

JOHN MILLER   July 3, 1869
Wife Catharine to have farm - then divide between 4 heirs: Elizabeth,
Mary, Nancy & Solomon. Executor: Zachariah Walker. Wit.: John Keys,
Jacob Leab. Probated August Term, 1869.
                                     Signed: John (X) Miller

JOHN JENKINS   November 18, 1865
Wife Prudence. Son Alfred. Three daughters: Nancy Howard, Elizabeth
Northington & Mary Ann Price. Jane Campbell - $1. Executor: Son Alfred
Jenkins. Wit.: William Gresham, John Gresham Jr. Proven September
Term, 1869.   Signed: John Jenkins

ISAAC KIZER   June 12, 1869
Wife Mary Jane. Daughter Maude. All my children. Wit.: Lewis & Adam
Cooper. Probated September Term, 1869.
                                     Signed: Isaac Kizer

CHARLES BASKET   May 26, 1857
Wife Sarah, son Manson - farm adjoining William Hughes which I purchased
of Joseph Clark. Son John - land adjoining Samuel Edwards, Henry Fox, I
bought of John McCracken. Son Charles Washington Basket. James M.
Basket, lawful heir of my son Charles. The graveyard. My lands adjoin-
ing Samuel Sherfey, Joseph Clark, Andrew Goodman, D.J. Carr, Samuel R.
Evans. Five sons of my son Charles Jr.: Charles Jr., James M., ?).
Mary Jane Basket. My dau. Sarah, Rachel Basket Gray, decd. Wit.:
Joseph D. Clark, George W. Maupen. Probated January 1860.
                                     Signed: Charles (X) Basket

CATHARINE CLOYD   October 24, 1868
Son Barten B. Cloyd - my estate real and personal, all debts, my brother
David Click decd. estate. To son Samuel - $1. Daughter Mary Ann Horton
- $1. Son Barton B. to maintain me. Test: W.S. Turnbull, W.A. Cloyd.
                                     Signed: Catharine (X) Cloyd

JOSEPH HUNTER   November 15, 1865
To daughter-in-law Elizabeth, wife of son Perry - land on south fork of
Cherokee Creek adjoining Matilda Hunter, Hartsell Love (183 acres) - to
her from the dominion of any other person including the payment of a
note ($400) executed by me to my son Joseph Hunter in 1858. Note to be
paid from my estate and whats left over to said Elizabeth solely for her
own use. Executor: Son Perry Hunter. Test: G.H. Range, B.F. Hankal.
                                     Signed: Joseph (X) Hunter

SUSANNAH KLEPPER   April 1868
To David Klepper - $16.16 2/3. Polly Ann Camel's legal heirs, Sarah Ann
Camel, Martin - $16.16 2/3. Same to my second daughter Elizabeth Eve
Range now living in California. To heirs of James Madison Klepper decd.,
who are living in Illinois. Third daughter Rebecca White living in
Sullivan County - $16.16 2/3. To Lucinda wife of Robert Young. My
youngest son A.J. Klepper has stayed with me, built me a house, barn etc.
- I give him my farm 150 acres on Beavers Creek on Watauga River adjoin-
ing Michael Bashor, Richard Bowman, Jos. White decd., Jacob Davault,
John Fulner Sr. & John Junr. My oldest children were raised while I was
a widow. Executor: George P. Ford. Test: G.H. Range, T.S. Galloway.
Probated _____.   Signed: Susannah (X) Klepper

ELISHA SMITH   September 9, 1865
Wife Nancy - decent support from my farm - daughter Nannie S. to take
care of her and to get my homeplace (123 acres known as Gamble Farm),
with all personal property. Other heirs Carolina Blevens & Finley
Smith decd. - have their part. Test: G.W. Kitzmiller, M. Kitzmiller.
Probated November Term, 1869. Signed: Elijah Smith

MRS. EMELINE M. DEADERICK   March 24, 1859
To children of my deceased sisters. Brother Joseph. Little nephew
Deaderick Anderson Gammon. Executors: Abram L. Gammon & James W.
Deaderick. Test: Stephen D. Stuart, Daniel P. Ford. Probated March
Term, 1870.   Signed: Emaline M. Deaderick

PETITION OF HANNA C. ANDERSON   February 7, 1870
Samuel Anderson was last an inhabitant of Sullivan County - died 1849 -
leaving will with John R. Fain Exec., who died 1869 leaving unsettled
the estate of Samuel Anderson. I Hannah C. am Samuel's widow. Samuel
Anderson's Will was destroyed by fire. Another will by people who
remember must be granted. Petition O.K.

SAMUEL ANDERSON
Leave and bequeath all my property of every kind to my wife Hannah C.
Anderson. Executor: John R. Fain.
                              Signed: Samuel Anderson

Our mother Hannah C. Anderson to be Executrix of above will. Wit.: H.C.
Fain, S.S. Mitchell.   Signed: John Fain Anderson
                                                R. Ellen Anderson

HENRY HALL   January 18, 1870
Wife Jane, son Thomas H. - the Isaac Hamilton Farm in District 12 adjoin-
ing S.B. Ellis, William C. Hale. Son Samuel - land and personal property.
Daughter Nancy Ruth Hale. Three daughters: Ellen Pherson, Mary Douglas
& Jane Biddles heirs & son William Hall. To dau. Martha wife of William
Hall. Grandaughter Mary Jane dau. of William Hall. Daughter-in-law
Martha Hall. Executor: Samuel B. Ellis. Wit.: William Ellis, William
P. Chester.   Signed: Henry Hall

JAMES M. CARR
Wife Emaline Carr. Children: Jacob T. Carr, Nancy M.E. Vines, William
C. Carr when he is of age $1000. Paper found in James M. Carr's effects
at his decease - Probated March Term, 1870.

F. W. LANE   February 3, 1870
Son-in-law Madison Barron has a contract for the farm this year (1870) -
at end of year everything is to be sold and debts paid. I owe G.W.
Telford which is to be taken from son Francis Lane's part. Executors:
Son-in-law Madison Barron, G.W. Telford. Wit.: J. Houser, John Kyker.
Probated April Term, 1870.   Signed: F.W. Lane

JOHN PHILLIPS   March 11, 1870
Wife Sarah. Elizabeth Miller, widowed daughter - to have all my estate.
Sarah for life, Elizabeth for 8 years. Other children: Isaac, Nancy
wife of Alexander Moore, Urias, the children of Augusta wife of James M.
Moore, children of Malinda wife of William Johnson. To Temanda wife of
Capt. Martin Moore - $1, her husband borrowed of me and never paid it
back. If Martin Moore will pay debt to Jno. Baster, Timanda may share
equal. Executor: James H. Dosser. Wit.: S.D. Slemons, John C. Cloyd.
Probated June Term, 1870.   Signed: John (X) Philips

SAMUEL CARRUTHERS   June 5, 1867
Wife Catharine - entire estate. Children: Liza Mulkey - $1, Manarva
wife of Phillip Duncan, 2 sons David Andrew & Jonathan Lafayette
Winfield. If one of my sons should die without heirs, Liza Mulkey's
children are to share. Executor: John White. Wit.: J.M. Carr, J.G.L.
White. Probated August Term, 1870.
                              Signed: Samuel Caruthers

NACKY ROBERTS   February 3, 1869
Grandson William Slemons. Granddaughter Nacky Ford. Daughter Nacky
Holtsinger. Executor: Rev. John Holtsinger of Greene County. Wit.:
Alex Mathes, Wellington H. Stepp_?_. Proven August Term, 1870.
                              Signed: Nackey Roberts

JOHN P. WALTERS   June 24, 1870
Wife Catharine - control of all my estate. Daughter Mary E. Walters.
My brothers & sisters: Elizabeth Painter, Jane Painter, Amos, George
W. & Robert Walters decd. Sister Sarah Housley - $5. James Hughes
appointed guardian of minor heirs of Robert Walter decd. Executors:
Wife Catharine, W.D. Copp. Wit.: George Copp, James Freeman.
Probated August Term, 1870.   Signed: John P. Walters

NANCY HARTSELL   December 4, 1868
Widow of Jacob Hartsell decd. I have money and personal property - pay
debts and divide between my children - dau. deceased. Executor: M.P.
Boring. Wit.: John W. Boring, William M.A.R. (X) Beamer. Probated
September Term, _____.   Signed: Nancy Hartsell

SAMUEL GEISLER   July 27, 1869
Son Daniel Geisler - 85 acres purchased from Thomas Arrington. Daniel
is to pay my 3 living daughters: Susann Bayles - $100, Rebecca Oliver -
$100, Elisabeth Dukst? - $100, Catharine Miller decd. heirs - $100.
Executor: Son Daniel Geisler. Wit.: Abraham Fine, Jno. R. White.
Probated November Term, 1870.   Signed: Samuel Geisler

ISAAC MORRELL   August 3, 1870
Wife Susannah. $5 to daughter Elzirah, Mary, son Eldridge, son Isaac.
Other children: Catharine, Rufus & Martha are to live with and take care
of me and my wife. Executor: Son Rufus. Wit.: P.H. Mallern, D.S.
Crumley. Probated November Term, 1870.
                              Signed: Isaac Morrell

JOHN BAYLES   September 10, 1870.
Wife Adaline. Son E.W. Bayles - 60 acres adjoining Philip Nelson,
Samuel, Mary & Henry Sligar. To son R.R. Robert Bayles - 60 acres
adjoining J.E.T. Haws & Henry Nave. To daughter J.E. Bayles - 70
acres adjoining R.M. Young & Henry Sligar. Grandson Nathaniel
Kenney. Executors: E.W. & R.R. Gayles. Wit.: J.E.P. Harris,
David Moore. Probated November Term, 1870.
                              Signed: John Bayles

CALVIN HOSS   May 3, 1870
Wife _____ to have 270 acres Leach Farm. My son Henry Hoss Jr. - to
cut logs on land for the mill. Unmarried daughters Fannie & Sarah Laws
are to be made equal in personal property with my other children.
Elizabeth wife of Calvin Jones - land in Warm Cove except 1 acre I sold
to George Story and 50 acres sold to George Whaley. Daughter Hannah M.
Nelson - 50 acres to be free from her husband William B. Nelson. Son
Henry Hoss to have farm where I live including ½ interest in the sawmill
and water power. To daughter Lucretia Garber - the Lemons Farm where
Rev. Stine now resides (89 acres). To Sarah Lewis Hoss - the 200 acre
Deakins Farm. To daughter Fannie C. Hoss - personal property at her
mother's decease. Money at 6% interest. Samuel (man of color) to stay
on farm if he chooses. Executors: Son Henry & son-in-law Calvin Jones.
Wit.: E.E. Hoss, Henry Hoss, George T. Hale.

If I could give them all an enduring heritage true and genuine Religion,
with this in their possession they would be rich without a cent, but if
they be destitute of this, the Gold of California and the pearls of the
ocean cannot make them wealthy.

Codicil - 7 October 1870 - James Leach & Eli Story owe me $240 or $250 for balance on the purchase money for 250 acres mountain land northside Ramsey Branch. I sold to the Big Faces of the same branch toward White Oak Flats. Land I bought of Philip Park. I change Henry's land of which I bought of Jas. E. Deakins - Beginning at Walters or Millers corner adjoining Asher, to big hill beyond Meeting House. Names included: Jacob Miller, Jesse Bacon, Hezekiah Bayles, Daniel Deakins, Kezee Bayles, Widow Lowery, Lemons Farm, Leach Farm, Andrew Lilburn. Wit.: E.E. Hoss, Henry Hoss, George F. Hall. Probated December Term, 1870.

DAVID BEALS   August 31, 1857
Wife Elizabeth. Three sons: Marshal, West & William M. Beals. Three daughters: Abigail, Nancy & Martha. Sons to have land and pay daughters $100 each. Other children: Thomas, David, Samuel, Caleb, Jacob, Isaac H. & Abram Beals & daus. Hannah, Rachel, Elizabeth, Catharine & Jerusha to keep what I have given them. Executors: Wife Elizabeth & her bro. William Mitchell. Wit.: R.S. Ferguson, Jeremiah K. Shipley. Proven January Term, 1871.   Signed: David Beals

RICHARD McLIN   January 27, 1870
Wife Rachel. Son Robert to have part known as Benjamin McLins part, which was Benjamin's part when he and I divided, on Miry Branch adjoining John F. Small. Two daughters at home: Elizabeth & Sophia to be made equal to other 2 daughters who are married, Lucinda & Frances. Executors: Wife Rachel, son Robert A. McLin. Wit.: S.E. Lyon, James A. Carson, W.B. Crookshanks.   Signed: Richard McLin

Codicil - 29 September 1870 - Daughter Frances E. Seehorn has been called to eternity. At my wife's death the division is to be between my 4 surviving children. Probated January Term, 1871.

SARAH SNIDER   October 11, 1849
Daniel Snider, son of my sister Isabella, is to be my Executor, pay my debts and have what is left over. Test: Hiram D. Hale, Harden Narice. Probated December Term, 1870.   Signed: Sarah (X) Snider

ABSALOM SCOTT   December 3, 1870
To wife Elizabeth - 100 acre farm on Knob Creek, 10th Civil District, known as the Mallonee Farm. To Nancy Scott Hipps my oldest child - 59 acre Cassada Farm and 4 acres timber adjoining on the Lyle Farm. To daughter Mary E. wife of David Slagle - 92 acres. To Riley Daniel Henson son and only child of Pinckney and Acksah Henson decd., my third daughter - $200 paid to Thomas Scott my son and Riley Daniel's guardian for his education. My real estate is Home Farm, William Andes Farm, where Thomas Scott now lives, Lyle Farm, Hunter Farm all containing 677 acres. To my children David & Thomas Scott, Sarah Jarves wife of A.M. Jervis, Isaac Scott, Margaret Melvina Scott, Daniel. Executors: Son Thomas & son-in-law A.M. Jerves. Test: W.H. Perkens, Jacob Perkens. Probated January Term, 1871.   Signed: Absalom Scott

DRURY MORROW   December 21, 1870   Non Cupative
To James H. Morrow - farm where he lives (Hysinger tract) adjoining Daniel Bowman, Mark Chase and others. To son John H. - 200 acres. Son Benjamin F. - 150 acres. To daughter Mary J. Campbell - 40 acres adjoining Slagles. To son-in-law Washington Kitzmiller husband of my daughter Sarah decd. - 80 acres, Buffalo Ridge District adjoining Martin, Roller and others, being a part of the old David Kitzmiller Farm. Granddaughters Elizabeth and Sarah Alice, daus. of my daughter Sarah decd. and Washington Kitzmiller - with resedence where they live, to be rented for their education. I borrowed a mare of Thomas Kell, which afterward went blind. I hold a note on Kell for $130 given in 1861 - he has married my niece. Give him my colt of said mare also the $130 note. Executors: Sons James H. & John M. Morrow. Wit.: James Moore, John R. Cosson. Probated February Term, 1871.

DANIEL BOWMAN   April 1, 1871
All lots I own in Johnson City - for use of family. Wife Catharine and
son Hiram - money in Government Bonds - to be divided equally - but not
to Hiram if he drinks Liquor. To Hiram's heirs. $6000 is due 8 April
1871 now in hands of Abraham H. Scypes, Race Street, Philadelphia,
Pennsylvania State be collected if possible and put on interest.
Executors: Daniel Geisler, Alfred Carr. Test: L. Bowens, L.H.P. Lush.
Probated May Term, 1871.   Signed: Daniel Bowman

T. L. YOUNG   March 20, 1871
My land be not sold until my three children come of age. I give my
Executors three years to settle my business. Test: L.H. Waddell and
Dr. W.R. Sevier. Probated May Term, 1871.
                              Signed: T.L. Young

JACOB MAYS   May 27, 1871
Son-in-law Abraham Huffine to have where he lives. Wife Mary H. May to
have rest her lifetime. Executrix: Wife Mary H. Mays. Test: D.W.F.
Peoples, Charles L. Keener. Proven July Term, 1871.
                              Signed: Jacob (X) Mays

DR. WILLIAM READ   July 14, 1871
Wife Marjery. Children: Delila Brown, Jane Felts, Elizabeth Booth,
Summerfield Read, Margaret & Julius Reed. My library to Summerfield
if he gets an education. Executors: Wife Mary, son-in-law J.F. Brown.
Wit.: T.J. Cloyd, G.W. Telford. Probated August Term, 1871.
                              Signed: William Read

THOMAS BACON   August 21, 1871
Executors: Jesse Bacon, H.M.M. Walker. Wife to have dowry and a child's
part. To Sarah A. Bacon - $200 more than the rest in lieu of her Hoss &
cow. Test: Nicholas Keefauver, Isaac Galloway. Probated October Term,
1871.   Signed: Thomas (X) Bacon

TERRY WHITE   January 24, 1870
Wife Mary. To William R. White - where we now live after our deaths.
To Edward (my servant of color) - house where he lives and maintenance
off the farm until death. Executor: William White. Test: Nancy E.
Gibson, James Crabtree. Probated November Term, 1871.
                              Signed: Terry (X) White

JAMES MULLINEX   April 6, 1871
Son John S. - land adjoining Murrell Moor, G.W. Vincent, son N.L.
Mullinex decd., Slatequine Ridge, W.M. Taylor. Son Isham D. Mullinex -
land on Long Ridge adjoining N.W. Bachman, John B. Hunt. Daughter Susan
Taylor wife of W.M. Taylor. Daughter Elizabeth - other lands and entire
stock of bees. To wife Mary and daughter Betty - cows, horses, etc.
Executor: _____. Wit.: J.N. Phillips, W.M. Basket, William Mullinex.
Probated February Term, 1872.   Signed: James (X) Mullinex

ELIZABETH BARNES   February 1, 1872
Husband John M. Barnes - to have all my property not willed to my sister
- she to have stone jar, sugar boll and wearing clothes. Husband to
have my interest in my father's estate. Test: Joseph Keebler, James M.
Grisham. Probated April Term, 1872.
                              Signed: Elizabeth (X) Barnes

DANIEL S. CRUMLEY   December 28, 1871
To my 3 daughters: Mary Ann Mottern formerly Crumley, Catharine Crumley
& Sarah J. Crumley - my entire tract of land - to them and the heirs of
their body, adjoining Garber, Gibson, Conley. My sister Martha Crumley

to live with my daughters Sarah J. & Catharine. Executors: Daughter
Sarah J. Crumley. Wit.: Joseph A. Conley, A.J. Smith. Probated May
Term, 1872. Signed: Daniel S. Crumley

HENRY FERGUSON   January 26, 1872
Wife - all my lands and personal property during her life - then to
Thomas and James B.O. Ferguson - if either falls to care for my wife
the other gets the property. Executors: George W. Ferguson, Robert
Conley. This will left with Audrey J. Brown. Wit.: Aaron Done, G.W.
Keys. Probated June Term, 1872.   Signed: Henry (X) Ferguson

DAVID BOLTON   January 7, 1870
Son Joseph Bolton and his wife Sarahphina - all lands in the county now
owned by me on Little Limestone. The children: Daniel A., John F.,
Elbert V., Henry W. & Susan Caroline Bolton & Alice Bolton. Grandson
Henry W. Bolton is to have $500 because he is afflicted and will
probably be an invalid. Executors: Grandsons David A. & John F. Bolton.
Wit.: E.D. Willet, Allen Stout. Probated June Term, 1872.
                        Signed: David Bolton

PHILIP HEYER   October 7, 1870.
To son George Frazer Heyer - all personal property including 3 promissary
notes on John H. Russell - $450 in all. Another note on Edward Bradshaw
of Tugg Co., Kentucky - now in hands of J.L. Lands of said county for
collection. Also a yearly income of interest on $1000, proceeds of a
scholarship at the Danville Theological Seminary, State of Kentucky.
Executors: Rev. James G. Mason of Jonesboro Tn. and he is to act as
guardian of my son. Wit.: William R. Sevier, Jno. F. Grisham. Probated
July Term, 1872.   Signed: Philip J. Heyer

WILLIAM H. YOUNG   June 11, 1872
My Joseph Leonard tract to be sold. I give to the Church House of Christ
in Johnson City the proceeds of 1 acre where I live. I have given to my
Christian Brother Maupin and S.H. Miller. To my daughter Sarah E.
Smithpeters - has received $165. Son John T. Oliver - to be made equal
with her because of the love and affection I have for him. Sell land
adjoining Samuel Melton and John Tyler to make heirs all equal. Seven
heirs: Sarah E. Smithpeters and her bodily heirs, Harriet J. Young,
Susan E. Hughes, Julia C. Young, Thomas A. Young, Mary E. Young & John E.
Oliver. To my wife Mary - balance of farm. Executor: J.C. Hardin.
Wit.: T. Jobe, S.N. Miller. Probated August Term, 1872.
                        Signed: W.N. Young

DR. DANIEL KINNEY   May 28, 1872
To Charles W. Meek - $100, Sarah A. Meek - $100. To Sallie Cecil (no kin
to me and not my child) age 6 or 7 years dau. of Julia Cecil - $100. To
George Kinney - twice the amount of the other heirs for living with and
taking care of me. Executors: George Kinney, Henry Hoss. Wit.: E.
Murray, G.F. Squibb. Probated October Term, 1872.
                        Signed: Daniel Kenney

J. C. GLASS   November 22, 1872
To wife Ophelia F. Glass - all my real and personal property except
$1000 gold which is for my daughter Mary Josepha, which is to be
invested in New Government twenty year 5 percent bonds with interest
payable in New Orleans to the child's mother or guardian, but registered
in the child's name. My one half interest in Michelberry Plantation
near Memphis, Tenn. to be sold and the proceeds given my wife except
$475, which is to be paid H.M. Nash of Stanton, Haywood Co. Tennessee
(This is the only debt I owe.). Sell my Glass Place in this county
near Leesburg, but dont sacrifice it. Give money to my wife.
Executor: My cousin J.C. Thompson. Probated December Term, 1872.
                        Signed: J.C. Glass

AMBROSE LAWING   July 12, 1872
To my imputed son Ulysses G. Metcalf - 75 acres in Washington County
District 18 on Devils Fork of Indian Creek adjoining E.M. Shelton, James
N. Carter. Sons: William W. & John W. Lawing. Wife Sarah. Executor:
Isaac Guinn. Test: W.E. Tilson, W.F. Guinn. Probated September Term,
1872.   Signed: Ambrose (X) Lawing

ABRAHAM JONES   January 29, 1873
Children: Amanda Douglass wife of William K. Douglass - the home fort
and is to support my wife Elizabeth comfortable furing her life and pay
each of 4 heirs of my son J.N. Jones decd. whose names are Margaret Gray
Hartman, B.R. Smith, Samuel B.R.K. Jones & Rachel E. Jones. To son
James K.P. Jones - my Jack Farm and strip of Grace Farm adjoining G.W.
Gray and S.B. Ellis - and he is to pay the heirs of Isaac N. Gray $700.
Their names Margaret N. Gray wife of Looney Gray, Barbara E.R. wife of
David Smith, Samuel N.K.B. Jones, Rachel Ellen Jones. To daughter
Elizabeth wife of John Hankle - the balance of my Grace Farm and pay
$500 to: Jerome Matlock, Josephine and James Matlock, heirs of my
daughter Sarah decd. wife of James Matlock. Daughter Edna decd.
Daughter Mary Jones - $50. Executor: Samuel B. Ellis. Wit.: John
Yoakley, Henderson J. Gray. Probated March Term, 1873.
                               Signed: Abraham Jones

HARRIET HALE   December 28, 1872
To my son F.D. Hale - all right and claim to my real property at Johnson
City his life time - then to my 4 sons. Administrator: Son William K.
Hale. Wit.: H.K. Chas, William G. Gorst. Proven March Term, 1873.
                               Signed: Harriet (X) Hale

ISABELLA SNIDER   October 11, 1849
Son Daniel Snider - all my land and livestock. To daughter Elizabeth
Hall. Executor: Son Daniel Snyder. Wit.: Hiram C. Hale, Hardin
Norris. Proven November Term, 1872.
                               Signed: Isabella (X) Snider

ALEXANDER M. WILSON   December 3, 1873
Wife Anna - my bureau and bookcase and ample maintenance furnished her
by Jasin A. Bradshaw from the proceeds of my farm. Son George W. Wilson
and my daughter Nance wife of William Hannah have been provided for. To
daughter Phebe M. wife of Jason Bradshaw - the farm where I now live by
their paying a note of mine due Col. George W. Telford for $500 - I was
security for my son George W. Wilson and I paid to bring Emma and
Tennessee A. Hannah, children of Nancy and William Hannah decd., from
near Fort Smith, Arkensaw to Washington Co., Tenn., near Washington
College. Executor: Isaac A. Bradshaw. Wit.: Adam Wagner, E.E. Mathes.
Probated March Term, 1873.   Signed: Alexander M. Wilson

JAMES Y. DEAKINS   March 26, 1872
Wife Thursa - 250 acres land, all personal property she brought here
with her, doil fan?, cows, horses, she hogs etc. her lifetime. To sons:
William W., James W. & John - each a bed and fixtures. To son Henry - 2
beds and fixtures, cow and calf. To son R.M.R. Deakins - 2 beds and
fixtures, cow and calf. Grandson George K. Brown - to go to school and
get an education. Clarrissa & Margaret Brown, daughters of Susanna
Brown my daughter. Son R.M. Deakins is to manage and transact business
for my son Henry Deakins. Sons R.M.R. & Henry to stay on my farm and
care for my wife. Executors: Sons John and R.M.R. Test: S.W. Brown,
Lydia Keys. Probated _____.   Signed: James Y. Deakins

RISPAH C. PARKER   February 13, 1873
To son R.F. Parker - my saddle and $5 in U.S. Currency. To son John F.
Parker - bureau, clocks and looking glass. Two sons R.F. and John F. to
have land and personal property and pay my son William P. Tilson $50 in

U.S. Currency. Executor: D.W.F. Peoples. Test: Henry Miller, John M.
Carr.
                                              her
                           Signed: Rispah C. (X) Parker
                                              mark

MARTHA BARCROFT   July 10, 1872
To Home Mission Board of the United Presbyterian Church - $50. To my
sister Mary Cowan and nephew Ambrose P. Bell - $20 each. To sisters
Jane & Elizabeth Barcroft - the remainder. Executors: Jane & Elizabeth
Barcroft. Wit.: S.E. Lyon, Amanda Lyon. Probated July Term, 1873.
                           Signed: Martha (X) Barcroft

GEORGE E. GRISHAM   August 3, 1873
(About 1150 words). Wife Margaret Jane - my homestead during her natural
life, then to my adopted daughter Lula Bell Grishem and the male heirs of
her body - If no male heirs then to her other children equally - If she
dies without issue then it is to go to the minor heirs of W.M. Gresham
named Mary H. & Blanch B. Grisham in Fee Simple. To my wife - the storehouse opposit the courthouse in Jonesboro - then to the oldest male heir
if any in the family. To my apprentice George S. Brown, during his lifetime - that vacant lot on Cherokee Road or Street adjoining Silas C.
Shipley. To George E. Blevins, son of sister Mary of Arkansas and to
George E. Clark, son of sister Elizabeth - all my interest in the Old
Homestead land near Buffalo Ridge Meeting House adjoining W.M. Gresham
and others. Sell 60 ft. lots on each side of the Academy on Cherokee
Street and purchase tombstones for my wife and me and enclose the old
family graveyard at the home near Buffalo Ridge. I will the remainder of
the Academy Lot to the Christian Church of Jonesboro, lately organized
and has no creed but the Bible, for the benefit of educating young men
for the ministry - Its trustees: C.L. Munday, W.G. Barker, William M.
Grisham. To my wife - the store Munday & Grisham, after deducting $130
my father George Grisham gave for tombstones for he and his wife Mary B.
Grisham. My interest in the Simpson saw mill to be sold and my wife to
put it on interest for my own child Lula B. & George E. Britton - 4 years
schooling each, and niece Fannie C. Barrett. Mrs. Sarah C. Obney to live
where she is 3 years - then the trustees of Old Martin Academy shall have
it for the church. Another lot to David Campbell, son of my sister
Eveline. Executor: My brother William M. Grisham. Test: W.R. Sevier,
E.L. Deaderick. Probated September Term, 1873.
                           Signed: George E. Grisham

BARBARA HARMON   May 15, 1873
To Elizabeth Jane wife of M.W. Broyles - all my personal effects for
taking care of me. To son Philip Harmon - $20 in gold. Put tombstones
at our father and mothers graves according to our standing in society.
Executor: George Copp. Test: Frances Copp, M.W. Broyles. Probated
October Term, 1873.   Signed: Barbara (X) Harmon

JOHN WALTERS   October 17, 1873
Son George F. Walters - 6¼ acres I purchased from Isaac Click. Exec.:
George F. Walters. Test: Jno. F. Harris, Elbert Miller. Probated
November Term, 1873.   Signed: John Walters

ELIZABETH McNEAL   December 10, 1873
My notes when collected and personal property be divided between my four
children: James P., William, Charlie & Mary McNeil. Executor: My
youngest brother William R. Miller. Test: James T. Hunt, S.H. Miller.
Probated January Term, 1874.

GREENBERRY BORING   March 31, 1858
Sons: Isaac, Madison, John. Wife Mary. Test: Abraham Gregg, James
Hodges. Probated February Term, 1873.
                           Signed: Greenberry Boring

REV. JAMES MILLER   February 18, 1874
Wife Elizabeth D. Miller - to have my house where we reside in Johnson
City, and at her death it is to descend to Christian Church of which I
am a minister and member, to be used as a parsonage. My other lot
Southeast of Main Street in Johnson City to be given for a comfortable
church if built in 6 years. My interest in N.A. Patterson's Improved
"Eagle Wing" Screw Propeller under letters patent of the Government of
Great Britain, The Dominion of Canada, France and Belgium shall be held
by my wife as agent for the Christian Church of United States of America.
To William Miller, a colored man - 10 acres of the "Coon" Tract in Dist.
No. 9 on the waters of Brush Creek in Washington County. Executors:
Wife Elizabeth D. Miller & John D. Reeves. Wit.: L.A. Faw, S.H. Miller,
Jacob McNees. Probated March Term, 1874.
                        Signed: James Miller

JONATHAN KILLEY   March 16, 1874
My wife Elizabeth to have the home farm and at her death, it is to go to
my son Jonathan P.B. Killey. Sell my Melvin Tract in District 10 to pay
my debts. $100 to be paid Barbary Bowman, my granddaughter, daughter of
David Bowman and my daughter Margaret deceased. Daughter Sarah wife of
Thomas Hale, son James F., dau. Mary Ann wife of Adam Fox, Elizabeth K.
and Sarah M. Edens children of my deceased daughter Barbary S. Edens,
dau. Matilda wife of John Eden & Dau. Minerva K. wife of Nathaniel Eden.
Executors: Thomas B. Stout, James M. Reeves. Wit.: William J. Stout,
N.A. Patterson, H.B. Hankal. Probated April Term, 1874.
                        Signed: Jonathan (X) Killey

JOHN H. BOWMAN   June 17, 1874
Bury me between my 2 wives Selina & Rebecca. Bury me in a plain Shroud
of white linen and put me in a black walnut coffin with a flat top. Son
Adam B. - 160 acre Homestead Farm, carpets on the floor and curtains at
the windows. Daughter Sarah R. Hendrex - $1000. Daughter Mary
Kitzmiller - $1000. Daughter Honora E. Mooman - $1000. Daughter Louise
Klepper - $1000. Daughter Loucindy N. Mooman - $1000. Daughters Salina
J. & Cordelia A. - $1000 each. Daughter Margaret A. - $1000. Lots in
Johnson City. My Home Farm near the Railroad Trestle where William
McCorkle now resides. My store goods that may be on hand. Pay to John
G. Dinn the worth of a horse, saddle and bridle worth $100. Divide money
from Adam Broyles Estate between my oldest daughters. Executors: Son
Adam B. Bowman & son-in-law David J. Kitzmiller. Wit.: C.C.C. Nelson,
W.F. Range. Probated July Term, 1874.

BENJAMIN FORD   December 10, 1866
Four girls now at home: Nancy, Cynthia, Martha & Susanna. Three sons:
Benjamin, Mordecai & George W. Daughter Roda Ford deceased. Sons John
A., William F. Ford. Daughter Elizabeth Ervin. Daughter Sabra Cornet
decd. her children William & Mary Cornet. Executor: Nathan Shipley.
Test: Elbert A. Shipley, James H. Jones. Proven August Term, 1874.
                        Signed: Benjamin (X) Ford

SARAH BASHOR   June 26, 1874
Five years ago my husband died leaving me with 9 children at home and
one married (Matilda). Benjamin has since married and moved to Virginia.
My husband's will left everything to me and the debts are still not paid
by maybe 300 or 400 dollars. I now have 8 children at home, Isaac &
Christly are my oldest and Michael age 6 is my youngest. I appoint sons
Isaac and Christly my Executors to have and hold all my real estate (199
acres) at the mouth of Boones Creek adjoining A.J. Klepper and others.
My girls are Mary, Nancy & Sarah M. My boys are David, James D. & Henry
Michael Bashor. Sons Isaac and Christley are to raise, school and care
for the 6 younger ones until they are of age. Farm, tanyard, water
power. Executors: Sons Isaac & Christley Bashor. Wit.: George P. Faw,
J.B. Garst, Christina Sherfey. Probated July Term, 1874.
                        Signed: Sarah (X) Bashor

ELIZABETH BAINS   February 24, 1873
Son Jesse J. Bains. Land descended to me by heirship from my brother
Nathan Jones in this county, between Fall Branch and Jonesboro adjoining
George Whitlock, Joseph Howe, David Gibson, now the heirs of Nathan
Jones decd., J.H. Crouch. Executor: Jesse J. Bains. Wit.: A.H. Pierce,
J.A. Shepherd. Probated _____. Signed: Elizabeth (X) Bains

JAMES GRAY   November 28, 1868
To son Anderson - 200 acres and to pay other heirs $12 per acre ($2400).
To son Robert H. - 53 acres adjoining James Hale @ $14 per acre ($742)
and the remainder @ $16 per acre to be surveyed. Sons George W. & Robert
H. Gray and daughter Harriet Hodges are to share equal in my estate. Son
Anderson has his part. Executor: Samuel B. Ellis. Test: Isaac Wine,
Samuel Wine. Probated October Term, 1874.
                        Signed: James Gray

WILLIAM MILLER   August 28, 1874
Sons James & Samuel - land where I reside and the tract given me by the
Rev. James Miller. To Jemima Smith - my bed. Sons James & Samuel to
care for my mother if she needs it. In consequence of the wilful and
malicious desertion of my bed and board by my wife Mary, without a just
cause, she receives no part of my estate. Wit.: L.L.C. Nelson, T.A.
Fare. Proven September Term, 1874.
                        Signed: William (X) Nelson

ADAM SELL   August 30, 1873
Wife Margaret. Children: Elizabeth Thornburg - $1, Joseph Sells, Sarah
Moore, Matilda Moore, Catharine Cruthers, Susannah Smith, George & Henry
Sells - to receive equally except Catharine Cruthers who is to receive
$100 more. Daughter Mary Prichet has her part. Executor: John White.
Wit.: H.H. Carr, L.A. Fan. Signed: Adam Sell

4 September 1873 - Margaret Sells adopted Adam's will as her own.
Probated November Term, 1874. Signed: Margaret (X) Sell

MISS MARGARET L. STEVENS   August 1, 1874
Sister Estella L. Cox wife of Mr. John C. Cox - all my estate including
¼ interest in the farm of my father Isaac Stevens decd. in Sullivan Co.,
Tennessee. My other sister and brother: Elizabeth M. and Hiram D.
Stevens. Executor: Brother-in-law John C. Cox. Wit.: J.M. Mitchell,
John F. Grisham. Probated November Term, 1874.
                        Signed: Margaret L. Stevens

JAMES KINCHELOE   October 21, 1867
Wife Louisa - 50 acres. Daughters: Emely McPherson, Louisa Odell,
Elivina Hulse, Sally Cochran, Eveline Martin, Loves Caroline Keen, Betty
Ship. Daughter Orlena Register's husband Gregg Register owes Nathan W.
Bachman $450 for which I am security. Two sons: Eldridge F. Kincheloe,
J.H. Kincheloe & grandson George F. Kincheloe to have no more of my
estate. Executors: Sons Eldridge & J.H. Kincheloe. Wit.: Nathan
Shipley, W.H. Gray, George W. Fry. Probated April Term, 1874.
                        Signed: James Kincheloe

NANCY BROYLES   September 25, 1868
Formerly Nancy Mitchell. Sons Samuel D. & William H. Mitchell - what
William Mitchell decd. left me. My wearing apparel to my 3 granddaus.:
Ann, Jane & Emma Allen. Grandsons William, George & Robert Allen - $10
each. Executor: Samuel D. Mitchell. Wit.: H.F. Bailey, J.M. Bayless.
Probated December Term, 1874. Signed: Nancy Broyles

JAMES VAUGHAN   December 21, 1874
Of District 11. Wife Matilda, oldest daughter Martha widow of Thomas
Crawford decd. with 2 small children. Youngest daughter Mary L. Vaughn

who is single and at home. My children now living: Joseph E. Vaughn, L.C. Vaughn, Martha A. Crawford, R.A. Vaughan, E.L. Vaughan now Temple & Mary L. Vaughan. Executors: L.C. Vaughan & George P. Faw. Wit.: Perry Hunter, T.J. Galloway. Probated January Term, 1875.
Signed: James Vaughan

HENRY HARRINGTON   No date
To Rachel Caroline Young - all my estate from Montgomery Hoss, Sq.? Ann Jones on south side of road. On north side of road to Harriett Young - if she dies without heirs, to Rachel Caroline Young. Executor: Strobie Young. Wit.: Alexander S. Brownlow, Jesse Duncan. Probated January Term, 1875.   Signed: Henry (X) Harrington

JAMES BIDDLE   September 23, 1874
Wife Elizabeth and daughter Mary Ann have a permanant home during Elizabeth's natural life. Sons J.N. & John Biddle have their part. . Other children: Washington, Nancy Good, Sarah Taylor, Mary Ann. Executor: J.N. Biddle. Test: T.P. Britton, J.L. Biddle. Probated February Term, 1875.   Signed: James Biddle

SIMEON BROYLES   March 27, 1852
Wife Mary. Son Archibald - land where we live adjoining Jesse Broyles, Alexander Broyles and others. Five daughters: Elizabeth wife of Brooks H. Bell, Sally wife of William Blackburn, Evy wife of Jacob Broyles, Eleanor wife of Nathaniel Broyles, Polly Ann wife of John Mauk. Three sons: Jesse, Jefferson & Jacob have their portion. Executor: Son Archibald Broyles. Wit.: W.H. Smith, Jas. M. Mauk. Probated April Term, 1875.   Signed: Simeon (X) Broyles

ABRAHAM SNAPP   September 6, 1873
To heirs of my son Samuel Snapp decd. late of Russellville, Tenn. to wit: John, Louvina & Edward - jointly $2000. To son Windle D. Snapp - farm where I now reside on the northeast bank of Nolachucky River in District 2 adjoining Samuel D. Waddle, containing 212 acres, and all my personal property, household, horses, cattle, hogs, sheep etc. Exec.: Windle Snapp. Wit.: A.S.N. Dobson, J.M. Bayless, J.G. Duncan. Probated May Term, 1875.   Signed: Abram Snapp

SARAH HUMPHREY   March 17, 1871
My horses to be used by James H. Wheelock and wife to raise and educate their children. To Hannah wife of James Whitlock - my Tennessee Beauty coverlet. To Sarah W. Whitlock - my calico quilt pieced in half squares. To John Anderson Whitlock - my bureau. To William Newton Whitlock - my coverlet called the Winding Vine. To George Washington Whitlock - cover- let called the Charriott Wheel. To my brother Elvin Whitlock - coverlet Winding Compass. To Martha daughter of Elvin Whitlock - my Big Wheel. To James M. Whitlock and wife - a note I have on Thomas Humphrey for $140, 3 notes on L.N. Humphrey and one on E.K. Hunt. My brothers: Edmond, William, Deyton B. & Elvin Whitlock. My Queens ware to Hannah Whitlock. Executor: R.S. Ferguson. Wit.: William W. Depew, Thomas (X) Ford. Probated May Term, 1875.   Signed: Sarah (X) Humphreys

DR. O. R. BROYLES SR.   April 15, 1875
State of South Carolina - Anderson County. To W.W. Humphreys Judge of Probate for the county and state aforesaid - the undersigned represents that her late husband Dr. O.R. Broyles died 25 February last leaving his last will and testament with two codicils. Sarah Ann Broyles widow was bequeathed the entire estate and was named Executrix. She asked that they be admitted for probate. His 3 sons: A.F., Charles E. & William H. Broyles to be Executors.
WILL - I bequeath to my wife Sarah Ann all my estate whether in South Carolina, Tennessee or elsewhere. Children: Augustus T., Charles E., Margaret Vanwyk, William H., Ozy R., Thomas F., John P., & Sarah A.

Williams 21 September 1868. Wit.: W.J. Lyon, Jon D. Taylor, Z.T.
Taylor.   Signed: O.R. Broyles
Codicil - 20 April 1871 - All children educated except son John P.
Another codicil - 28 January 1874. Probated 15 July 1875 in South
Carolina.

JOHN KING   January 29, 1875
Of Johnson City. To James Miller - my watch. To Joseph McKasson - my
shawl. To Mary Hyder - my bed. To AME Zion Church - $5 to buy wine for
the Sacrament. To Samuel Weeks - all the rest of my estate. Executor:
Daniel Weeks. Wit.: George Phillips, Alfred Hyder.
                              Signed: John (X) King

JORDON LOVEGROVE   June 17, 1875
To wife Elizabeth - the Jordan Lovegrove farm adjoining David and Samuel
Murr and William Lovegrove. My children to live with their mother while
they are single. Son James to cultivate the farm. My children: John,
David, Katharine Ann, William, Henry, Mary Eliza, Hannah Eliza, James
Franklin and Susan Estaline and their heirs. Executors: Sons William
Henry & James Franklin Lovegrove. Wit.: K.R. Carmack, P.N. Mottern.
Probated July Term, 1875.   Signed: Jordan Lovegrove

ELIZABETH KEY
I owe J.M. Hoss, son Landon has made a payment on note. Two children,
Minerva Myers and Landon Keys to have my entire estate, equally divided.
Executor: Enos Kincheloe. Test: W.R. Sevier, John Allison, Jr. Proven
July Term, 1875.   Signed: Elizabeth (X) Keys

MARTHA H. WYLY   May 10, 1875
To my adopted son Joseph A. Wyly - books from my husband's library. To
my son Charles H. Wyly - all the remainder of my personal property. My
father Joseph Henderson to be my sons guardian. Executor: My brother
Finley Henderson of New York City. Wit.: A.E. Jackson, Joseph
Henderson. Probated July Term, 1875.
                              Signed: Martha H. Wyly

RACHEL O. McLIN   December 29, 1874
Widow of Richard McLin, decd. Children: Robert, Elizabeth Ann, Locind
Carson and Sophiah C. My daughter Elizabeth Ann has died, her husband
Alexander Carson helped us divide. All property I have in my own right
is to go to Sophiah C. for caring for me. Executor: John B. McLin.
Wit.: M.B. Crookshanks. Probated July Term, 1875.
                              Signed: Rachel (X) McLin

JACK GILLESPIE   August 14, 1875
To daughter Hattie - 2 acres of land where we live which I bought of M.F.
Jerolds, corn on Isaac Broyles farm, pay B.B. Broyles for borrowed wheat.
Persons mentioned: Isaac Barkley, Mary Hansford. Have my brothers
Washington and Preston to bury me in the meadow near the Old Gillespie
Homestead. To son James, daughter Marthy. Test: E.S. Malles, Isaac
Broyles, James McAllister. Proven September Term, 1875.
                              Signed: Jack (X) Gillespie

JAMES CAMPBELL   April 5, 1860
Son Madison got more than an equal share. My children. Executors: Son
John & son-in-law Jacob Bowman. Wit.: W.W. Mullendore, John B. McLin,
J.F. Mahoney. Probated November Term, 1875.
                              Signed: James (X) Campbell

JOHN JONES   December 15, 1875
To my wife _____ Jones, George A., C.E., L.N., E.J., S.D. & J.F. Jones -
all to live together until the youngest comes of age. Pay James M. Jones
$100. To Mary E. Jones if her Onkel Elsy, who she lives with, does not
make her an heir. Executor: My brother James H. Jones. Probated
February Term, 1876.   Signed: John Jones

GEORGE WALTERS   September 17, 1875
Wife Susannah. Daughter Clara Miller and her heirs. Land I bought of
John Tabor. My grandchildren viz: George F. Walter, Fannie Dulaney,
Laura C. Walter, Isaac N. Walter and Margaret E. Keener - lawful heirs
of my son John Walter decd. Daughters Catharine, Margaret Rubble's
heirs, her husband Henry W. Ruble. Executor: Grandson George F. Walter.
Probated May Term, 1876.   Signed: George Walter

JOHN T. SMITH   December 11, 1875
Wife Mariah - all real estate and personal property after debts.   To
Samuel F. Smith, my son - equal shares in my home farm adjoining Bacon,
Garber, Mathes and Smith, and all personal property at Mariah's death,
but he is to pay expenses. Executors: Wife Mariah & W.H.M. Smith.
Wit.: Samuel H. Garber, Samuel E. Morrell. Probated May Term, 1876.
                          Signed: John T. Smith

CHASE HALE   April 27, 1872
Wife Clary - everything as long as she lives. Heirs: Margaret Jackson
wife of John W. Jackson - an equal share to be paid to her alone, dau.
Susan Hale - to have an equal part, Elizabeth Hale wife of my son William
deceased - $1 - she has since intermarried with a Steel man and moved to
Illinois leaving no heirs by my son William, Polly An Jackson, Hannah
Cox, Ruth Mitchell and Nancy Jobe - equal shares. Heirs of my son George
deceased to have his share. James W. Cox son of Sally Cox decd. - her
share. Heirs of Betty Jackson decd. - a share. Executor: Nathan Shipley.
Wit.: William Ford, Chase Mitchell. Probated May Ter, 1876.
                          Signed: Chase (X) Hale

NANCY McCLUNG EARNEST   July 3, 1876
50 acres where I have lived for several years adjoining David Dewald,
J.H. Collom, David Haga and others to my two daughters: Amanda Marilla
and Margaret Melvina Earnest and they are to care for their father
Josiah W. Earnest his lifetime. The estate willed to me by my uncle
E.L. Mathes decd. - to my daughters: Jane Anna McCurry, Amanda M.
Earnest, Margaret M. Earnest, Nancy L. Harrison will share at the death
of her father Josiah W. Earnest. Executor: Jacin A. Bradshaw. Test:
James Patton, James M. Bayless. Probated August Term, 1876.
                          Signed: Nancy (X) McClung Earnest

REV. JOHN WRIGHT   September 18, 1874
Rev. John Wright and Margaret of Johnson City, Tennessee. To our son
George Washington Wright - our lot in Johnson City where we live adjoin-
ing Dr. Mongh, Main Street & J.H. Hail's lot. Our son John James Wright,
a cripple, is to be cared for of his ½ interest in lot. Daughter
Catharine Range. Executor: Son George Washington Wright. Wit.: Mont
Hoss, Jacob McNeec. Probated September Term, 1876.
                          Signed: John Wright
                                  Margaret (X) Wright

WILLIAM H. COWAN   May 9, 1875
Wife M.A. Cowan. Children: J.M., Sallie H.C., M.J.C., J.I.C., F.A.C.,
L.A.C., W.P.C., E.M.C. Children to finish their education. Executors:
My wife M.A. Cowan & son J.M. Cowan. Test: G.W. Telford, W.E. Mathes.
Probated September Term, 1876.   Signed: W.H. Cowan

CHARLES BACON   January 29, 1873
Wife Elizabeth. Son Preston Bacon - to have the 180 acre farm we live
on adjoining Endymon Yoakley and William Hickman. He is to care for his
mother and have all land but 25 acres. Son Jonathan - $400. I hold a
note on E. Carey for $600. Daughter Dela Ellen Moore and her heirs -
$400. Daughter Nancy Jane Bacon - to stay on here while she is single
and have $400. If necessary sell land adjoining Henry N. Bacon, E.
Conly and Jonathan Hartman. It is well understood by me that Temander
Carey, Louisa Carey and Henry N. Bacon and Sylvenous Bacon has got their
$400 paid to them by me. Executors: Elijah Carey, Sylvenius Bacon.
Test: Nathan Shipley, George W. Galloway. Probated March Term, 1876.
                        Signed: Charles Bacon

SAMUEL GARST   April 21, 1869
Wife Susannah, children to all share equal. Executor: Son-in-law
William A. Sherfy. Wit.: C.T.C. Deake, J.F. Grisham. Proven November
Term, 1876.   Signed: Samuel (X) Garst

JOHN WILLIAMS   October 10, 1876
Wife _____. To daughter Anne - 30 acres over and above what she is to
receive of her mother's estate. To daughter Mary B. & Theophiles A.
Williams - 36 acres that formerly belonged to John Williams Sr. To son
George W. - 25 acres. Son James - $150. To son John L. & daughters
Caroline, Sarah & Sophronia - $50 each. Executor: Son George W.
Williams. Wit.: Thomas L. Williams, Samuel Arnold. Proven November
Term, 1876.   Signed: John Williams

JOSHUA HENLEY   January 2, 1864
Wife _____. Children: Rebecca Henley, Suaphine Graham - 2/3 my estate
free of their husbands. To son John - the remaining one third. To
support their brother Theodore. I have provided for my other children
not named in this will. Executor: John S. Henley. Wit.: James E.
Deakins, Samuel E. Graham. Proven November Term, 1876.
                        Signed: Joshua Henley

JOHN W. LANE   June 14, 1875
Wife Sarah Jane Lane. Children: George A., Armah Lane, Sarah Lane my
youngest daughter, Mary Treadway & Louisa May Lane. Executors: William
A. May & George A. Lane. Wit.: Alexander McCall, John T. Partien.
Probated December Term, 1876. Signed: John W. Lane

JACOB RANGE
Daughters: Louisa - $1000, Susan - $500, Elizabeth Rankin, Eliza Miller
& Nancy Hoss. Son George - $5. Sons Peter & Jacob to have my plantation
and Louisa and myself are to have a room or rooms and furnish us with
what is necessary. Executors: Sons Peter & Jacob Range. Test: Joseph
Bowman, Jasper N. Christy, Henry P. Settens. Probated December Term,
1876.   Signed: Jacob Range

ARTY M. TREADWAY   February 1, 1876
Heirs: David B., William M., Martha L. Cloyd, Mary Luttrell, Sarah P.
Haynes, Elizabeth More, Nancy C. Crumly, Lovina Graham, Daniel B., Eliza
Brown, Heirs of John Treadway. Executor: Iranius Keicher. Wit.: A.V.
Thompson, Iranius Keicher. Proven January Term, 1877.
                        Signed: Arty M. Treadway

ABSALOM GOFORTH   October 30, 1876
Wife Mary Emeline. Children: Josephine, James M., Lucindy Cloyd,
Thomas J., Sabra More, Andrew J., Mary A. Rutland, William N., Lorra A.,
Ellen, Lewis S. & Charles G. Goforth. Executors: Wife Mary Emeline &
son William N. Goforth. Wit.: J.A. Conley, Anderson Reep. Probated
February Term, 1877.   Signed: Absalom (X) Goforth

BENJAMIN SHERFY   December 1, 1864
Wife Barbary - to have 180 acre home tract I bought of Jones Hunt Martin
for 5 years after my death, then lay off 80 acres for her with improve-
ments and sell the rest. Note on Samuel Miller - to my wife. I want
John Willcox to stay on farm with Barbary. I raised my brother's son
John B. Sherfy, he is to heir equally in my estate. Executor: Son-in-
law John Wilcox. Wit.: J.M. Bayless, F.W. Done. Probated February
Term, 1877.   Signed: Benjamin Sherfy

WILLIAM MIDDLETON   August 30, 1867
Wife Ann Middleton. All the heirs. Executrix: Wife Ann Middleton.
Test: J.J. Yeager. Probated March Term, 1877.
                               Signed: William Middleton

ELIZABETH D. MILLER   December 21, 1876
Widow of Rev. James Miller, decd., see his will. To my friend Sarah J.
Miller - all my household and kitchen furniture. All the gold I have
both what is in the house and what is loaned out. She stayed with and
helped care for my husband James Miller and me. My library and secretary
holding it to the Christian Church of Johnson City, of which I am a
member. To my sister Mary wife of William P. Reeves - $1000 in cash.
To my sister Matilda C. wife of Peter M. Reeves - $1000 in cash. To
Lizzie Miller Patterson daughter of Susan Patterson - $100. Money to
the heirs of my 2 sisters equally. To Sarah Miller Coonty - bonds worth
$2000. Executor: My nephew E.C. Reeves. Test: J.F. Grisham, S.H.
Miller. Probated March Term, 1877.
                               Signed: Elizabeth D. Miller

JOHN MOORE   April 27, 1875
Wife Margaret and daughter Nancy M. Moore - land known as the Sarah
Tucker interest in the Nicholas Tucker Farm adjoining David Murs, D.A.
Thompson, Elizabeth Thompson and heirs of Dr. William Reed decd. Dau.
Nancy is notable fisically to support herself. My heirs: James W.,
& Elie Moore, Sarah E. Cane wife of John Cane & Rebecca wife of J.W.
Reed. Executor: J.F. Brown. Wit.: David Mizer, David A. Thompson.
Probated March Term, 1877.   Signed: John (X) Moore

CLARA MILLER   March 22, 1877
Six children: James M. Miller, Mary A. Kilby, Sarah C. Loyd, Susan M.
Kilby, Melissa J. Miller & Sophronia C. Miller. Two youngest daughters
Melissa & Sophronia. Each child got a straw bed. Executor: Henry Hoss
Junr. Wit.: John T. Parker, Joseph Booth. Probated March Term, 1877.
                               Signed: Clara Miller

JAMES A. DILLWORTH   October 1, 1876
Wife Mary Charlotte. Heirs: Caroline Fleming, Mary wife of Oscar
Dillworth, Virginia McPherson, Mary Sparks & Charles E. Dillworth.
Executor: Dr. M.S. Mahoney. Wit.: Hugh D. Hoss, Charles C. McPherson.
Probated May Term, 1877.   Signed: J.A. Dillworth

NANCY FORD   April 28, 1877
Buffalo Ridge, Washington County, Tennessee. To my brother G.W. Ford -
some personal property. To my sister Cintha Ford - 4 hogs, mare, colt.
Note on Joseph Dove, Note on Grant Ford. Note on G.W. Kitzmiller also
my interest in land willed me by my sister Cintha Ford in District 12
adjoining G.W. Kitzmiller, Jonathan Ford, William Hall and Samuel
Chapman. Wit.: James H. Ford, Grant Ford.
                               Signed: Nancy (X) Ford

ABRAHAM SAYLOR   November 6, 1876
Wife Abigail Saylor - to have control during her life. Son Isaac - to
remain on farm and care for his mother. Son Isaac and all my legal heirs

to divide at my wife's death. Executor: Son Isaac. Wit.: D.P. Hunt,
A. Carr. Probated June Term, 1877.

Signed: Abraham Sailler

JOHN BRADY   July 1877
Wife ____ and her daughter Sarah to remain on the place until October
1 - then it is to be sold. My children who I understand are in America:
John, Biddy, Micha & Patrice Bracy - my former wife to be made equal
with the 4 children. Executor: J.E.T. Harris. Wit.: F.W. Dove,
J.E.T. Harris. Probated August Term, 1877.

Signed: John (X) Brady

B. F. TEMPLIN   June 10, 1877
My wife Rebecca to have all my land and personal property. Have good
substantial pailings built around the graves of my children, made of
cast or wrought iron and set on a rock wall. Executrix: Wife F.
Templin. Test: Thomas J. Wilson, E.E. Wilson. Probated August Term,
1877.

Signed: B.F. Templin

JAMES CRABTREE   June 19, 1877
To son Terry Crabtree - ½ my land where I now live. To daughter Martha
Arnold - the remaining ½, then to her son Junie. Martha and Terry are
to both have access to the water. My wife Jenny (Jane) to live with
either child she chooses. Other children: Margaret Workman, Elbert
Crabtree, J. Crabtree - $30 each. Executor: ____. Wit.: O.H.
Kirkpatrick, William R. White. Probated August Term, 1877.

Signed: James (X) Crabtree

CHINOWTH HALE   April 22, 1877
To my son Harvey N. Hale - the farm where I live and he is to care for
my wife Nancy Hale and pay $25 apiece to my other children: Thomas &
Harriet Hale, Fannie Curtis, Louise Sells and Rena Hale. Executor:
John F. Grisham. Test: Robert Dyer, David Fox. Proven August Term,
1877.

Signed: Chinowth (X) Hale
Nancy (X) Hale

GEORGE BALLARD   August 4, 1876
Wife Elisa Jane & son John A. Ballard to have land during her natural
life and raise my minor children. Heirs: John, Stephen, grandchildren
Heily F., William and Hattie May Seevers - 1/6 said realty - said child-
ren are of my daughter Harriet Seevers decd. Executor: Son John
Ballard. Test: F.D. Crumley, Sam Williams, G.M. Murrell. Probated
September Term, 1877.

Signed: George W. (X) Ballard

HARRIET WALL   March 28, 1873
My present husband Armistead Wall made an agreement when we married that
we would each retain and control our own property as we saw fit. My
property real and personal. I give my house and lot on Main Street in
Jonesboro where I have lived for many years and which I inherited from
my grandmother Susan Woodson at the death of my mother Elisa C. Jackson
- to my daughter Elisa Gamble and Cordelia May and to my 2 grandchildren
Hattie Benson & Oliver Eugene Ross (by right of their father James B.
Ross decd.) children of my former husband. Each daughter to possess 1/3
interest and my grandchildren the other 1/3. If my daughter Cordelia
mae dies without issue - her part to go to equally divided between Elisa
Gamble if living or her son Augustus Gamble, Hattie Benson & Oliver
Eugene Ross. To Augustus Gamble - I give the portrait of my first
husband Oliver B. Ross and to grandson Oliver Eugene Ross - the portrait
of his grandfather James Ross. Collect note due me from John W. Lampson
and pay debts. The foregoing disposition of my real estate is in
accordance with the spirit of my grandmothers will (and understand it)
from whom this property was derived. My daughter Elisa Gamble has
visited and cared for me while sick this past year. Wit.: H.C. Jackson,

L.E. Jackson. Probated September Term, 1877.
                    Signed: Harriett Wall

MARY ANN AIKEN   February 15, 1878
Husband James Aiken to have a home while he remains single and lives
with the children. My children: Mary C., Elizabeth A. and Peter.
Sell land and pay my debt to Martha J. Humphres. Executors: Solomon
Miller & Richard Armentrout. Wit.: J.K. Armentrout, William E. Miller.
Probated April Term, 1878.   Signed: Mary A. Aiken

REV. GEORGE GRISHAM   September 15, 1877
Age 82 years and upwards. Daughter Sarah is without husband or heirs
because of her peculiar situation in life - my son William M. Grisham
is to make her a deed for a life estate in the homeplace on the road
leading from Boons Creek to Buffalo Ridge Meeting House. Other children: Albert Hiram Grisham, Evelina Campbell (Abney lot in Jonesboro &
note on P.H. Grisham for $100). Daughter Elizabeth Clark, son Jno. F.
Grisham, son Peter H. Grisham, daughter Mary widow of W.H. Blevins now
living in Arkansas. Son William M. Grisham - a note on C.L. Mundy for
a balance on the Christian Church of Jonesboro, I have given this to
the church to be taken from his part of my estate. Executor: Son
William M. Grisham. Wit.: J. Hoss, J.M. Johnson.
                    Signed: George Grisham

RICHARD CHINOWTH   April 24, 1878
To Emeline wife of my son William Chinowth and her heirs - my house and
lot in Johnson City situated on King's Street adjoining Dr. E.S. Miller.
My farm in Buffalo Ridge adjoining George Gray, Chamberlain Hale - to be
sold and proceeds given to grandson Daniel Fox. Addy and Robert Dyer,
Amanda Hughes, Elizabeth Dyer and the heirs of Martha Chase decd. -
equal shares of the rest of my estate after paying debts. Pay John
Chinowth, release a debt from the estate of my son James M. Chinowth
decd. Son James heirs: Emeline, Daniel Fox, John C. Son-in-law Nelton
Chase is in no way to have any part of my estate. Wit.: W. Hodges,
James Seaver. Probated July Term, 1878.
                    Signed: Richard Chinowth

REBECCA CARTRIGHT   May 5, 1878
I will one quilt to each one of my brother George Hamilton's girls. To
my brother George Hamilton - one $300 bond from my husband William
Cartright decd. estate. Executor: William N. King. Test: Albert
Thomas Brown, G.W. Fitzmiller. Probated August Term, 1878.
                    Signed: Rebecca Cartwright

SAMUEL E. EDWARDS   January 14, 1878
Wife Mary Edwards - the farm as a dower for life to raise and educate my
youngest son Samuel Judson Edwards. Land bounded by Carr, J.D. Fox and
Dr. A. Martin. To my daughter Mary Elizabeth Edwards & son Joshua Polk
Edwards - the west end of the old Joshua Edwards farm in Sullivan County,
containing 138 acres adjoining Bullock, Jones, Rader, Longacre, Rutledge,
Owen Edwards & Joseph Longacre including the Edwards brick home and log
barn. These children are to pay me $100 each. To my daughter Eliza Ann
Morrell and son Abel Washington Edwards - the remainder of the farm above
by their paying me $200 each beginning January 1, 1879. David K. Edwards
wants nothing disposed with, I grant him his wish. I will to my seven
children (David K. included) in common 300 acres on Sharp's Creek in
Sullivan County. Wit.: D.K. Edwards, John W. Morrell, A.W. Edwards.
Probated October Term, 1878.   Signed: S.E. Edwards

ESTELLE COX (born Stephens)   September 12, 1878
Husband John C. Cox - my right and title to my late father's estate, also
that bequeathed me by my sister Margaret Stephens decd. My 3 surviving
children. Wit.: Lawrence Bowers, Lavina Walters. Probated October Term

94

Signed: Estelle L. (X) Cox

JONATHAN HARVEY COLLOM   October 10, 1878
Wife Nancy. Sons: R.N. Collum - $115, J.P. & E.M. Collum - each $130 to
make them equal with my other children. Executor: Son R.N. Collum.
Wit.: A.S.N. Dobson, David Dewald. Probated November Term, 1878.
                                   Signed: Jonathan H. Collum

ELIZABETH MARSH   November 14, 1874
Sister Hannah Jones - both personal and mined estate so sister Hannah's
2 children Mary E. Bacon & John A. Jones can share equal. Executor:
Henry M. Jones. Wit.: S.P. Martin, E.A. Ferguson. Probated January
Term, 1879.   Signed: Elizabeth (X) Marsh

DANIEL SHERFY   March 16, 1878
Wife Mary. Two grandsons: James H. and Daniel B. Sherfy whom I have
raised - to cultivate farm and take care of Mary. My heirs: Samuel A.,
Joseph B., Andrew, John A., & 2 grandsons James H. & Daniel B. Sherfy.
Executor: J.F. Grisham. Wit.: Joseph B. Sherfy, William Chase.
Probated February Term, 1879.   Signed: Daniel Sherfy

MARGARET MAY   April 10, 1879
Three daughters living: Mary A. Peoples, Margaret L. Henley, Malinda C.
Beard. Son Samuel May. Son Isaac, Martha A. May. Executor: D.F.W.
Peoples. Wit.: John P. Miller, Jeff Sligar. Probated May Term, 1879.
                                   Signed: Margaret (X) May

EMALINE GOFORTH   March 16, 1879
Children living with me: William, Alice, Ellen, Lewis, Charley Goforth -
my homestead right in the land where we live - due me by the Homestead
Act. Son Thomas, daughter Saber wife of William Moore, Mary Ann wife of
_____ Rutland & Andrew J. Goforth. Executors: J.A. Conley, William
Goforth. Wit.: Anderson Rupe, James W. Goforth. Probated May Term,
1879.   Signed: Mary (X) Emaline Goforth

ANNA HISE   October 7, 1879
My husband _____. Daughter Elizabeth to live where we live and care for
her father. Granddaughter Hannah Jane Hise. At my husband's death the
farm is to be sold and the money divided equally. Wit.: John Killey,
James M. Miller. Probated November Term, 1879.
                                   Signed: Anna (X) Hise

R. C. LOVE   October 13, 1879
Each child to receive $204.69 - that is M.E. Love, S.L.G. Love, M.M.
Moorfield (formerly Love), H.G. Love & M.V.V. Love. Money in Greenback.
To wife Elizabeth - all personal property. Executrix: Wife Elizabeth.
Wit.: John H. Denton, James M. Love. Probated November Term, 1879.
                                   Signed: R.C. Love

SUSANNAH TRUXELLS   February 19, 1878
To daughter Virginia E. Sherfy for taking care of me - all my estate
consisting of my house in Fall Branch, Tennessee. She is to pay my
funeral expenses, tombstones to mine and my granddaughter Maria Katharine
Gardner's graves, and a note to my son James E. Truxell. Executrix:
Virginia E. Sherfy. Wit.: George R. Duncan, Abraham G. Cox. Probated
December Term, 1879.   Signed: Susannah Truxell

MARY EDNA COPP   July 25, 1878
To be buried at Philadelphia Church with a marble monument at my grave.
Thank God I owe no debts. My husband Jacob F. Copp - all my estate.

Executor: Bruce Broyles. Wit.: Bruce Broyles, James Freeman.
Probated March Term, 1880.   Signed: Mary Edna Copp

HENRY DENTON   March 5, 1880
Three children: D.B. Denton, John F. Denton & Amanda Denton Huffine -
to sell real estate and divide equally. To son William Denton - $50.
To Louisa Denton Saymore - $50. Executor: D.W.F. Peoples. Wit.:
Jesse Slagle, Daniel Huffine. Probated April Term, 1880.
                              Signed: Henry (X) Denton

JOHN PIERCE   June 2, 1879
To Elizabeth Brown for her amicable qualities and service to my family,
she has been a good girl - $500. Wit.: Jno. S. Biddle, Samuel Kelsey.
Probated April Term, 1880.   Signed: John Pierce

SALLIE JANE MILLER   June 6, 1880
To Matilda C. wife of Peter M. Reeves - clothes. To Mary wife of William
P. Reeves - silverware. To Mary wife of N.A. Patterson - my chair. To
Lizzie A. Reeves - my delf ware. To 4 sisters: Elizabeth Lane, Martha
Rezor, Mary Kooz & Margaret Ann Melvin - all that I received from my
father's estate. To Trustees of Methodist Episcopal Church of Johnson
City - $1000 for the erection of a church. The balance to Heirs of
Peter M. Reeves (John D., Elbert C., James M., George A. & Lizzie A.
Reeves & Mary S. Patterson). Executor: James M. Reeves. Test: James
S. Hunt, E.S. Miller. Probated July Term, 1880.
                              Signed: Sallie Jane (X) Miller

NATHANIEL T. BROWN   January 2, 1879
Real Estate where I live to son H.N. Brown and daughter Roena A. Smith -
lying on road Mauk's Ford to Jonesboro to river - to maintain and support
my widow and pay my daughter Mary J. Hankle $500 and money after to
educate her children. To son W.N. Brown. Executors: Wife Pheuetta
Brown & H.H. Ruble. Wife to remain until W.N. Brown becomes of age.
Wit.: R.M. Chase, D.J. Kitzmiller. Probated July Term, 1880.
                              Signed: N.T. Brown

DANIEL FRANCIS   December 24, 1879
Son Jacob H. Francis - to have my real and personal estate if he takes
care of me my lifetime and assumes and pays my debts. He is never to
allow a distillery for making liquor on the farm. Wit.: T.T. Price,
H.L. Price. Probated September Term, 1880.
                              Signed: Daniel (X) Francis

HUGH P. YOUNG   October 10, 1877
To 5 children by my last wife Latitia M. Young to wit: Ellen C., George
W., Susan E., Julia F. & Barbara A. Young - 130 acres where I live and
what I purchased of the Kwuse Farm. Daughter Emeline is still single.
To son-in-law Alfred Crouch and wife Rebecca - 11 acres adjoining saw-
mill property with mill race and water power adjoining Caruthers & James
Crumley. To children of my first wife: Robert W., John, Joseph, Emeline
Young, Mary Bacon, Sarah Klepper, Elizabeth Hale's heirs, Isabella Jones
- land in District 10 adjoining William P. Reeves and Daniel Bowman. My
son William Young is deceased without heirs - his widow Susan Young
married _____ Jones - to her $1. Son Hugh P. Young is dead, to his son
Robert Young - $1. Executor: Son John C. Young. Wit.: George C.
Bowman, Christena Sallenbarger. Probated August Term, 1880.
                              Signed: Hugh P. Young

HENRY LINEWEAVER   February 11, 1875
Have lived over 3 score and ten years. Wife Catharine to have comfort-
able support on my Home Farm adjoining Alfred Martin, Henry Fox, John
Curtis, George C. Bowman, George P. Faw & William B. Bowman. The Eutau

Place near Brickers District adjoining John Reedy, Dr. Jeralds and others.
We raised 6 children: Elizabeth wife of John Bottles and lives in Va.,
Catharine widow of Daniel Ragan living in Kansas, Susannah who first
married James Bottles - now married to Addison Huffman, John B. Lineweaver living in Kansas, Sarah and Margaret now at home. Son John B.
left me in time of war. Executors: William B. Bowman & George P. Faw.
Wit.: Solomon Hyllow, J.H. Bacon. Probated October Term, 1880.

Signed: Henry (X) Lineweaver

NICHOLAS KEEFHAVER   May 23, 1879
Wife Decy. Two sons Shelton and Abraham Keefjaver are willed my land and
care for Dicy. Land adjoining Jesse Bacon, James Keebler, Samuel Miller
decd. Son Henry Keefhauver, Mary Bacon decd. heirs are to have one share,
Nancy Squibb, Delila Martin, to share in money on hand and from the
personal property sale. Executor: Henry Keefauver. Test: Nathan
Shipley, Samuel C. Nave. Probated October Term, 1880.

Signed: Nicholas Keefhaver

GEORGE G. KING   April 30, 1877
To Montgomery Broyles - 25 acres adjoining Thomas King and Jacob Range
on Jonesboro to Davaults Ford road. To son George King if he has legal
heirs. Montgomery Broyles to pay my debts to Oliver Broyles and John
White. My wife Argille. To daughters: Sara Broyles, Martha Range and
Rosa Buckner - $50 each. To grandchildren of Joseph and Margaret Crouch
- $1, and those of Benjamin and Jane Kelley - $1. Executors: George
King & Montgomery Broyles. Test: H.H. Carr, John White.

Signed: George G. (X) King

Cidicil - To Montgomery Broyles 45 or 50 acres instead of the 25 acres
above - on Great Road (Jonesboro to Davaults Ford on Watauga River)
adjoining Azariah Peoples 6 November 1880. Probated December Term, 1880.

EDWARD WEST   December 28, 1880
Wife Isabella - farm adjoining Peter Northington, William Hoss and others,
to be managed by D.R. and E.H. West. She is to receive $100 per year.
To sons David R. and Edward H. West - the farm where I live adjoining
William Tyler, Nolachucky River, C. Ward, Charles Beard and James
Stephens, H.H. Ruble - at the death of my wife. Daughter Isabella Ruble.
Son James A. West. To grandson Samuel M. Russell's guardian. To
Benjamin West (a boy of color) - $100 when he is 21. To Northern Pres.
Board of Home Missions - $200. To granddaughter Nora Ruble Mathes -
$200. Sell my Roger Farm and personal property. Executor: Edward H.
West. Wit.: J.S. Henley, A.C. Broyles. Probated January Term, 1881.

Signed: Edward West

WILLIAM ELLIS   May 15, 1877
Only son Samuel B. Ellis. Granddaughter Mollie E. Ellis. Daughter
Elizabeth Hamilton - $500. Malinda Ellis __?__. Wit.: Isaac Wine,
Samuel Wine. Probated February Term, 1881.

Signed: William Ellis

ELIZABETH BACON   December 28, 1880
Daughters: Tymeander Cary, Louisa Carey, Delia E. Moore, Nancy Jane
Ferguson's 3 children (William, Virga & Cora Ferguson). Son Jonathan
Bacon, Sylvenous Bacon, Preston Bacon, Henry U. Bacon, Nancy Jane
Ferguson's heirs. Executor: Henry F. Carey. Test: Elijah Cary, S.H.
Murray. Probated March Term, 1881.

Signed: Elizabeth (X) Bacon

ELISHA FINE   April 9, 1881
My money is in hands of Vinett Fine my Executor. Use $30 for tombstones
at mine and my wife's graves, $6 to enclose them and the rest of my
estate to my daughter Margaret Ellen Thornburg and her heirs. Test:

M.J. Peoples, H.R. Fine. Probated March Term, 1881.
                                    Signed: Elisha (X) Fine

WILLIAM HAWS   March 14, 1866
Wife Amanda Jane - maintenance to be ample in kind and quality until her
death or marriage. To daughter Marietta Evans - land adjoining John
Brabson heirs and John & Thomas Williams, and to share my railroad stock.
Pay debt I owe my wife of $60. Executors: 2 sons H.M. Harrison &
Shadrack W. Haws. Wit.: Alexander Mathes, John Aston Sr. Probated May
Term, 1881.   Signed: William Haws

LUCINDA F. HANNAH   June 27, 1877
Nieces: Margaret Cowan, Nancy Telford, Fannie & E.J. Telford, Emma C.
McClure, Alice Barkley, Lucinda Oliphant and Eva A. West. I have 2/3
interest with G.W. Telford in notes and claims against Robert and John
Payne, Estate of Alexander Wilson decd. and Mitchell Workman. My 2/3
interest in the Hannah Farm near Washington College - to my nieces. My
sister Esther Hannah decd. left land to me (not recorded). I made a
former will to Amanda Telford now decd. - to be revoked. Executor:
E.G. McClure. Wit.: N.A. Telford, A.S.N. Dobson, C.M. Harlow.
Probated June Term, 1881.   Signed: L.F. Hannah

JOHN MOORE   January 23, 1880
Sons: Simeon - $1, Dave S., William M., James M., Alexander. Daughters:
Polly Ann wife of William Husk, Lizzie Jane wife of John Lovegrove, To
Ebenezer L., to all - $1 each. I will all the rest of my estate to my
son Landon Taylor Moore or his heirs - for the care and kindness he has
shown me over the past eleven years. Executor: J.F. Brown. Test:
Alfred F. Brown, John S. Rothrock. Probated July Term, 1881.
                                    Signed: John Moore

W. P. RANKIN   June 19, 1881
All my real estate and interest to my mother ____?____ during her lifetime, then to my sister Emma L. King and brother Robert J. Rankin. My
stock of leather and hides at the Tanyard. Executor: Brother Robert
J. Rankin. Wit.: E.C. Reeves, A.B. Bowman. Probated July Term, 1881.
                                    Signed: W.P. Rankin

MICAJAH HODGES   May 1, 1880
To 2 sons William W. & George W. Hodges - my plantation. Other children:
Robert G. Decd., Nancy M., Sarah H., son Mahlon M. decd., Emily S.,
Elizabeth M., John C., Edna P. & Orlena Josephine & Abby Jane. Executor:
W.G. Gray. Wit.: P.H. Boring, Fred Devault. Probated August Term, 1881.
                                    Signed: Micajah (X) Hodges

CHARLEY SLAGLE   February 3, 1879
At wife Eliza's death - divide equally among my children. Test: John
Preston Slagle, David E. Slagle. Probated September Term, 1881.
                                    Signed: Charley (X) Slagle

DAVID S. GUINN   August 21, 1880
Brother Matthew S. Guinn and Elizabeth Jane his wife. Land where my
brother and I now live and which belonged to our father Thomas Guinn
decd. Executor: Joseph D. Lyon. Wit.: Jasper N. Lewis, Esther M.
Osborne. Probated September Term, 1881.
                                    Signed: David S. Guinn

CYNTHIA FORD   September 16, 1881
To George W. Ford - all notes and money. $1 to John, W.T., Nelson Crows
heirs, Sarah Caswell's heirs, Patsy Hall, Smith Ford, Price Ford and
Susan Chapman. Witnesses: Cynthia (X) Ford, John (X) Ford. Probated

MARY KEEBLER   April 24, 1881
My niece Mary Ann Barkley and her 4 children: Kittie Brabson, Samuel K.,
John & William Barkley a minor. My brother Samuel Keebler and I never
married - lived together, never divided up. Niece Marietta Eames - a
bed, to her daughter Kittie Brabson - my chest. Wit.: H.H. Ingersoll,
W.A. Crockett. Probated December Term, 1881.
                              Signed: Mary (X) Keebler

ISAAC TAYLOR   November 15, 1880
Daughter Sarphina J. Strain - all notes I hold on J.B. Strain. Grand-
sons: William T., Samuel H., David A. & Melvin A. Strain - all the
right to farm to hold for ever. I hold notes on my son D.C. Taylor for
$2400. Granddaughter Nancy Jane Strain - my interest in Taylor and
Jackson Stoneware Factory (1/3 the factory and all mushinery). To Mt.
Lebanon Church - $400 for which J.B., H.T. to give $100 each. To be
paid the Elders as long as it is Presbyterian. Executor: Joe B. Strain.
Wit.: J.U. Baker, David Decker. Probated February Term, 1882.
                              Signed: Isaac Taylor

SAMUEL DOUGLAS   February 28, 1876
Property to be sold and divided between the following heirs: James H.,
Elbert S., Preston & John C. Douglas, daus. Uriah, Eliza, Elvirah Hall,
Elizabeth, Sary, Mary, Julian, Harriet & Elvinia. Wit.: E.R. Chinouth,
James H. Jones, William H. Deakins. Probated February Term, 1882.
                              Signed: Samuel Douglas

LEMUEL KEEBLER   December 20, 1881
Wife Bethena. Daughters: Mary Jane & Cynthia. Son Samuel R. to manage
and tend farm, provide for his mother and sisters and Willie A. Gray
until he is 21. At Bethena's death Samuel R. is to receive deeds from
and pay for: A.C. Keebler - $400, Liza R. Bacon - $200 - land adjoining
Robert E. Hunt, Joseph H. Martin, W.W. Deakins, Jacob Bacon, Amanda
Stafford. Wit.: Jacob Bacon, J.J. Deakins. Probated February Term,
1882.   Signed: Lemuel Keebler

AMOS BIRD   January 25, 1882
Wife Lucinda. All heirs to share equally. Wit.: J.M. Seaton, E.E.
Mauk. Probated April Term, 1882.   Signed: Amos (X) Bird

ALLEN BARENS   April 15, 1882
Bury me in Family graveyard. Wife Martha. Four youngest children:
Martha A., Virginia F., Addie E. & Rutherford B. Hays Barens. Six
children: Susan E., Martha A., Virginia F., Addie E., Rutherford B.
Hayes Barens & Analiza L. Stepp. Executrix: Wife Martha. Wit.:
A.B. Bowman, John H. Stephens. Probated May Term, 1882.
                              Signed: A.L. Barens

ELIZABETH BARCROFT   August 3, 1881
To Ambrose Bell - $50, he is in the State of Iowa, is the son of my
sister Alice decd. To Josiah and Samuel Alexander sons of John and
Martha Alexander decd. I give to the Presbyterian Church at Leesburg,
now in the course of erection - $25. To sister Jane Barcroft - $200.
Three Presbyterian Churches were destroyed by the storm in 1881 - in
Illinois, Kansas & Iowa - $200 to each. Remainder of my estate to
Presbyterian Church U.S.A. Executor: James W. Duncan. Wit.: John
Davault, F.R. Davault. Probated September Term, 1882.
                              Signed: Elizabeth (X) Barcroft

MARGARET S. HORTON   February 8, 1882
Widow of Joseph Horton. To step son William Horton and wife Malinda -
all my estate to take care of me. Wit.: George R. Duncan, William R.
White. Probated September Term, 1882.
                                   Signed: Margaret S. Horton

WILLIAM JENKINS   July 21, 1882
My wheat is in J.F. Grisham's barn - undivided - give to daughter Sarah
Curtis to support my sife Eliza Jenkins. I owe Susan Crouch and John
Curtis. Executor: J.F. Grisham. Wit.: J.E. Harwood, Abner Hankal.
Probated September Term, 1882.   Signed: William (X) Jenkins

JOHN ALLISON   June 20, 1881
Daughter Hannah Eliza Deakins formerly Allison. Daughter Mary Cate who
married first Wright Smith. I gave to Susan Allison $1000 Confederate
Dollars. Daughters: Ellen Jane Keebler decd., Florence Davault, Alice
Allison Cox - I gave property of her mother my second wife - also $1100.
Executors: A.B. Cummings, Valentine Davault. Wit.: H.E. Mathes, John
Allison Jr., M.S. Mahoney. Probated November Term, 1882.
                                   Signed: John Allison

WILLIAM T. ELAM
Pay about $90 I owe to James H. Dosser & Co. Pay E.H. Mathes, pay M.S.
Mahoney, Pay Dr. E.T. Deaderick. Col. R.H. Duncan was to furnish me
money for my business, repay him, My niece Mrs. Mary Alice Cox - $100.
All the balance and residue I bequeath to Mrs. Eliza A. Elam wife of my
brother Robert H. Elam, I am a member of their household. My $2000
policy in Knights Honor is paid. Executor: Dr. M.L. Maloney. Wit.:
A.J. Blevens, R.M. May. Probated November Term, 1882.
                                   Signed: W.T. Elam

NANCY J. NELSON   December 22, 1882
To sister Sarah R. Bacon - all personal estate. To brother Elbert H.
Nelson - land I inherited from my father John Nelson decd. adjoining E.E.
Shipley, Sevier, Martin & others. Brother Elbert H. Nelson to care for
my afflicted brother James H. Nelson and give him a home. Sister
Susannah R. Bason. Single brothers & sister. Executor: Brother John
H. Nelson. Wit.: S.P. Martin, Joseph M. Bacon, Uriah H. Hunt. Probated
March Term, 1883.   Signed: Nancy J. Nelson

HENRY SLIGER   March 29, 1883
Wife Catharine. Divide my estate equally at my wife's death. Charge my
son H.M. Sliger $100 I advanced him. Executor: Samuel Keplinger. Wit.:
Charles Gookin, A.R. Piper. Probated May Term, 1883.
                                   Signed: Henry Sliger

WILLIAM T. COX   March 29, 1883
To all my children an equal share: James T. Cox, Sary Mandy, Martin,
Charles Cox, George B., William H., Isaac C., Jesse M. Cox, Mary Jane
Hite. Jesse to care for my wife and his mother. Jesse Martin to have
one bed so he will be equal to the rest of the heirs. Executor: Son
Charles. Wit.: E.R. Chinowth, Calvin R. Cox, James H. Jones. Probated
June Term, 1883.   Signed: William T. Cox

SARAH A. BOWMAN   October 24, 1871
Nancy Anna my youngest daughter - personal property including grave
shovel. To Samuel Hysinger & Thomas Hays - $1. To Samuel March and
wife Hannah - $5, Robert S. Bowman - $2, Haney Elkins - $1, Margaret
Amanda Halti? - $10, Hannah Emily Phelps - $10, Samuel David Bowman -
a copper kettle. Executor: William H.M. Smith. Wit.: John C. Smith,
John A. Jones. Probated July Term, 1883.
                                   Signed: Sarah (X) Bowman

LAWRENCE V. BROYLES   July 19, 1883
Wife Frances L., 3 brothers: Isaac N., James W. & William M. Broyles.
Executor: H.F. Bailey. Test: J.M. Seaton, Augustus Holt. Probated
August Term, 1883.   Signed: Lawrence V. (X) Broyles

R. G. BENSON   January 8, 1883
Wife Nancy J. Three single daughters: Altie, Laura & Cora - land
adjoining James H. Beard, Pritchett, Jacob Aldin. Daughter Sally
Harwood - land adjoining J.S. Grisham - 12 acres firewood and rail
timber. Daughters Ellen & Mattie - remainder of my land. Three
grandchildren heirs of my daughter Minnie Allison decd. Executor:
Nathaniel Galloway. Att.: Charles E. Dosser, J.F. Gresham. Probated August Term, 1883.   Signed: R.G. Benson

M. S. MAHONEY   July 10, 1883
Close my mercantile business at least cost to the estate. Wife Margaret
G. - 1/3 of estate and whatever personal property she may want, piano,
library and watch. Daughter Dora Frank Kirkpatrick Mahoney - 1/3 part of
my estate. Other 1/3 to my brother Josiah Mahoney and his wife Mary A.
Mahoney. Trustee Henry M. Walker. Wife Margaret G. to be guardian of my
daughter. Executors: R.M. May, J.A. February. Wit.: S.J. Kirkpatrick,
A.W. Stuart.   Signed: M.S. Mahoney

Codicil - The Executors I appointed do not wish to serve, therefore I
appoint E.A. Shipley and Margaret Mahoney my wife. 17 August 1883.
Wit.: R.H. Dungan, J.C.H. Smith. Probated September Term, 1883.

JAMES M. FULKERSON   November 8, 1882
To sons: Gregory & Crockett Fulkerson - all my real estate in 7th Civil
District adjoining Jasper Dukes, S.V. Hunt and others - they are to pay
son Elihu $300, dau. Virginia Pierce $100 and a horse, and take care of
my wife (their mother) Nancy Fulkerson during her life. Executor:
Gregory B. Fulkerson my son. Wit.: A.R. Moulton, George R. Duncan.
Probated October Term, 1883.   Signed: James M. Fulkerson

JOHN FULWER   April 14, 1881
Wife Rebecca, sister Susannah - 137 acres farm where I now live adjoining
Jackson Kleppers widow, Oliver and others, also what I purchased of Thos.
and Nat Galloway in District 11. Son George Fulwer, my second cousin
George Goodman - $200. To Angelina Fulwer widow of John Fulwer decd. my
son - they have no heirs. Put tombstones at our graves. Executors:
Son George W. Fulwer, Perry Hunter. Wit.: J.C. Smith, John B. Shipley,
D.P. O'Brien, J.H. Peoples. Probated December Term, 1883.
                              Signed: John (X) Fulwer

SAMUEL McCORKLE   November 22, 1883
Daughters Martha J. Williams, Eliza E. Fagin - borrow made by Rev. W.P.
Maupin. Note on J.M. Fagan. Six children: Mary C. Webb, William M.
McCorkle, Martha J. Williams, J.J. McCorkle, Susan M. Hughes, Nancy H.
Williams. Wit.: James M. Crockett, Samuel Williams.
                         Signed: Samuel McCorkle

ISAAC C. HACKER   July 22, 1881
Daughter Miriam - 1/3 of estate. Five remaining heirs: Robert,
Alexander, Newton, Marietta & Catharine - each to share equal in the
remaining 2/3. To Melvin Bitner heir of my daughter Martha Bitner -
$1. Attest: J.M. Seaton, I.N. Broyles. Probated December Term,
1883.   Signed: J.C. Hacker

J. C. HURDI   December 4, 1883
Of legal age. To my wife - my house and lot. To son Wesley - house and
lot after her death. Children: Jonathan, Rosecrans, dau. Adah, Mollie.

Executor: Son Wesley. Test: E.S. Browning, J.M. Keplinger.

MATILDA FREEMAN   September 29, 1883
Two grandsons William & Wallace Freeman sons of my daughter Jane Freeman
(now Jane Smith Peters) and Joseph F. Freeman son of Madison Freeman -
the farm where I live in the 8th District adjoining D.W.F. Peoples,
Widow Walters and others being 44 acres I purchased of E.W. Walker, when
they are 21. Until my grandsons reach 21, my son Madison and daughter
Jane are to have the use and benefit of the farm. Son Madison has cared
for me and I will continue to depend on him. Executor: J.C.H. Smith.
Wit.: E.A. Shipley, J.C. Low. Probated March Term, 1884.
                              Signed: Matilda (X) Freeman

JOSEPH WOOLF   January 12, 1872
Executors: Nephew John S. Woolf & Samuel C. Nave (who married my niece
Margaret Woolf). John S. Woolf's 2 children Manervia Elizabeth and
Joseph John and their heirs - all my knob land, 8 shares railroad stock
and $700 of my best notes plus interest. Alice and Elizabeth Nave,
daughters of Samuel C. Nave and wife Margaret - to have my Old Farm
where I live. Eliza daughter of Henry Saylor - good horse. Margaret
Nave widow of Margaret & Samuel C. Nave's son that died - a horse.
David Saylor and his wife Hannah - to stay with me and have all personal
property. Wit.: W.T. Range, A.B. Bowman. Probated June Term, 1884.
                              Signed: Joseph (X) Woolf

JAMES FORD   December 15, 1870
Wife Sarah. To all my brothers and sisters - $1. Executrix: Wife
Sarah. Test: Nathan Shipley, M.S. Mahoney. Probated April Term, 1884.
                              Signed: James Ford

AMOS WALTER   September 15, 1878
Wife Elizabeth - farm on Nolachucky River until the younger child becomes
of age. My children: O.P., Tennessee Louise M., Mary L., William D.,
John G., G.C. & Margaret L. Walter. Son Joseph E. Walter has all I
intend for him to have. Executors to be court appointed.
                              Signed: Amos Walter

Codicil - I want my son Joseph E. Walter to share equal but he owes me
$1000. Wit.: W.D. Coff, J.C. Glaze. Probated May Term, 1884.

ELIZABETH NELSON   March 13, 1884
Bury me in the graveyard near Cherokee Baptist Church with my husband
P.P.C. Nelson and little son Judson. Put tombstones at graves and
enclose in iron railings. To Baptist Church on Cherokee - $50 to help
build a new church. Pay it out of my Calvin Jones note. To daughter
Hassie Campbell - note I hold on Prof. R.J. Lusk. To son-in-law John C.
Campbell - 3 acres near Mr. Wellborn. To granddaughter Alice Campbell -
3/4 acres. To grandson Nelson R. Campbell - house and lot near Jobe
Spring on Cherry Street known as the office of my husband. I give to my
daughter Hassie and John Campbell - my mountain land in Carter County.
Executor: John C. Campbell.

Codicil - Rents on lots willed above are to go to my Executor and be
used to educate the children. 19 March 1884. Wit.: A.B. Bowman, E.S.
Miller. Probated June Term, 1884.

SOPHIA CUNNINGHAM DUNCAN   January 30, 1884
Of Jonesborough. Of interest due me in Knoxville April 1883 pay $20 to
Presbyterian Church Fund of Jonesboro. In case I leave a child - my
Executor C.E. Lucky of Knoxville is to invest my funds for the best
interest of the child. To Foreign Mission of the Presbyterian Church -
$500. To Home Mission of the Presbyterian Church - $500. To the
Western Few? Seminary in Oxford, Butler County, Ohio - $300 - the
interest on which is to pay tuition for a young lady unable to attend

school。 My mother - my clothing。 My husband C.A. Duncan has enough and
will have a living in his Priest Office。 Plain neat stones to be put at
graves in our square that is: Aunt Jane Davis, Pa Samuel B. Cunningham,
Ma A.D. Cunningham and myself。 Wit.: D.J. Gibson, C.A. Duncan, Nathan
Bachman。 Probated July Term, 1884。

Signed: Sophia C。 Duncan

W. N. BROWN (William Nathaniel)   April 18, 1884
Wife Hassie - land in District 2 Washington County conveyed to me by my
father N.T. Brown decd。 Sister M.J. Hankle & mother Pleuetta Brown。
Executor: Maj。 James E。 Deakins。 Wit.: J.W.H. Smith, Harvey Pritchard。
Probated August Term, 1884。   Signed: W.N. Brown

RICHARD NORTHINGTON   November 10, 1883
Daughter Mary Jane Johnson, son David, heirs of my daughter Susan Jones
decd。, son Jno. S。, daughter Elizabeth Caruthers。 Wife _____。 Nine
grandchildren: Willie Johnson son of Mary; John Alfred son of David;
Eddie son of James S.; John, Lillie & Mollie Caruthers children of
Elizabeth and the 3 boys of Susan Jones。 Executor: James H。 Dosser。
Wit.: J.N. Dosser, J.D。 Slemons。 Probated September Term, 1884。

Signed: Richard Northington

J. F。 DEADERICK   August 2, 1884
Three daughters: Susan, Eliza & Kate - my dwelling and lots in Jonesboro, back of Joseph February adjoining S.J. Kirkpatrick and J.S. Mathes
- 2 store houses on Main Street occupied by A.G. Mason & Son and Dr。 D.J.
Gibson。 Daughter Susan L。, son David - 97 3/4 acres on Knob Creek
surveyed by Nathan Shipley, County Surveyor。 Son Eugene。 Six children
of my deceased son William V。 to wit: Eugene, Laura, Henry, Edward,
Claude & Charles。 To Cora Brown - $1。 To Frank second son of William
V。 - $1。 Eight children and two children of my deceased daughter Isadore
- share and share alike (Susan, Fannie, David, Eugene, Eliza, Isadore's
children Sue & Carrie, Kate, Thomas O。 & Vina Gleem。 Executor: Son
Eugene L。 Deaderick。 Wit.: Margaret Brown, Charles E。 Dosser。 Probated
October Ter, 1884。   Signed: J.F. Deaderick

SARAH J. C. SMITH   July 25, 1884
Daughter Hassie Brown to be guardian to my younger children。 Husband
Dr。 William Smith。 30 acres in District 2 adjoining Peter Northington,
formerly owned by John Smith Esq。 and purchased by me of Elizabeth
Smith now Mrs。 James E。 Deakens。 All my children adult and minor。
Executors: Dr。 William Smith my husband, S.J.C. Smith。 Wit.: J.B.
Deakens, J.N. Tucker。 Probated December Term, 1884。

Signed: S.J.C. Smith

JOHN BOWMAN   September 13, 1862
Wife Eliza。 Children: Nancy, Ann, Theodore, Archibald, Elizabeth,
Daniel J。, Mary C。 Executors: Wife Eliza, son Theodore。 Wit.: Hardin
Hopper, Daniel Smith, D.J。 Bowman。 Probated December Term, 1884。

Signed: John Bowman

SUSANNAH C. BAYLESS   July 23, 1884
Husband Robert B。 Bayless - property in District 10, my interest in my
mother's estate。 Wit.: J.A. Pritchett, William Melvin。 Probated
February Term, 1884。   Signed: Susanna C。 Bayless

THOMAS N。 ELIS   January 11, 1885
Executor: H.B. Hankle。 Sell land in 9th District adjoining S.H. Miller
and Thomas Young。 Six children: son H.H. Elis, oldest son W.L. Elis,
oldest daughter Mary Elis, Mandy J。 Elis, J.H. Elis, Cordelias Elis。
Wit.: T.A. Young, Rufus Taylor。 Probated February Term, 1885。

Signed: Thomas N。 (X) Elis

THORENTINE HUGHES
Wife Saly Hughes - personal and real property - 4 acres adjoining M.S.
Crouch, J.H. Crouch, J.M. Barnes and John Hilbert. At wife Saly's death
the above property to go to Mary Crawford and her heirs absolutely.
Executor: J.L. Clark. Wit.: J.L. Clark, C.C. Crawford. Probated
March Term, 1885.   Signed: Thorentine Hughes

YOUNG BAYLESS   May 27, 1880
Wife Naomi C. Bayless - all personal property except blacksmith tools.
My farm in District 8 adjoining Joseph Price, Trusten Leach, Thomas
Saylor and James S. Beard - 100 acres. Sell blacksmith tools. Naomi
to have house where I live in Jonesboro. Executor: Samuel M. Pate.
Wit.: W.E.S. Armstrong, D.G. Laine.
                        Signed: Young Bayless   Probated April Term, 1885.

W. W. WORLEY   June 9, 1884
Of Johnson City, Tennessee. Wife N.D. Worley - tract of land in Woodruff
County State of Arkansas - see deed executed from G.R.W. Martin. To
daughter Emma - lot in Johnson City bought of J.J. Adams, at her death
to W.W. Worley, at his death to revert to our estate. To daughter Emma
and wife N.D. - my brick store and dwelling in Johnson City known as
John Johnson property and bought of me from J.P.McCall and W.W. James,
also the track of land on Bruch Creek in Johnson City. Children: Emma,
W.W. Jr., James B., Adie, Tilly, Dora & Bessie Worley. Executors: E.S.
Worley of Sullivan County, dau. Emma Worley. Wit.: E.H. Harr, Isaac
Harr. Probated April Term, 1885. Signed: W.W. Worley

LIZZIE M. EDWARDS   March 2, 1885
Brother A.W. Edwards - money and pay interest for 16 years and 18 months
to Baptist Churches Missionary and Sunday Schools. Sister A.E. Morrell
and heirs. Sister Nannie L. Edwards. Brother A.W. Edwards to sell land
in Sullivan County. Executor: Bro. A.W. Edwards. Wit.: A.W. Edwards,
Jno. W. Morrell. Probated May Term, 1885.
                        Signed: Lizzie M. Edwards

SARAH P. ROBINSON   March 24, 1874
Of Baltimore, State of Maryland. Husband William Writ Robinson - all my
estate. Wit.: J. Lawrence Campbell, Fielder C. Stingluff, Charles D.
Greenfield.   Signed: Sarah P. Robinson

Baltimore City - SS - Sarah P. Robinson died 4 April 1874 - J. Harmon
Brown - Register of Wills. Probated in Washington County, Tennessee
May Term, 1885.

NELLY HELMS   February 12, 1881
Of Jonesboro. Granddaughter Louvena Russell daughter of Amanda Helm
decd. - lot on Water Street in Jonesboro adjoining Cosson, A.E. Jackson
and R.W. Fenk. Also to Louvena - all my personal property, notes, money
and other assets free from the control of her husband. To my daughter
Lowinda Crusins? - remainder of my lot, at her death to go to Louvenia.
Executor: Barney Cunningham. Wit.: J.F. Grisham, J.A. Grisham.
Probated June Term, 1885.   Signed: Nelly (X) Helms

ABSOLOM THOMPSON SR.   May 30, 1885
Sons: William & Winfield. Daughters: Martha & Catharine. I am
interested in the Ross Deed of Trust which is $2300 - $2800 in Greene
County provided they pay all my just and honest debts. Test: T.T.
Broyles, N.V. Gammon. Probated July Term, 1885.
                        Signed: Ab Thompson Sr.

JOSEPH HUNTER   June 20, 1879
Daughters Alice Hunter & Ann Mariah Broyles - my lands adjoining John
Walter decd. Daughter Eliza M. Saylor, sons Eugene and James P. Hunter.

Son John C. Hunter to be given land at John C. Harris decd., if the rest of the heirs are willing. John C. Hunter moved to Arkansas. Laura Hunter heir of my son Joseph L. Hunter. Heirs of Sallie L. Broyles, sons E.E. and J.P. Hunter, heirs of Eliza M. Saylor decd. Executor: E.E. Hunter, Test: Jacob Perkins, J. Hardin Jones. Probated July Term, 1885.
Signed: Joseph Hunter

JOHN C. D. BUCHANAN   June 22, 1885
My mother M.A. Buchanan - to have all my real and personal property as long as she lives, at her death it is to go to my sisters son J.A. Rogers. My brother Frank Buchanan and sister Sarah J.A. Rogers to have my trunk. Executors: W.S. Strain, A.S.N. Dobson. Propounded for probate in Anson County, N.C. September A.D. 1885.   Signed: John C.D. Buchanan

NATHAN JOBE   July 7, 1885
Sisters: Nancy & Lydda Jobe - all my personal property. Nephew W.P. Jobe. Nancy and Lydda to live in my house and have a support and maintenance out of my real estate. Executors: Grant Ford, Jonathan Ford. Wit.: G.W. Kitzmiller, James H. Ford. Probated October Term, 1885.
Signed: Nathan P. Jobe

MARCELLUS M. MARTIN   September 1, 1885
Now residing on Boones Creek. Sister Ida E. Martin - all property (real, personal or mixed) her lifetime and at her death to be equally divided between heirs of my brother William H. Martin deceased. Executor: A.C. Bowen. Wit.: S. Miller Senr., George C. Bowman. Probated _____.
Signed: Marcellus E. Martin

DAVID GARST   September 3, 1885
Son Thomas C. Garst - 160 acres surveyed by Nathan Shipley to take care of, maintain and support my wife and me. Daughter Eliza D. Garst - $100. Son William G. and wife Sarah - the tract of land known as the David Mainers Farm. Grandsons David Bashor and wife Martha, Isaac Bashor and wife Mary. To daughter Susan wife of James Conner - land in Sullivan County. To grandson Benjamin Garst an illigitimate son of Susan Conner - $300. Son Isaac. Son Hiram went before M.M. Duncan of Macompen County, Illinois and said he wanted none of my estate. Executor: Dr. J.L. Clark. Wit.: J.F. Grisham, R.B. McConley. Probated October Term, 1885.
Signed: David Garst

JACOB MURRAY   October 14, 1885
Wife Mary E. to have all she brought with her when she married me and what she has made since and 1/3 of all my property or be paid $100 by Samuel G. Murray. Executor: Nephew A.H. Murray. Wit.: S.P. Martin, Elijah Carey. Probated November Term, 1885.
Signed: Jacob Murray

JOHN LONGMIRE SR.   March 17, 1875
Wife Elizabeth - to have all real and personal estate during her life, then divided among my heirs: Joseph A., John R., William, Montgomery & Alexander Longmire, Abigail Pinner & Hannah A. Long. Executors: Sons John A. & Alexander C. Longmire. Wit.: D.W.F. Peoples, J.H. Peoples. Probated November Term, 1885.   Signed: Jno. Longmire

MARK PENNYBACKER   February 10, 1872
Two daughters: Sarah Mitchell & Catharine Pennybacker - 240 acres where I live adjoining David Garst and E.S. Cox. Grandchildren Isaac S., Susan & Lizzie Pennybacker heirs of my son George Pennybacker - my interest in land Joseph Kratzer gave to Simon Kratzer his son for the time of his natural live - 270 acres - my part being ½ of same. Son John - my interest in the Trust Fund in the hands of Lawrence Bowens, Trustee - this cannot be obtained until Simon Kratzers death. Executors: son-in-

law John M. Mitchell. Wit.: Perry Hunter, Richard Northington.
Probated January Term, 1886.   Signed: Mark Pennybacker

PETER HARRINGTON   August 12, 1885
Three sisters: Ann Jones, Mary Crumley & Christian Crumley - 1/3 to
each one of money derived from the sale of land given me by me deceased
father adjoining J.M. Reeves, C.L. Gilmer, heirs of John Little, heirs
of Richardson Harrington & Henry Harrington. Executor: Dr. E.S. Miller
Jr. Wit.: H.H. Lusk, E.S. Miller Senr. Probated January Term, 1886.
                              Signed: Peter (X) Harrington

GEORGE W. GRAY   May 19, 1883
To son L.G. Gray - the Hacker and Thomas Dyer land. Daughter Mary Hodge
to have use of house, barn, lot and spring during my life. Sons Nelson
A. Gray, James Gray, L.G. Gray. Wit.: John Maden, A.C. Fox. Probated
February Term, 1886.   Signed: George W. Gray

Names mentioned: John Hankel, J.P. Adams, James Fitzgerald, Hunterson
Hale of color, Joseph Chinouth.

WILLIAM BEALS   October 24, 1885
Brother West Beals - residue of my personal property after debts are
paid and all real property. Sister Polly Ann alias Mary Ann Sherfey.
Executors: J.M. Bayless & James Wilcox. Wit.: S.P. Martin, John
Wilcoxen. Probated February Term, 1886.
                              Signed: William (X) Beals

S. K. H. PATTON   January 31, 1886
Children: Mary E. Cowan, Ann B. Evans, Sue O. Willard, Landon H. Patton,
John A. Patton, Henry W. Patton, Nannie A. Hunt, Will C. Patton, Jesse W.
Patton, Cordia F. Vincent, Samuel F.N. Patton Jr., Mary E. Cowan or Sue.
Willards heirs. Wit.: E.S. Depew, William C. Patton. Probated March
Term, 1886.   Signed: S.K.N. Patton

WINNIE DEAKINS   March 10, 1886
In extreme old age. To Samuel Templin, a colored boy now living with me
- all my estate, but he is to remain here and live with me when I demand
it and wait on me. Executor: R.M. May. Wit.: W.T. February, E.A.
Shipley. Probated April Term, 1886.
                              Signed: Winnie (X) Deakins

DANIEL DEWALD   February 4, 1882
Daughters: Mary Ann Dewald, Elizabeth Dewald & Margaret Thomas and 2
children - 70 acres adjoining Great Road, J.W. Earnest. Other children:
Catharine Walter, Julia Galloway, William V. Dewald, James M. Dewald.
If Catharine's grandchildren die without heirs - her part is to revert
back to the others. Executor: James M. Dewald. Wit.: Alexander
Mathes, James M. Bayless. Probated May Term, 1886.
                              Signed: Daniel Dewald

MARY E. BARNES
Executor: Joseph Barnes. Tina & Hannah Barnes - my real estate, and
pay a note to Jane Kash by Joseph Barnes. Wit.: John B. Chase, R.W.
Chase. Probated May Term, 1886.   Signed: Mary E. Barnes

JOHN KYKER   May 10, 1886
Wife Malinda - personal property. Children: Elizabeth, Margaret, Sarah
Jackson and Elbert heirs, John Reed my grandson - my watch. Executor:
Jacob J. Reed. Wit.: E.L. Browning, J.L. Dillow. Probated August Term,
1886.   Signed: John Kyker

NANCY M. COX   April 2, 1886
Brother G.W. Hodges, Elizabeth Adams daughter of Martin Adams - bed now
in possession of my husband James Cox. All the rest to be divided between John C.C. Hodges, G.W. Hodges, heirs of Elizabeth Shanks and heirs
of Josephine Adam wife of Martin Adams. Executor: Fred Davault (son of
Samuel Davault). Attest: P. Yoakley, G.F. Hodges.
                                   Signed: Nancy M. (X) Cox

JAMES HALL   September 1, 1886
To son Ebenezer - land in 11 Civil District adjoining Whaley, Samuel Hall,
Snider - to pay $335 for my daughters. To son Samuel - land in District
11 adjoining Nathaniel Hall, Snyder, Ebenezer Hall - to pay $375 for my
daughters. To son Nathaniel - land adjoining Watauga River - to pay $375
for my daughters and sence he got the mansion house, he is to provide a
reasonable and comfortable for my daughters: Elizabeth & Sarah Jane as
long as they remain single. To son Robert - land adjoining bank of
river - $375 for my daughters. Married daughters: Ibby Friday & Sarah
J___he?. Executor: John H. Saunders of Sullivan County. Wit.: James
White, David J. Bowman. Probated October Term, 1886.
                                   Signed: James (X) Hall

A. A. BAYLESS (Adeline A. Broyles?)   September 24, 1885
Two sons: E. Ward & R.R. Bayless, daughter J.E. Buckwell. Mrs. E.W.
Bayless - all household and kitchen furniture. Grandsons, sons of E.W.
Bayles - all my cattle. To Angie & Gertrude Bayles, granddaughters -
all my fowls. To son E.W. Bayles - 2/5 of my real estate. To son R.R.
Bayles - 2/5 of my real estate. To daughter J.E. Brockwell - 1/5 of my
real estate. Executors: Sons E.W. & R.R. Bayless. Test: D.W.T.
Bayles, J.D. Burwell. Probated October Term, 1886.
                                   Signed: A.C. Bayles

WILLIAM M. McKEE   November 25, 1885
Wife Phebe J. - all property, to educate my 4 youngest children: Bell
Jane, Willie Van Buren, Henry Edgar & baby not named. Phebe is in charge
- no one is to interfere. My daughter Perine M. McKee shall have a home
with my wife so long as she remains single and they can agree. Wit.:
Wellington H. Stepp, John W. Stepp. Probated November Term, 1886.
                                   Signed: William M. McKee

WILLIAM MATHES   March 14, 1885
Wife Elenore Mathes. To my daughter Emily Mathes - 20 acres adjoining
John C. Smith, Samuel F. Smith - plus personal property. To Sarah
Estelle, daughter of Emily Mathes. Heirs: John C. Mathes, Margaret L.
McAdams, Elina Ann Squibb, grandchildren Lucky Dosser, Luella and John
William Bales - heirs of my daughter Mattie Bales deceased. William
Franklin and Robert Lee McRoberts deceased, Mary Huffman. Executor:
W.H.M. Smith. Wit.: P.A. Miller, John C. Smith. Probated January Term,
1887.
                                   Signed: William (X) Mathes

HANNAH RIGGS   February 6, 1883
Brothers: William H. Humphrey & Jesse Humphrey. Joseph H. Nelson and
wife Hannah Lisa Nelson to have my property and pay my bills. Test:
E.K. Hunt, W.H. Hickman. Probated February Term, 1887.
                                   Signed: Hannah (X) Riggs

GRANT FORD   December 23, 1886
Three sisters: Roda Fitzgerald, Frances Ford & Eliza Louiza Ford -
during their life, then to my nephew Richard Nelson Brown. Executor:
Nelson A. Gray. Test: Joseph H. Martin, L.G. Gray. Probated February
Term, 1887.
                                   Signed: Grant (X) Ford

RICHARD CHENOWETH   April 27, 1878
To Emeline wife of my son William - my house and lot in Johnson City on
Kings Street occupied by Dr. E.S. Miller. Sell my farm in Buffalo Ridge
adjoining George Gray and Chambdin Hale - divide with grandchildren:
Daniel Fox, Addie & Robert Dyer, Amanda Hughes, Elizabeth Dyer and the
heirs of Martha Chase. John Chinoweth heirs, release a debt on son James
M. Chinoweth. Divide the remainder in 4 parts and pay to: Addie &
Robert Dyer, Amanda Hughes, Elizabeth Dyer, heirs of Martha Chase. In no
way is Nelson Chase to have any part of my estate. Wit.: W. Hodges,
James Seaver. Proven February Term, 1887.
                                        Signed: Richard Chenoweth

SUSANNAH ARCHER   July 29, 1871
Daughter Catharine Archer - to have all real and personal property.
Son J.M. Archer. Daughter Martha Milhorn - have their part. Executor:
James M. Grisham. Wit.: Francis M. Walker, John F. Grisham. Probated
February Term, 1887.   Signed: Susannah Archer

THERSA DEAKINS   December 16, 1886
Note on John H. Gibson - $800, William A. Sherfy - $200 and one on L.H.
Bachman - $125 - be collected and divided between: James Deakins little
son of Nelson Deakins decd. & Mrs. Jane Deakins widow of Nelson Deakins,
sister Rachel Deakins, nieces Susannah & Emeline Deakins. I married
James Y. Deakins. Note on J.C. Martin - to step son Henry Deakins, his
brother R.M.K. Deakins with whom I expect to spend the rest of my life.
Executor: E.A. Shipley. Wit.: Jno. W. Bayless, S.H. Sherfey. Probated
February Term, 1887.   Signed: Therza Deakins

FANNIE HUFFMAN   March 9, 1887
Husband W.T. Huffman - real estate I'm to fall heir to of my father Hiram
Mulkey decd. estate. Executor: Husband W.T. Huffman. Wit.: H.E. Clark,
Levi H. Markwood, John Bacon. Probated May Term, 1887.
                                        Signed: Fannie Huffman

BENJAMIN HOSS (Col.?)   April 9, 1878
My entire estate to Emma Jane, a daughter born to my wife before our
marriage, but has since adopted my name and is known as Emma Jane Hoss,
free from the influence of any husband she might have. Executor: Landon
C. Hoss. Test: A.F. Hoss, W.F. Young. Probated April Term, 1887.
                                        Signed: Benjamin Hoss

SUSAN HOSS   February 22, 1887
My house where I now live in District 9 adjoining Thomas Wilburn, Jacob
Smith & Caruthers - to Benjamin Boren. Executor: J.M. Carr. Wit.:
L.C. Hoss, J.D. Weaver. Probated June Term, 1887.
                                        Signed: Susanna Hoss

WILLIAM GIBSON   March 6, 1884
Wife Hannah - to have all my estate her lifetime, then it is to be
divided among my heirs: daughters Minerva C., Abigail J. & Harret E.
Gibson. Land adjoining E.T. Virginia & Georgia Railroad. Son T.J.
Gibson and daughter Maggie Hodge. Executor: Son T.J. Gibson. Wit.:
S.M. McKenney, Joseph J. Woolf, John S. Woolf. Probated June Term, 1887.
                                        Signed: William Gibson

GEORGE W. TELFORD   April 8, 1885
My present wife _____ to own in her own right a house and lot northside
of Brown's Branch adjoining Robert Reed - house to be built at $300 -
with furniture and a roll of carpet plus interest on money. To my granddaughter Mrs. Mary Bayless (wife of Mc Bayless) daughter of Robert
Earnest and Jane Earnest formerly Jane Telford. Executors: E.H. West &

F. W. Earnest. Wit.: J.N. Black, J.W. Brown. Probated May Term, 1887.
Signed: G.W. Telford

SUDIE E. HUNT   July 21, 1887
Husband W.C. Hunt - personal property including one factory blanket.
Sisters: A.E.L. Stepp, Mattie Madden, Jennie Thomas (her son Eddie
Thomas), Virgie Martin, Addie Tucker, brother R.B.N. Barnes, niece
E.L. Stepp, J.M. Hunt. To Mora E. Hunt - $5. To my mother - my
jersey sack and blue silk handkerchief. Sisters Eliza Stepp, Mattie
Madden, Addie Tucker & Jennie Thomas - to have money from sale of my
farm in District 9, from my father's estate. Executor: R.M.K. Deakens.
Wit.: Isaac Harr, T.C. Murray. Probated August Term, 1887.
Signed: Sudie E. Hunt

HARVY K. CHASE   April 20, 1887
Wife Elizabeth - 250 acres with full control to support my 3 daughters
Mattie, Fanny & Dolly Chase during their natural lives. Sons Andy S.
Chase & Chester Chase. Executors: Wife Elizabeth & Dr. J.L. Clark.
Wit.: C.O.M. Beals, J.K. Weems. Probated June Term, 1887.
Signed: H.K. Chase

WILLIAM M. FLEMING   October 4, 1887
Wife Caroline S. - all my property - daughters Kate R. & Mary V. to have
a home as long as they are single. Other children well provided for.
Grandchildren. Executrix: Caroline S. Fleming. Wit.: S.J. Kirkpatrick,
E.J. Baxter. Probated November Term, 1887.
Signed: William M. Fleming

MARY VAUGHN AIKEN   March 19, 1883
Husband John Chapman Aiken - all my estate. Executor: Husband John
Chapman Aiken. Test: Jno. B. Shipley, Fanny S. Matthews.

Codicil - Pay my sister Mrs. Mattie Crawford $100 and to each of her
children, R. Dalla M. Crawford & Charles T. Crawford. Sister Ellen L.
Temple. To Foreign Missions of Southern Baptist - $100. All this
property came from my father's estate. Wit.: Jno. B. Shipley of
Knoxville, Tenn. & Fannie E. Matthews of Knoxville, Tenn. Proven
October Term, 1887.
Signed: Mary Vaughn Aiken

ELIZABETH CAULEY   November 8, 1887
My land - partly owned by my father Jacob Keebler - my portion decreed
by County Court. Land adjoining Alpheus Keebler, Conrad Bashor and
others. Sell land and pay Doctor Bills and debts. Three oldest child-
ren: David J.G. Conley, Samuel R. Conley & Joseph Conley. Land in
District 15 - to my husband Joseph A. Conley and my 2 youngest children,
Lafayett & Alexander C. Conley. Executor: E.L. Deaderick. Wit.:
Conrad Bashor, Robert Bates. Probated December Term, 1887.
Signed: Elizabeth (X) Cauley

R. K. COLLINS   August 5, 1887
Of Johnson City. Everything to wife S.M. Collins. Executrix: Wife
S.M. Collins. Probated February Term, 1888.
Signed: R.K. Collins

HENRY SWADLEY   August 11, 1886
Wife Mary. Heirs: George E. Swadley - where he lives in Unicoi County,
son John W. Swadley - $2000 in tanyard stock and $1200 in notes, daughter
Virginia W. White wife of James M. White - a farm in Sullivan County
where they live, son David C. Swadley - knob land, daughter Susan A.
Swadley - $2000, daughter Barbara A. Swadley - $2000. My niece Ann E.
Nead daughter of Daniel Nead. Executors: Sons John W. & David C.
Swadley. Wit.: A.B. Bowman, S.H. Ponder. Probated April Term, 1888.
Signed: Henry Swadley

SARAH SQUIBB   June 23, 1882
Nephew Henry Clay Keebler - all my property after debts are paid - 130
acres in District 14. Executor: Henry Clay Keebler. Wit.: J.F.E.
Morrell, Reece B. Stone. Probated April Term, 1888.
                              Signed: Sarah Squibb

SUSAN EMELINE FORD   March 18, 1888
Daughter Mary Elizabeth Clemons - my Singer Sewing Machine. George
Washington Ford - 1 fiddle. William A. Ford. To my 3 children just
mentioned above I leave my land in the 10th District adjoining Range.
Executor: W.S. Porch. Probated April Ter, 1888.
                              Signed: Susan Emeline (X) Ford

JOHN S. KEPLINGER   January 14, 1888
Wife Elizabeth F. Keplinger and son William R. Keplinger - the residue
of my estate. Executor: My father Samuel B. Keplinger. My heir William
Rhea Keplinger's inheritance to be held in trust until he is 21 or
married. I have 350 acres in Washington County, Virginia adjoining Col.
J.G. Haynes, D.E.P. Campbell, Jordan Fleanor, Gus Mass. Wit.: John P.
Blair, T.D. Keplinger, James N. Peoples. Probated April Term, 1888.
                              Signed: John F. Keplinger

DAVID MAYS   March 7, 1888
To my daughter Mary and her husband James Deakens and their children and
heirs: Veina, Hester, Floyd, Will, Carl, Liza, James Jr. & Maggie.
Executor: Grandson H.F. Deakens. Wit.: W.F. Simpson, James (X) Whaley,
Francis Rackett. Probated April Term, 1888.
                              Signed: David (+) May

E. SMITH MATHES   June 6, 1888
Son Mack M. Mathes - all my real estate where I now live including the
Bone Mill, the Bricker Lot and woodland near Thomas Cloyds. My carding
machine now in Moors Mill. My organ and library of books - to be divided
between my four children: Mack M., Alex P., Rollee J. & Adda M. Mathes.
Organ to Mack's 2 daughters Birtie and Mamie Mathes. Pay the heirs of
Thomas Riddle, if they can be found the amount due them per the will of
Alexander Mathes Senr. decd. Grandchildren: Effie D. & Frank S. Mathes.
To Old School Presbyterian Church Home & Foreign Missions - $50 each.
Executor: Son Mack Mathes. Wit.: Ez. S. Mathes, James M. Argenbright.
Probated July Term, 1888.   Signed: E. Smith Mathes

JAMES HODGES   January 14, 1881
Wife Mary. Sell personal property to pay debts. Four daughters:
Elizabeth Smith, Susan Cox, Hannah White & Louisa Kidwell. Grandson
Joseph K. Hodges, only child of my son Joseph - $400 and like sum to
my granddaughter Mary Hodges, the only child of my son John decd. The
above will be equal to my other children: Joseph K. Hodges and Mary
Hodges, Martin, Henry, Kenedy, Rollen and Mary Range - to whom I made
advances years ago. Executors: Sons-in-law Richard Kidwell & Landon
White. Wit.: A.G. Pickens, E.C. Reeves. Probated July Term, 1888.
                              Signed: James Hodges
     J.K. Hodges
     Chattanooga, Tenn.
     Room #6 Tenns Building

REBECCA KEEN   May 17, 1888
If they can agree - debts to be paid and a division made between Vansant
Keen, Enoch N. Keen, Ester W. Duncan & Amanda M. Moulton & George S.
Whitlock. Executor: John P. Duncan Esq. Wit.: Ambrose Gibson, Robert
McCulley, W.A. Robeson. Probated July Term, 1888.
                              Signed: Rebecca (X) Keen

W. H. HUMPHREYS   March 28, 1888
Daughters: Edith and Anna Humphreys - to have all my property. Three
sons: David J., John and William Humphreys. Wit.: John B. Chase, P.M.
Chase. Probated August Term, 1888.
                         Signed: W.H. Humphreys

M. P. CHASE   January 2, 1888
Daughter Elmira Chase - to have 50 acres of my land and be my Executrix.
Daughter Tennessee & son Dan Chase to live with Elmira and do as Elmira
says. Other heirs. Sons Mat Chase & Dan Chase to farm land. Attest:
John B. Chase, R.M. Chase.   Signed: M.P. (X) Chase

Codicil - Children: John B. Chase, Elizabeth Dickinson. Probated August
Term, 1888.

ELLEN W. MARTIN   July 22, 1888
To Anna Mary Martin - house and lot in Johnson City 9th Civil District
adjoining Nannie Riley. Son John A. Martin, daughter Sue McAnderson,
Juliet E. Plemmons & Anna Mary Martin. Executor: Ike T. Jobe. Test:
George S. Galleher, A.C. McNeese. Probated August Term, 1888.
                         Signed: Ellen M. Martin

ALFRED LYLE - Johnson City   May 15, 1888
Wife Rebecka Lyle - land in Johnson City adjoining Miller Brothers
Foundry during her life - at her death, to my children. Wit.: Jas.
Sutton, K.J. Miller. Probated September Term, 1888.
                         Signed: Alfred (X) Lyle

SAMUEL E. LYON   June 29, 1887
Wife Nancy J. Lyon. Executor: Joseph D. Lyon. Wit.: W.L. Lyon, W.S.
Strain. Probated September Term, 1888.
                         Signed: S.E. Lyon

State of Texas, Dallas County appeared J.A. Lindsey, J.P. & exofficio
Notary Public in and for Dallas County, Texas. W.S. Strain swore that
the above was a true will - 5 September 1888. Proven September Term,
1888.   Signed: W.S. Strain

THOMAS C. PATTON   March 30, 1885
Of Rheaton in the County of Greene, State of Tennessee. Three daughters
of my brother James: Mary Bell, Margaret Edney & Nola Elizabeth - ½ my
undivided interest in 100 acres in Landall County, Kentucky on waters of
Little Raccoon Creek adjoining Charles Scovell, Richard Pursley & Nosic
Black. To brother George - other ½. Executor: Brother James Patton.
Wit.: G.N. Shoun, W.D. Good. Probated (date not given - had to be 1888).
Witnesses were dead, proved by Newton Hacker and A.W. Mettelel.
                         Signed: Thomas C. (X) Patton

ELIZA C. SEATON   July 21, 1888
My husband W.B. Seaton - to have my farm in Eastern Suburbs of Jonesboro
during his natural life. Daughter Maggo Seaton - to have a home with my
husband. At their death property is to be sold and pay James L. Goodson
- $800 I owe him on land, also to my two sons William H. and Charles E.
Seaton - $300 each. Give to James L. Goodson, William H. & Charles E.
Seaton - 1 bed each. To Ellen Stanfield, Jamie Broyles, Virgie Hett.
Executor: E.A. Shipley. Wit.: J.M. Campbell, W.E. Hankal. Probated
February Term, 1889.   Signed: Eliza C. Seaton

SARAH MILLER   June 11, 1886
Granddaughter Maggie - 12 acres adjoining James Barnes. Grandson William

Miller and great grandson Charles Isenbarger. Wit.: David Barnes, T.H.
Barnes, T.L. Hale. Proven January Term, 1889.
Signed: Sarah (X) Miller

MARY M. MAUPIN   November 14, 1887
Son James Henry Maupin - only heir. Suit pending in Chancery Court at
Jonesboro in regard to Pension Money. I will to my son money said - be
paid to John F. Gresham for my benefit by David Erwin from the Baker
estate, if it can be collected. If my husband John A.P. Maupin should
survive this son, all to revert to him. Wit.: David G.W. Barnes, John
W. Leab. Probated January Term, 1889.
Signed: Mary M. (X) Maupin

Humphreys Glaze et al vs. William B. Glaze et al - Moses Glaze, Laurence
Glaze, Caroline Morrison, Wilson Moore & David Moore. Non Cupative Will
- 20 January 1889. By order of Circuit & Supreme Court the will of
David O. Moore decd. to be recorded.
Signed: Lewis Cooper,
Circuit Court Clerk

DAVID O. MOORE   Non Cupative
On the 26 day of June 1887 - David O. Moore died between 8 & 9 A.M. at
the home of Mark Seaton in the First District of Washington County where
he had been suddenly taken ill and had lived for 10 days. We were
called into the room where the deceased was lying by H. Glaze. Mark
Seaton came in first and when H. Asten came in said H. Glaze spoked to
said David O. Moore as follows: "Davy I will state the matter over in
the presence of these witnesses as you have first stated it to me and
you can answer. You say (addressing deceased) that if you dye you do
not want that note to come against me and you want me to have one of
your mules." Deceased David O. Moore replyed, "yes if I die I dont want
that note I hold against you to ever come against you and I want you to
have one of my mules." The said David O. Moore died on the 27 day of
June 1887. Written and signed by us July 5, 1887.
M.S. Seaton
Henry Aston

Humphreys Glaze says this is the will - David and Wilson Moore says this
is not the will of David O. Moore. Jury trial - Jurors: James Brobeck,
H. Campbell, W.A. Headrick, P.H. Mottern, C. Smith, T.J. Gibson, E.
Davidson, J.W. Sherfy, R.W. Morrell, James Hale, S.B. Slaughter & W.M.
Cooper - tried on Friday - to render verdict tomorrow.

Monday April 23, 1888 - Jury came and found in favor of plaintiff - that
the paper does contain the non cupative will of David O. Moore decd.
Contestants: David Moore & Wilson & R.G. Moore to pay the costs.
Plaintiff to pay witnesses: A.B. Graham, W.N. Broyles, A.F. Mauk.
Motion for a New Trial
Moved to Supreme Court of Tennessee at Knoxville, the second Monday in
September. Will upheld. Moores to pay Humphreys Glaze - the costs of
surety bond. 7 November 1888 Supreme Court upheld decision of Circuit
Court. Moores to pay costs of the appeal. Circuit Court - Jonesboro
January 30, 1889 - upheld will. Signed: Lewis Cooper, Clerk

G. W. KITZMILLER   April 25, 1888
Wife Margaret J. - all property of all kinds, to raise my children.
Each child to have a Bible costing $2 each. At her death all property
to be divided equally. Executrix: Wife Margaret. Test: P. Yoakley,
L.H. Bachman. Probated February Term, 1889.
Signed: G.W. Kitzmiller

SARAH A. BROYLES   June 19, 1885
Of Anderson County, South Carolina. Son Augustus - 1/8 part of my silver
and mahogany dining table. Son Edward - gold watch, son Henry, daughter
Margaret, son Robert, daughter Sarah Anne and her daughter Maggie, son
John. My plantation on Chucky River, Washington County, East Tennessee
- to be divided in equal parts running from the river to the mountain.

Divide in 3 parts — the west tract down river adjoining Mrs. Broyles — to daughter Sarah A. Williams. The tract up river where the brick house is located — to my son Thomas. Middle tract — to son John. The Bayles tract to son Robert. John's may take the Laurence place in South Carolina, if he does, the Tennessee place must be sold to pay Augustus what is due him from his father's estate. Two daughters: M.C. Van Wyck & Sarah A. Williams. Land valued at $26.50 per acre. Wit.: J.C. C. Featherton, R.E. Belcher, W.C. Andrew. Probated 22 August 1888 in Anderson County, South Carolina — then 15 November 1888.
Signed: Sarah A. Broyles

Personal property included silver, 1/8 to each heir. 7 large silver candlesticks, Brussels Carpet, mahogany furniture, gold broaches, linen sheets, trifle dishes, cellery stands, decanters, gilt china, quilts made by my own hands.

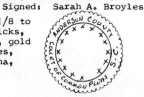

JOHN L. MURRAY   October 8, 1881
Land along railroad — west side for son Thomas — eastside for daughter Nancy Ann. Wife Rebecca L. to be cared for. Executor: Thomas C. Murray. Wit.: A.J.F. Hyder, E.P. White. Probated February Tern, 1889. Land adjoining Hodges, railroad and had a sawmill.
Signed: John L. Murray

ALBERT KING   March 29, 1882
All property to be divided between the heirs of my wife: Lafayet, William C. & Mary. My daughter Caroline — $100. Executor: My son Lafayet King. Wit.: John Saylor, Joshua Boring. Probated March Term, 1889.   Signed: Albert King

JOHN N. STEVENS   February 9, 1889
Of Johnson City. Wife Nancy C. Stevens. Six children: Alfred J., Masonri Dove, John C., Levance, Oswego & Samuel J.T. Stevens. Executor: Calvin Bowman — Executed 9th Civil District. Wit.: N.T. Nave, J.L.W. Caruthers. Probated March Term, 1889.
Signed: John Stevens

MRS. FANNIE R. HUNTER   September 1, 1888
To sister Mary B. Sparks — all my estate, money, notes, accounts, furniture etc. Executor: My father J.F. Broyles. Test: J.S. Broyles, Maggie Sheecraft. Probated November Term, 1888.
Signed: Fannie R. Hunter

FETHIAS SMITH   February 7, 1889
To daughter Mary A. Bayless — to give me a decent maintenance during my natural life. My 160 acres in the 3rd District of Loudon County, Tenn. to be sold. Wife Malinda decd. Pay Alexander H. Smith and Jacob Warren what I owe. Divide the remaining between all my children. Executors: E.A. and Thomas Taylor. Wit.: William R. Thompson, W.S. Thompson. Proven May Term, 1889.   Signed: Fethias Smith

MANERVA GIBSON   November 19, 1866
To my brother Pearce Gibsons heirs — $1. Sister Elizabeth Gibson — land from my father Thomas Gibson (25 acres). Sister Peneasa wife of John S. Woolf — the remaining land. To brother Pleasant Gibson — $1. Brother Caswell Gibson — $1 and to his heirs — $1. To brother William Gibson — $1. Executor: John S. Woolf. Test: Francis (X) Williams, David A. Feathers. Probated June Term, 1889.
Signed: Manerva (X) Gibson

DANIEL CLARK   March 4, 1887
Wife Loretta A. Clark. To Clark Kebler, son of Susannah Kebler formerly

Dove — $200. **Brothers** and sisters $5 each. Executors: Joseph Miller, son of Jacob Miller, decd. Wit.: F.M. Stout, Joseph Bowman. Probated January, 1889.

Signed: Daniel Clark

J. F. GILLIAM   13 August 1888
Executor F.A. Stratton to have my real estate in Tennessee, Virginia, Indiana and other states as well as stock, bonds and all insurance policies. To be used for the support of my wife and children. Wit.: Jesse Bean, A. R. Wing. Probated August 1889.

Signed: J. F. Gilliam

JOHN BEALS   9 August 1889
Wife Sarah Ann to live where we do now and be supported by my 3 sons: Joseph E., James H. D., and Isaac S. Beals during her lifetime. To son Joseph E. — the Susannah S. Beals tract. Sons: William K. Beals and John K. Beals. Daughters: Susannah Done, Martha E. Motern. Land bought of old Joseph Archer. Tools: double shovel plow, grain drill, reaper, thrashing machine. Executor: Joseph E. Beals, my son. Witnesses: S.P. Martin, S.L. Dishl. Probated September 1889.

Signed: John Beals

STEPHEN P. SMITH   8 September 1889
To my mother Sallie C. Smith eleven shares of the Capital Stock of the Crandall — Harris Tobacco Warehouses, shares are $100 each, one policy in Northwestern Mutual Life Insurance Company, Milwaukee, Wisconsin for $3000 bought December 11, 1882. Executrix: My mother, Sallie C. Smith. Witnesses: R.A. Wood, F.K. Mountcastle. Probated October 1889.

Signed: Stephen P. Smith

MARY ANN DEWALD   5 September 1889
Of Brownsboro. My undivided interest in 70 acres land in District 2 Washington County, Tennessee willed to me by my father Daniel Dewald to: Sister Betty Dewald, niece Mary Jane Thomas and nephew D.A. Thomas. To Sister Bettie Dewald — 1 rose bud quilt and glass tumblers and other things. To Mary Jane Thomas — 2 quilts (Mo. Rose and Tulip) and other things. To sister Julia Galloway — 1 satchel. Executor: David D.A. Thomas. Witnesses: A.S.N. Dobson, James Kimery. Probated October 1889.

Signed: Mary Ann (X) Dewald

Compiled by
Ella E. Lee Sheffield
Texas City, Texas

ABIGAIL, Abraham 16
  Job 16
  John 16
  Joshua 16
  Phebe 16
  Rebecca 16
  Sarah 16
ADAIR, Ezekiel 20
  Hannah 20
  James 23
  James, Senr. 20
  Jane 20
  John 20
  Polly 20
ADAM, Josephine 107
  Martin 107
ADAMS, Agnes 10, 24
  Alexander 30, 72
  Alvin 72
  Elizabeth 107
  J. J. 104
  J. P. 106
  Jannet 24
  John 5, 7, 12, 24
  Lydia M. 72
  Margaret 10
  Martin 107
  Martin K. 72
  Mary 24
  Mary J. 72
  Mary Jane 72
  Samuel Hanly 24
  Sarah 6
  Sarah F. 72
  William 10, 24
ADLER, Jacob 76
AIKEN, Adelaide 44
  Elizabeth 44
  Elizabeth A. 94
  James 14, 94
  John 21
  John A. 14
  John Chapman 109
  Margaret 44
  Mary A. 94
  Mary Ann 94
  Mary C. 94
  Mary Vaughn 109
  Peter 94
  Vance 24
ALDIN, Jacob 101
ALEXANDER, Elizabeth 77
  James 20
  Jane 20
  John 23
  Josiah 77
  Margaret M. 62
  Martha 77
  Samuel 77
  Susannah 66
  Suzan 77
ALLEN, Ann 87
  Catharine 52
  Emma 87
  George 87
  Harvey 73
  James 37
  Jane 87
  Margaret 25
  Robert 72, 87
  Samuel 52
  Serephina 72
  William 73, 87
ALLGOOD, Manly 25
ALLISON, Alice 100
  Alphia 64
  Ann 4, 16
  Archibald Chester 64
  Deborah 64

ALLISON (cont.)
  Elinor 45
  Elizabeth 5
  Ellen Jane 100
  Esther 5
  Florence 100
  Frank 5
  G. W. 64
  George 64
  Hannah 16
  Hannah E. 36
  Hannah Elija 12
  Hannah Eliza 74, 100
  Hugh 13
  James 5
  James H. 55
  Jane 4, 5, 12, 24, 36
  Jesse 61
  John 4, 55, 64, 100
  John, Jr. 89, 100
  Julia 71
  Martha 64
  Mary 64, 100
  Minnie 101
  Nancy 12
  Polly 4, 16
  Polly Ann 25
  Polly Anna 12, 16, 36
  Rachel 12, 16
  Robert 4, 5, 8, 11, 13,
    16, 24, 55, 63, 64
  Robert, Jr. 74
  Robert, Senr. 12
  Ruth 55
  Susan 100
  Susannah 45
ANDERSON, Adaline 67
  George 77
  Hanna C. 79
  Henry 77
  James 14
  James V. 12, 20
  John 4, 65
  John Fain 79
  Miriam 40
  Nancy 77
  Patsy 11
  R. Ellen 79
  Ruth E. 77
  Samuel 79
  William 14
  William T. 20
ANDES, Abraham 41, 58
  Allen 58
  Ann 29
  Barbary 29, 58
  Catharine 29, 58
  Debroah 29
  Elizabeth 29
  Frederick 29
  Hally 29
  Henry 59
  John J. 58
  Katharine 54
  Levina 58
  Mary 58
  Phoebe 29
  Rebecca 58
  Ruth 58
  William 58
  William D. 58
ANDREW, David 79
  W. C. 113
ANON, Mary
ANTWIL, Emily 69
ARCHER, Benjamin 14, 72
  Catharine 108
  Elijah 57, 72, 75
  Elizabeth 72

ARCHER (cont.)
  J. M. 108
  Joseph 72, 114
  Jonathan 72
  Jurial D. 72
  Looamy 72
  Martha 108
  Mary Ann 72, 75
  Nancy 72
  Silas 72
  Susannah 72, 108
  Thomas 72
  William 64, 72
ARGENBRIGHT, James M. 10
ARMENTROUT, Catharine 68
  Frederick 68
  Hiram 68
  J. K. 67, 94
  J. R. 68
  Layamora 68
  Michael 68
  Philip 68
  Richard 94
  Smith 72
ARMSTRONG, E. 77
  Edmund 40
  Edward 40, 72
  Margarim 18
  Sarah 77
  W. E. S. 104
  William 6
ARNOLD, Emanuel 39
  Junie 93
  Martha 93
  Samuel 91
ARRINGTON, Thomas 80
ASHER, -- 81
  Agnes 61
  William E. 61
ASTEN, H. 112
ASTON, Henry 112
  John, Sr. 98
ATKINSON, Wilton 33
BACHMAN, L. H. 108, 112
  N. W. 82
  Nathan 103
  Nathan W. 87
BACON, -- 90
  Abigail 24
  Catherine 19, 63
  Charles 19, 24, 37, 62,
    76, 91
  Dalooney 59
  Deborah 63, 68
  Delia E. 97
  Dicey 63
  Dorcas 50
  Edmund 73
  Elijah 59
  Elizabeth 19, 34, 59,
    63, 68, 91, 97
  Ellendlind 63
  Henry N. 91
  Henry U. 97
  Isaac 24
  J. H. 97
  Jacob 19, 41, 99
  Jacob B. 48
  Jane H. 58
  Jemima 50
  Jeremiah 65
  Jesse 59, 71, 81, 82,
    97
  John 24, 30, 59, 63,
    108
  Jonathan 24, 52, 63,
    91, 97
  Joseph 24, 63
  Joseph L. 59

BACON (cont.)
Joseph M. 100
June 59
Lear 50
Liza R. 99
Louisa 97
Lyddian 63, 68
Malinda 59
Marls 58, 59
Martha 63
Mary 96, 97
Mary E. 95
Mary Nancy 58
Nancy 19, 24, 63
Nancy Jane 91, 97
Polly 19
Polly Ann 59
Preston 91, 97
Rachel 50
Robert Shelton 58
Sarah 63, 68
Sarah A. 82
Sarah R. 100
Sileta 59
Sylvenous 91, 97
Thomas 24, 82
Tymeander 97
BAILEY, H. F. 87, 101
BAINS, Elizabeth 87
J. W. 76
Jesse J. 87
BAKER, -- 112
J. U. 99
BALCH, John K. 20
BALES, John 107
Luella 107
Mattie 107
Solomon 23
William 107
BALL, Joseph 26
Martha 6
Nancy 38
Rebecca 26
Samuel 26
Thomas 26
BALLARD, Elisa Jane 93
George 93
George W. 93
Harriet 93
John A. 93
Stephen 93
BALLENGER, B. 52
Bluford 37, 38
James 37
Polly 37
BALSER, Joseph 72
BANCROFT, Ambrose 45
Elizabeth 45, 59
Jane 45, 59
Jonathan 35, 45
Martha 45, 59
Mary Ann 59
BANNER, Ann 34
Catharine 34
Elizabeth 34
Ephraim 34
Henry 34
Judy 34
Lewis 34
Mahaly 34
Mary 34
Phillip 34
BARCROFT, Alice 99
Elizabeth 85, 99
Jane 85, 99
Martha 85
Mary 85
BARDING, Desa A. 70
James 48, 70
James D. 70
John M. 70
Louisa H. 70
Louisiana G. 70

BARCROFT (cont.)
Loutisha 70
Stephen P. 70
William Chester B. 70
BARELL, W. W. 38
BARENS, A. L. 99
Addie E. 99
Ellen 99
Martha 99
Martha A. 99
Rutherford B. Hays 99
Susan E. 99
Virginia F. 99
BARGER, Christiana 35
Jane 51
Wyland 46
BARKLEY, A. B. 70
Alice 98
Andrew H. 53
Blanche Jane 76
D. B. 64
Daniel 31, 43, 53, 67
Daniel B. 53
Delila Tennessee 43
Ebenezer 42, 43, 53, 54, 58
Elizabeth 43
Emaline 43
Henry P. 54
Isaac 89
Jacob 53
Jacob C. 53
Jacob E. 53
James M. 76
Jane 53
John 43, 53, 99
John K. 54
Kittie 99
Margaret 40, 47, 53
Margaret Carolina 76
Mary Ann 99
Mary Louisa 76
Polly 58
Samuel K. 99
Sarah 43, 53
Sarah Jane 43, 54
Susan 53
Susannah 43
W. G. 85
William 99
William S. 53, 76
BARNES, David 112
David G. W. 112
Elijah 31
Elizabeth 21, 82
Hannah 106
J. M. 104
James 8, 21, 22, 111
James M. 106
Jenny 8
John 62
John M. 62, 82
Joseph 12, 106
Madison M. 62
Mary 12, 21
Mary E. 106
Nathan 18, 26, 37
Peggy 8
Polly 8
Samuel W. 52
T. H. 112
Thomas 28
Tina 106
BARNET, Lavinia 37
Polly 16
BARNS, Els 29
BARRETT, Fannie C. 85
BARRIT, J. D. 69
Jane 69
BARRON, Ann 5
Daniel 37, 68
Henry 5
Jacob 68

BARRON (cont.)
James 5
John 5, 68
Joseph 5, 10
Madison 79
Margaret 5
Mary 5, 10
Peggy 28
Polly 28
Sarah 5, 10
Thomas 68
Walker 5, 28
William 5, 10
William P. 73
BASHER, Elizabeth 49
Henry 49
John M. 62
BASHOR, Benjamin 86
Catharine E. 70
Christly 86
Conrad 109
David 86, 105
Henry 49, 86
Isaac 86, 105
James D. 86
Martha 105
Mary 86, 105
Michael 75, 77, 78, 86
Matilda 86
Nancy 86
Sarah 77, 86
Sarah M. 86
BASHORE, Anna 70
Christley 70
Henry 51
Isaac 70
John 70
Margaret 70
BASKET, Charles 14, 78
Charles, Jr. 78
Charles Washington 78
James M. 78
John 14, 78
Manson 78
Mary Jane 78
Michael 14
Nancy 14
Polly 14
Rachel 14
Richard 14
Sarah 78
W. M. 82
William 14
BASON, Susannah R. 100
BASS, Matthew 6
BASTER, Jno. 79
BATES, Margaret 4
Robert 109
W. H. 66
BATTS, Susanna 61
BAXTER, E. J. 109
Sarah 36
BAY, Elizabeth 4
Thomas 4
BAYLES, -- 113
A. C. 107
Abram 51
Adaline 80
Alice 21
Angie 107
Ann 7
Anna 70
Bethmoth 59
Cynthia 70
D. W. T. 107
Daniel 7, 21, 25
E. W. 80
Eleanor 51
Eliza 70
Elizabeth 21
F. S. 74
Gertrude 107
Hannah 12, 21

BAYLES (cont.)
Henderson 21
Hezekiah 20, 21, 81
Isabel 70
J. E. 80
Jesse 30
John 7, 21, 70, 80
Julia 74
Kezee 81
Lemander 28
Luthy 25
Margaret 25
Martena 21
Matilda 21
Martin McAmish 70
Mary 5, 12, 80
Mary Louisiana 51
Nancy 30
Phebe 21
Polly 21
R. R. Robert 80
Rebecca 25
Reese 70
Reuben 19, 21, 25, 33,
35, 40
Reubin 6, 12
Samuel 21, 28, 30, 80
Samuel G. 60, 64
Sarah Ann 49
Sileta 59
Susan 51
Susann 80
Susannah 21
Thomas 74
William 11, 12, 13, 20,
21
William A. 35
William E. 51
Wilson 63, 66
Young 45, 53
BAYLESS, A. A. 107
Alfred G. 73
Barton 68, 74
Billy 57
Bird D. 73
Daniel L. 73
E. W. 107
E. Ward 107
Eliza 73
Elizabeth 73
Hiram 74
J. E. 107
J. M. 87, 88, 92, 106
James M. 90
Jno. W. 108
Mary 108
Mary A. 113
Mc. 108
Naomi 104
R. R. 107
Robert B. 103
Samuel G. 74
Susannah 103
William M. 73
William R. 77
Wilson 71
Young 104
BAYLEY, Lucy 3
Mary 3
Sarah 3
Walter 3
BAYLIS, Ann 19
Anna 19
Daniel 19
George 19
John 19
Martinen 19
Mary 29
Rees 19
Samuel 19
Sarah 19
BEALS, Abigail 81
Abram 81

BEALS (cont.)
C. O. M. 109
Caleb 27, 81
Catharine 81
David 27, 31, 81
Elizabeth 27, 81
Hannah 75, 81
Isaac 23, 75
Isaac H. 81
Isaac S. 114
Jacob 81
James H. D. 114
Jerusha 81
John 57, 75, 114
John K. 114
Joseph 23, 75
Joseph E. 114
Marshal 81
Martha 81
Martha E. 114
Mary 75
Mary Ann 75
Nancy 81
Polly Ann 106
Rachel 75, 81
Samuel 27
Sarah Ann 114
Solomon 31, 75, 81
Susannah 75, 114
Susannah S. 114
Thomas 81
West 81, 106
William 106
William K. 114
William M. 81
BEAMER, William M. A. R.
80
BEAN, George 1
Jesse 114
Liddy 1
Robert 1
Russell 1
William 1
BEANE, Edmund 11
Margaret 11
Rosamond 6
BEARD, Betsy 32
Charles 97
David 70
Edia 20
Edith 70
Emeline 70
Esther 32
Eugene 67
George C. 62
Isabella 32
James 28, 32
James H. 101
James S. 104
Joseph 32
Malinda C. 95
Margaret 67
Marth 32
Mary 50
Matilda 70
Mattie 32
Nancy 32
Robert 32
Robert E. 67
Robert Emmerson 67
Sally 32
Samuel 32, 70
William 26, 32, 70
BEDDEL, Jane 53
BEEDLES, William 46
BEELE, Levi 13
BELCHER, R. E. 113
BELL, Aily 45
Alice 99
Ambrose 45, 59, 99
Ambrose P. 85
Brooks H. 88
David 4, 54

BELL (cont.)
Elizabeth 4, 46, 47,
88
Frederick 57
George 4, 11, 17, 23
Hally 29
James 4, 57
John 4, 45
Mary 4
Sarah 4, 57
Thomas 4, 46
William 4
BENSON, Altie 101
Cora 101
Ellen 101
Hattie 93
James H. 101
Laura 101
Mattie 101
Minnie 101
Nancy J. 101
R. G. 101
Sally 101
BENTON, Isaac 5
BERRY, Tilburn 63
BERRYMAN, Samuel 11
BEUTS, James H. 66
BEWLEY, Sarah 29
BIBLE, George 23
BIDDLE, Elizabeth 25, 57,
71, 88
Hugh 25
J. L. 57, 72, 88
J. N. 88
J. S. 73
James 25, 88
Jane 79
John 25, 46, 57, 88
Jno. S. 96
Margaret 57
Mary A. 57
Mary Ann 88
Nancy 25, 88
Peggy 25
Samuel 21, 25, 38
Samuel D. 57
Sarah 25, 88
Thomas 8, 25, 57
Washington 88
BILLINGSLEY, Mary 41
Nancy 25
Sarah 41
BIRCH, Joseph 45
BIRCHFIELD, Ez 54
BIRD, Amos 99
James 30
Lucinda 99
BITNER, Katharine 39
Margaret A. 17
Martha 101
Melvin 101
Samuel K. 46
Thomas 65
BLACBURN, Ann 4
Archibald 4, 20
Benjamin 3, 4, 20
Betsey 20
Elizabeth 4
Isbell 20
John 4
Mary 3
Nathaniel 20
Polly 20
Robert 4, 14
Rosannah 20
Samuel 4, 20
Thomas 20
William 20
BLACK, J. N. 109
Nosic 111
BLACKBURN, Sally 88
William 88
BLAIR, -- 53

BLAIR (cont.)
  Anna 8
  Blair 40
  Brue 9
  David 8
  Hannah 17
  Hugh 17
  Isabel 8
  J. 58
  James Buoin 8
  James H. 53
  James Moore 9
  Jean 8
  Jenny 9
  John 8. 9, 10, 15, 17,
    28, 34, 36, 37, 40,
    42, 63
  John, Jr. 14, 15
  John, Sr. 15
  John B. 46
  John P. 110
  Jonah 17
  Joseph 17
  Margaret 18, 53
  Martha 8, 17
  Mary 8
  Nancy 10
  Polly 17
  R. L. 58
  R. L., Jr. 62
  Rachel 17
  Robert 8, 9, 51
  Robert L. 74
  Samuel 9, 17
  Susannah 10, 15
  Thomas 17
  W. K. 40
  William 9, 17
  William K. 37, 45, 58,
    62
BLAKELY, Daniel 27
  James 27
  Jno. 18
  John 20, 27, 38, 41
  Lydia 27
  Martha 27
  Matthew 38
  Robert 27
  Thomas 27
  William 27
BLEAKLEY, John 7
BLEAKLY, Robert 4
BLEVENS, A. J. 100
  Carolina 78
BLEVINS, George E. 85
  Mary 94
  W. H. 94
BLYE, Deborah 29
BOGART, Elizabeth 33
  Hannah 56
  Jeremiah 33
  Lemuel 26, 56
  Mary 15
  Rachel 26
  Samuel W. 45
BOLLEN, John 26
BOND, Charles 60
  Mary 60
BOOLL, Ebenezer 77
BOLTON, Alice 83
  Daniel 54
  Daniel A. 83
  David 83
  Elbert V. 83
  Henry 54
  Henry W. 83
  John 54
  John F. 83
  Joseph 83
  Magdalena 54
  Sarahphina 83
  Susan Caroline 83
  Valentine 54

BONELL, William 44
BOOTH, David 9
  Elizabeth 9, 54, 82
  Jane 9
  Jemima 9
  John 9, 54
  Joseph 9, 92
  Mary 26
  Phebe 9
  Rachel 9
  Sarah 9
BOOTHE, Madison 39
BOREENG, Vincent 62
BOREN, Abrrodla 6
  Absolem 6, 14
  Benjamin 108
  Carolina 47
  Casandra 40, 47
  Chana 40
  Chance 40, 41
  Chaney 6, 19
  Elijah 16, 26, 31, 40
  Greene 14
  Hezekiah 15
  James 6
  Jane 40, 47
  John Dopon 6
  John Dorsey 41
  Lauretta P. 41
  Loretta 47
  Loretta P. 40
  Lucinda 47
  Martha 6
  Nancy 14
  Nicholas 41
  Rachel 6
  Sabrina 47
  Sabrina A. 41
  Sarah 6
  Tempereace 6
  William 6
BORING, Greenberry 85
  Isaac 85
  John 85
  John W. 80
  Joshua 113
  M. P. 80
  Madison 85
  Mary 85
  Montgomery P. 69
  P. H. 98
  Vincent 57, 64, 71
BOTLES, Zachariah M. 35
BOTTEL, Elizabeth 35
  Henry 35
  Jacob 35
  John 35
  Joseph 35
  Mary E. 35
  Sarah 35
  William 35
BOTTLES, Elizabeth 33, 97
  Henry 33
  Jacob 33
  James 97
  John 28, 33, 97
  Joseph 33
  Mary 31
  Mary E. 33
  Sarah 33
  Susannah 97
  William 33
BOWENS, L. 82
  Lawrence 105
BOWERS, Abraham 15
  Henry 12, 15
  John W. 68
  Joshua 15
  Laurence 42
  Lawrence 94
  Leah 15
  Levi 15, 41
  Lourane 15

BOWERS (cont.)
  Nancy 15
BOWMAN, A. B. 98, 99, 102,
    109
  A. C. 105
  Adam B. 86
  Ann 42, 103
  Archibald 103
  Barbary 45, 86
  Barnet 12
  Benjamin 40
  Calvin 113
  Catharine 33, 49, 82
  Christena 49
  Cordelia A. 86
  Corneleus 3
  D. J. 103
  Daniel 11, 24, 33, 40,
    49, 81, 82, 96
  Daniel J. 103
  David 86
  David J. 107
  Elias 45
  Eliza 60, 103
  Elizabeth 45, 49, 60,
    103
  Eve 40
  George 45
  George C. 71, 96, 105
  H. 49
  Haney 100
  Hannah 100
  Hannah Emily 100
  Hiram 82
  Jacob 33, 40, 49, 65,
    76, 89
  James 76
  James K. O. 71
  John 15, 31, 35, 40,
    45, 64, 68, 103
  John, Jr. 35
  John A. 42
  John H. 49, 73, 86
  Joseph 15, 40, 49, 71,
    91, 114
  Katherine 40
  Loucindy N. 86
  Madison 40
  Madison M. 45
  Margaret 76, 86, 100
  Margaret A. 86
  Maria 45
  Mary 15, 40, 45, 49, 86
  Mary C. 103
  Nancy 103
  Nancy Anna 100
  Peter 12
  Rebecca 33, 40, 86
  Rebecka 24
  Richard 78
  Robert S. 100
  Salina J. 86
  Samuel 33, 40, 42
  Samuel David 100
  Sarah 40, 49, 76, 100
  Sarah A. 100
  Sarah R. 86
  Selina 86
  Susannah 33, 49
  Theodore 103
  William B. 96, 97
  William D. S. 40
BOWSER, Elizabeth 43
  Harrison 43
  John 43
  Martha 43, 44
BOYD, Betsy 38
  David 38
  Daniel 38
  Elizabeth 38
  Hannah 38
  Henry 38
  Jacob 38

BOYD (cont.)
Jeremiah 55
Margaret 38
Mary 38
Nancy 38
Rosannah 38
Susan 38
William 38
BOYLES, Christian 46
BRABSON, A. B. 55, 66
Alexander A. B. 55
Alexander Crutchfield
46
Alexander W. 46
Alfred 46
John 98
John M. 46
Kittie 99
Mary 46
Mary S. 46, 66
Oscar 46
Thomas 25
Samuel Powell 46
BRACY, Patrice 93
BRADLY, Elizabeth 35
Jonathan 35
BRADSHAW, Edward 83
Isaac A. 84
Jacin A. 90
Jason 84
Jason A. 84
Phebe M. 84
BRADY, Biddy 93
John 93
Micha 93
Patrice 93
Sarah 93
BRANSON, Margaret 14
William 14
BRAY, Ordena 16
BREWER, W. P. 59, 61, 63
William P. 67
BRICHER, John 17
BRIGHT, Sarah 29
Sarah Jane 43
Susan 53
William 53
BRISON, Samuel 5
BRIT, James 43
Nancy 43
BRITAIN, Eliza 58
BRITTEN, Joseph 8
BRITTIN, J. 8
Joseph 6, 9, 10, 11
BRITTON, George E. 85
Lula B. 85
T. P. 88
BROBECK, James 112
BROCKWELL, J. E. 107
BROOKS, George W. 73
Jane 7
Liles 7
William E. 73
BROTHERS, Miller 111
BROWN, -- 108
Abigail 68
Albert Thomas 94
Alfred 66
Alfred F. 98
Alis 5
Ann 28, 31
Anne 1
Aseneth 68
Audrey J. 83
Benjamin 9
Bird 34
Casander M. 66
Catherine 16, 25
Clarissa 48, 84
Colwell 29
Conrad 26
Cora 103
David 4, 20

BROWN (cont.)
Delila 82
Eliza 91
Elizabeth 21, 25, 26,
27, 29, 34, 48, 61,
96
Elizabeth C. 66
Ellendlind 63
Elvira 48
Emeline 72
Eveline P. 62
Fanny 29
G. W. 77
Gabriel 28
George 25, 38, 48
George K. 84
George S. 85
H. N. 96
Hannah 21, 25
Harriet 34
Hassie 103
Henderson 21
Hezekiah 21
Hugh 12
J. F. 82, 92, 98
J. Harmon 104
J. W. 109
Jacob 13, 25, 28, 30,
34, 38
Jacob Davis 34
Jacob G. 52
Jacob K. 34
James 33, 61, 67
Jane 29
John 7, 12, 25, 29, 38,
68
John L. 68
John W. 38, 48
Jonathan 65
Julia C. 66
Lemander 28
Leneas B. 48
Liza 48
Louisa 44
Lucinda 66
Lydia 3
Malinda 34
Mandy 48
Margaret 38, 48, 67,
68, 84, 103
Martena 21
Martha 48
Martha Ann 68
Mary Ann 38, 55, 68
Mary Ann 48
Mary J. 96
Matilda 68
Michael 25
N. T. 96, 103
Nancy 38
Nathaniel T. 96
Nervy Jane 48
Patrick 34
Peter 7
Pheuetta 96
Phoebe 29
Pleuetta 103
Polly 21, 34
Rachel 66, 68
Rebecca 34
Reese 21
Reuben 21
Richard 38
Richard Nelson 107
Roena A. 96
Ruth 34
S. W. 84
Samuel 21
Samuel A. L. 66
Sarah 25, 27, 58, 68
Sary 48
Stephen 31
Susanna 84

BROWN (cont.)
W. N. 96, 103
William 28, 34, 48
William Nathaniel 103
Wyley 38
Zachariah 68
BROWNLOW, Alexander S. 88
BROWNING, E. L. 106
E. S. 102
BROYLES, -- 113
A. A. 51
A. C. 97
A. F. 66, 88
Aaron 1
Adam 1, 68, 86
Adam, Sr. 46
Adeline A. 107
Alexander 72, 88
Amanda 72
Ann Mariah 106
Anne 1
Archibald 88
Augustus 112, 113
Augustus T. 88
B. B. 89
Bruce 96
Catharine 32
Charles E. 88
Edward 112
Eleanor 88
Eliza 70
Elizabeth 23, 88
Elizabeth Jane 85
Ellender 37
Ephraim 37, 72
Evy 88
Fannie R. 113
Frances L. 101
Henry 112
I. N. 101
Isaac 68, 89
Isaac N. 101
J. F. 113
J. S. 113
Jackie 72
Jacob 37, 88
Jacob F. 37, 43
James, Senr. 27, 37
James W. 101
Jamie 111
Jesse 88
John 37, 112, 113
John P. 88
Joshua 1
Julius 46, 72
Lawrence V. 101
Lewis 37
Louise 72
Lucinda 72
M. C. 113
M. W. 85
Maggie 112
Malinda 37
Margaret 88, 112
Marilla 37
Mary 1, 88
Mary Ann 72
Mary B. 113
Mathia 1, 37, 52
Michael 23
Michael, Senr. 23
Milla 1
Mima 1
Montgomery 97
Moses 1
Nancy 68, 87
Nathaniel 88
Nerza 72
O. R. 88, 89
O. R., Sr. 88
Oliver 97
Ozy R. 88
Philip 72

CARSON (cont.)
  Richard 38
  Robert 4, 9
  Sarah 17, 48
  Sinthy 51
  Susanna 9
  Synthy 51
  William 3, 9, 17
CARSWELL, Sary 39
CARTER, Dicey 67
  Eliza Jane 65
  Emanuel 2
  James N. 84
  John 2
CARTRIGHT, Rebecca 94
  William 94
CARUTHERS, -- 108
  Elizabeth 103
  J. L. W. 113
  James 7
  Jane 7
  Jenny 9
  John 103
  Jonathan 14
  Lillie 103
  Mollie 103
  William 9
CARY, Elijah 97
  Tymeander 97
CASH, Asbury 11
  Benjamin 11
  James 2, 11
  John 11
  Leonard 10
  Margaret 11
  Patsy 11
  Sally 11
  Thomas 11
  William 11
  Zachariah 11
CASHADY, Elizabeth 12
  John Rader 12
CASHEDY, Marth 4
  Robert 4, 7, 19
CASSADY, Abram 57
CASSIDY, William 52
CASSON, Mary E. 40
CASWELL, Sarah 98
CATE, Mary 63, 100
  William 55, 63
CAULEY, Elizabeth 109
CECIL, Julia 83
  Sallie 83
CHAMBERLAIN, James 9
CHAPMAN, Samuel 92
  Susan 98
CHARLETON, -- 39
  John 19
  Pointer, Jr. 19
  Pointen 19
  Polly 19
  Rebecca 19
  Simpson 19
  Thomas 19
CHARLTON, Emaline 33
  John 20
  Margaret 21
  Mary 21
  Pointen 20
  Rebecca 21
  Susan 58
  Thomas 20
CHASE, Andy S. 109
  Chester 109
  Dan 111
  Dolly 109
  Elizabeth 32, 109, 111
  Elmira 111
  Fanny 109
  H. K. 57, 84, 109
  Harvy K. 109
  John B. 106, 111
  M. P. 111

CHASE (cont.)
  Margaret 68
  Mark 81
  Martha 94, 108
  Mat 111
  Mattie 109
  Nelson 94, 108
  P. M. 111
  Polly Ann 59
  R. 63
  R. M. 63, 96, 111
  R. W. 106
  Shadrack 68
  Tennessee 111
  Walter 32
  Walter J. 47, 48
  William 95
CHASTIN, James 5
CHENITH, Lucy 26
  Nicholas 26
  Richard 26
CHENNETH, Henry 18
  Joseph 18
  Nicholas 18, 19
CHENOTH, Barbary Ellender 75
CHENOWETH, Emeline 108
  Richard 108
  William 108
CHESTER, Casander Rebecca 66
  Catharine 64, 66
  Elizabeth C. 66
  John 10, 28
  John P. 34, 40
  Mary 64
  Sam G. 30
  Samuel G. 69
  T. G. 32
  Thomas R. 45
  William 66
  William P. 66, 79
  William P., Jr. 34
CHINOWTH, Agnes 50
  Archibald 50
  Daniel Fox 94
  E. R. 99, 100
  Elizabeth 50
  Emeline 94
  Ezekiel R. 50
  Henry 50
  James 94
  James M. 68, 94, 108
  John 50, 94, 108
  John Addison 50
  John C. 94
  Joseph 50, 106
  Martha Ann 68
  Nicholas 50
  Nicholas H. 50
  Richard 50, 94
  Ruth 50
  William 94
CHRISTIAN, -- 28
CHRISTY, Jasper N. 91
CLACK, William 51
CLARK, Ann 49
  Daniel 113, 114
  Edward W. 63
  Elizabeth 85
  George C. 63
  George E. 85
  H. E. 108
  Henry 1
  J. L. 104, 105, 109
  John N. 31
  Jesse 9
  Joseph 14, 78
  Joseph D. 78
  Loretta A. 113
  Mary 9
  Mary A. 63
  Mock H. 63

CLARK (cont.)
  Nancy 9
  S. P. 63
  Susan F. 63
  Susan P. 71
  Susan Penelope 63
CLAWSON, Peggy 19
CLEMONS, Mary Elizabeth 110
CLICK, Fanny 28
  Isaac 85
CLINE, Harriet 61
  Mary 61
  Michael 61
CLOUSE, Aaron 9
  George, Sr. 9
  Jacob 9
CLOYD, Barton B. 78
  Catharine 78
  David 78
  J. P. 61
  James 60
  James B. 30, 34
  James W. 60
  Jenny 60
  John 60
  John C. 79
  John P. 60
  Lucindy 91
  Martha L. 91
  Mary 38
  Mary Ann 78
  Samuel 11, 60, 78
  T. J. 82
  W. A. 78
  William 60
CLOYDE, Barton B. 60, 64
  James 60, 64
  James B. 64
  Jenny 64
  John 64
  John P. 64
  Samuel 64
  William 64
CLOYDS, Thomas 110
COCHRAN, Angeline 42
  Daniel 42, 43
  Franklin 42
  Franklin D. 43
  George 42, 43
  Jacob 42
  Jacob C. 43
  John 42, 43
  John B. 43
  Nancy Jane 42
  Rebecca 42, 43
  Sally 87
  Samuel 42
  Samuel C. 43
  Sarah 42, 43
COCKRAN, Rebecca 54
COFF, W. D. 102
COILE, Henry 30
COLES, John 28
COLLAR, John S. 62
COLLETT, A. 68
  Elizabeth 68
  Jesse 66
  Margaret Ann 66
COLLINS, A. C. 61, 72
  Jno. 40
  Margaret 68
  R. K. 109
  S. M. 109
  Thomas 27
COLLOM, J. H. 90
  Jonathan Harvey 95
  Nancy 95
  R. N. 95
COLLUM, E. M. 95
  J. P. 95
  Jona 17
  Jonathan H. 68, 95

CROOKSHANK (cont.)
George 24, 33
George Campbell 33
M. B. 89
Montgomery Henderson 33
Nancy Ann 33
Sarah 33
Sarah Keyes 33
Samuel McSpadden 33
W. B. 81
William 23, 33
William Boule 33
CROSSWHITE, Jesse 69
CROUCH, Agnes Range 74
Alfred 96
Amy 41
Caroline 42, 72
Elbert 74
Elizabeth 71, 74
George 29, 31, 41, 42,
44, 50, 71
George P. 71
J. H. 87, 104
J. K. 41
James 42, 49
Jesse 10, 29, 41
Jesse Hale 41
John 9, 29, 42, 48
John H. 74
Joseph 8, 12, 18, 21,
29, 35, 41, 48, 56,
63, 65, 74, 97
Joseph, Jr. 74
Joseph, Sr. 74
Julia 71
M. S. 104
Margaret 29, 97
Martha 29
Martha Jane 74
Martin 74
Mary 29
Mary Chester 64
Rebecca 96
Sarah 71
Susan 100
Susan Rebecca 64
Susannah 49, 71
T. H. 64
Thomas H. 35, 42
W. H. 59
W. W. 66
William 31, 48, 71
Wiloiam H. 41, 64
William Stevenson 41
CROUSE, Daniel 34
John 34
Michael 11
Rebecca 34
Solomon 34
CROW, George 22
John 22
CROWE, John 45
CROWS, Nelson 98
CRUMLEY, Carolina 73
Caruthers 96
Catharine 74, 82, 83
Christian 106
D. S. 80
Daniel S. 82, 83
F. D. 93
James 74, 96
Martha 82
Martha Ann 74
Mary 106
Mary Ann 74, 82
Mary E. 74
Sarah J. 82, 83
CRUMLY, Nancy C. 91
CRUSINS, Lowinda 104
CRUTHERS, Catharine 87
CULBERTSON, Andrew 7
James 7
Jane 7

CULBERTSON (cont.)
Joseph 7
Josiah 7
Mary 7
Samuel 7
CUMING, Samuel B. 51
CUMMINGS, A. B. 100
CUMTABLE, Hannah 31
CUNNINGHAM, A. D. 103
Aaron 2
Alexander Newton 12,
20
Ann 2, 74
Anna A. D. 73
Barney 104
Christopher 2, 3
Cornelius Eugene 74
David 2, 39
E. J. 12, 20, 21
E. John 12
Elinor 2
Elizabeth 2, 3
George 37
Jacob 2
James 4
Jane 2
Jane McLin 20
Jenny 12
John 2, 9
John W. 20
John Whitfield 12
Joseph 2
L. B. 21
Lyddia 2
Martha 12, 20, 21, 46
Martha Rowe 12, 20
Matthew 2
Mary 2, 3, 8
McCardle 37
Moses 2
Samuel 74
Samuel A. 76
Samuel B. 12, 20, 21,
23, 37, 50, 53, 63,
73, 103
Sarah 2
Sarah Jane 74
Sophia Mody 74
Susannah 2, 3
William Madison 12, 20
CURRIER, Jonathan 1
CURTIS, Fannie 93
John 96, 100
Sarah 100
DANIEL, Alice 8
Ann 8
Jemima 8
John 8
Mary 8
Phebe 8
William 8
DAREAN, Joseph 12
DARYWORTH, Charles 12
DASHAL, Thomas 15
DASHOR, Michael 48
DAVAULT, Amanda 52
F. R. 99
Frederick 63
Jacob 78
John 99
Mary 60
Peter 66
Valentine 64
DAVIDSON, E. 112
DAVIS, Agness 4
Ann 1
Daniel 28
Etheldred 3
Elizabeth 1, 10
Esa 1
Isaac 1
James 1
Jane 11, 74, 103

DAVIS (cont.)
Mary 1
Nathaniel 1, 4, 5, 16
Rebecca 58
Robert 1
Samuel 9, 12
Thomas Rutledge 12
William 6
DEADERICK, Amanda F. 20
Blair 36
Charles 103
Claude 103
David 12, 20, 103
David A. 20
Dew 53
Duncan 36
E. L. 85, 109
E. T. 100
Edward 103
Eliza 103
Elizabeth R. 20
Emeline M. 79
Eugene 103
Eugene L. 103
Fannie 103
Frank 103
Henry 103
Isadore 103
J. F. 70, 103
James W. 60, 79
James William 20
John F. 20, 36, 57, 65
Joseph 79
Joseph A. 20
Kate 103
Laura 103
Margaretta 20
Susan 103
Susan L. 103
William V. 103
DEADRICK, David 14
G. A. 32
James W. 44
John B. 55
John F. 44
Margaret 44
Rebecca 44
DEAKE, C. T. C. 91
DEAKENS, Ann 43
Carl 110
Daniel 32
Daniel M. 25
Elizabeth 103
Floyd 110
H. F. 110
Hester 110
J. B. 103
James 110
James, Jr. 110
James E. 103
Liza 110
Maggie 110
Mary 110
R. M. K. 109
Veina 110
Will 110
DEAKINS, -- 80
Ann 43
Charles 21, 39
Daniel 81
Emeline 108
Hannah Eliza 100
Henry 84, 108
J. J. 99
James 7, 21, 59, 108
James E. 81, 91, 103
James H. 70
James W. 84
James Y. 84, 108
Jane 108
John 68, 84
Louisa 68
Mary 68

DUNCAN (cont.)
  Telema 55
  William 15, 16, 73
DUNCOME, Charles 21
  John 21
  Joseph, Jr. 21
  Joseph, Sr. 21
  Melven 21
  Mowel 21
  Rice 21
  Stacy 21
DUNGWORTH, Charles 22
DUNHAM, -- 41
  Thomas 39
DYER, Addie 108
  Addy 94
  Amanda 94
  Elizabeth 94, 108
  Hacker 66
  Robert 93, 94, 108
  Thomas 106
EADS, Nancy A. 69
EAGAN, Susannah 22
EAJAN, Susannah 6
EAKIN, Mark Ann 70
EAMES, Marietta 99
EARNEST, Amanda M. 90
  Antamond 37
  Axley 37
  Elizabeth 37
  F. W. 109
  Felix 23
  Hannah 29, 37
  Henry 5, 25
  Isaac 27
  J. W. 106
  Jacob B. 37
  Jane 108
  Jane Anna 90
  John G. 31
  Jonah W. 37
  Josiah W. 45, 90
  Lavinia 37, 75
  Lawrence 37
  Lawrence W. 37
  Margaret M. 90
  Margaret Melvina 90
  Marilla 37
  Mary 108
  Nancy 75
  Nancy L. 90
  Nancy M. 44
  Nancy McClung 90
  Peter 27, 46
  Polly 29
  Rebecca 37
  Robert 108
  Syntha 37
  Wesley 29, 37
  William S. 37
EASLEY, Nancy 67
EASON, John G. 36
EDEN, John 86
  Matilda 86
  Minerva K. 86
  Nathaniel 86
EDENS, Barbary S. 86
  Elizabeth K. 86
  Sarah M. 86
EDMUNDS, James 47
EDWARDS, A. W. 94, 104
  Abel Washington 94
  D. K. 94
  David K. 94
  Eli 9
  Eliza Ann 94
  Elizabeth 45
  John 34, 45
  Joshua 94
  Joshua Polk 94
  Lizzie M. 104
  Mary 45, 94
  Mary Elizabeth 94

EDWARDS (cont.)
  Matilda 45
  Nannie L. 104
  Owen 94
  S. E. 94
  Samuel 78
  Samuel A. 76
  Samuel E. 94
  Samuel Judson 94
  Thomas 45
  Thomas P. 75, 76
  W. T. 76
ELAM, Eliza A. 100
  Robert H. 100
  W. T. 100
  William T. 100
ELKINS, Haney 100
ELIS, Cordelias 103
  H. H. 103
  J. H. 103
  Mandy J. 103
  Mary 103
  Thomas N. 103
  W. L. 103
ELLET, George 30
  Jane 30
  John 30
  Mandy 30
  Mary 30
  Margaret 30
  Patrick 30
  Sarah 30
ELLIS, Clark 11, 31
  David 62
  Edmund 49
  Elijah 11, 38
  Elizabeth 97
  Hannah 75
  Jacob 11, 31, 43
  James 11, 19, 26
  Jane 29
  John 11, 31
  Letitia 31
  Malinda 97
  Margaret 11
  Martha 11
  Mollie E. 97
  Polly 29
  Robert 31
  S. B. 79, 84
  Samuel B. 74, 79, 84,
    87, 97
  William 11, 31, 50, 79,
    97
ELLISON, Polly Anna 16
ELSEY, George Crow 22
  John 22
  Thomas 22
ELSY, Onkel 90
EMBER, Isaac 9
EMBREE, Charles 50
  Elbert L. 50
  Elbert S. 50
  Elihu 9, 18, 50
  Elijah 25, 30
  Mary Elizabeth 50
  Nancy 18
  Susan Marie 50
EMMERSON, Adaline B. 61
  Arthur 36
  Catharine 36, 61
  Eliza C. 42
  Eliza T. 42
  Judge 65
  Thomas 36
  Thomas B. 36, 42
ENGLISH, Agnes 11
  Alexander 11
  Andrew 11
  Anna 60
  Elizabeth 11, 14
  Henry 3
  James 62

ENGLISH (cont.)
  James H. 55
  Jane 11
  John 11, 14, 21, 60
  John, Sr. 11
  John W. 60
  Malinda 62
  Margaret 60
  Nathan 76
  Nathan J. 60
  Robert 3
  Samuel 76
  Samuel H. 58, 60
  Sarah 11
  Thomas 11, 14
  William 2
ENSON, George W. 46
  Martha 46
  Sara 46
  Thomas 8
  Thomas P. 46
  W. T., Sr. 36
  William T. 46
  William T., Sr. 34, 46
  William B., Jr. 46
EPPERSON, Lear 68
  Nancy 68
  Thomas 68
ERVIN, Elizabeth 86
ERVINE, William S. 30
ERWIN, Andrew 15
  David 112
  Francis 14
  J. B. 73
  M. T. 44
  Mary 54
  Rebecca 26
  Samuel 54
  William 26, 30
ESTES, Eliza 77
ETON, Mary 6
EUTZLER, Catharine 67
  Elizabeth 67
  Frances Edna 67
  John 67
  Mary Jane 67
  Noah 67
EVANS, Ann B. 106
  Archer 3
  Charlot 3
  Malvina 66
  Marietta 98
  Marth Adelaid 66
  Mary Malvina 66
  Samuel R. 78
  Sarah 23
EWING, Robert 6
FAGAN, J. M. 101
FAGIN, Eliza E. 101
FAIN, Agnes 2
  Betsy 14
  David 14
  Eberneza 14
  Fain 2
  H. C. 79
  Hugh E. 77
  James 77
  John 2, 14, 77
  John H. 77
  John R. 77, 79
  Nancy 14, 77
  Polly Ann 14
  R. S. 77
  Rosanna 14
  Rosannah 2
  Ruth 2
  Samuel 14, 15
  Sarah 11
  Sally 14
  Thomas 77
  William 14, 15
  William, Sr. 11
FAIR, John 9

GREEN (cont.)
  Allen 42
  Amanda 46
  Amanda E. 46
  Charles 42
  Eliza C. 42
  Eliza T. 42
  Elizabeth 42
  Evaline 42
  George 42
  Ira 46, 68
  J. N. 46
  James R. 53, 55
  John 42
  Joshua 35, 40, 44, 47,
    53
  Malinda J. H. 46
  Mary 42, 46, 68
  R. B. 46
  Rosannah 46
  Susan 35
  Susannah 46
  Thomas 42
  Tolbert 42
  William W. 53
  Willie W. 47
GREENE, Joshua 39, 53
  Susan 53
GREENFIELD, Charles D.
  104
GREENWAY, Anna 35
  Eliza 48
  Elizabeth 35
  George 35
  Hannah 35
  Jesse H. 35, 48
  John H. 35, 68
  John McCracken 62
  Martha 35
  Mary Ann 35
  Matilda 48
  Patsy 35
  Pleasant 48
  Pleasant W. C. 48, 51
  Polly Ann 35
  Richard 35, 48
  Sally 48
  Susan 35
  Susan M. 48
  William 35
  William G. 62
GREER, Catharine 30
  Charles 4
  David 3, 4
  Hulda 4
  John 32
  Joseph 3
  Samuel 25, 32, 69
  Samuel, Senr. 32
  Thomas 32
  Thomas D. 32
GREGG, Abraham 64, 85
GRESHAM, Anna 9
  Betsy 9
  Dorcas 9
  Fuller 9
  George 18
  J. F. 77, 101
  John 9
  John, Jr. 78
  John F. 70, 72, 112
  Preon 9
  Rhoda 9
  Simeon 9
  Susannah 9
  Thomas 9
  W. M. 85
  William M. 75
GRIER, Hulda 4
  James 4
  Mary 4
GRIMSLEY, J. M. 48
  Lofton 22

GRIMSLEY (cont.)
  William 17, 21
GRINDSTAFF, Isaac 3
  Jonn 3
GRISHAM, Albert Hiram 94
  Elanch B. 85
  Elizabeth 85
  Evelina 85, 94
  Rev. George 94
  George E. 85
  J. A. 104
  J. F. 91, 92, 95, 100,
    104, 105
  J. S. 101
  James M. 82, 108
  John 75, 83, 87, 93,
    108
  Lula B. 85
  Lula Bell 85
  Margaret Jane 85
  Mary 85, 94
  Mary B. 85
  Mary H. 85
  P. H. 94
  Peter H. 94
  Sarah 94
  William M. 85, 94
GROSS, Mr. -- 46
GROVE, Christian 28
  Jane 28
GROVES, Catharine 33
  Christian 33
  Jane 33
  Susan 33
  Thomas 33
GUESS, Joseph 41
  Nancy 41
GUIN, David 63
  John 54
GUINN, Andrew 56
  David 56
  David S. 56, 98
  Elizabeth Jane 98
  Henry 56
  Isaac 84
  Isaac Newton 56
  James 56
  John 56
  Josiah 56
  Lise 56
  Margaret 56
  Mary Ann 71
  Matthew 56
  Matthew S. 56, 98
  Polly 56
  Thomas 56, 98
  W. F. 86
  William 56, 71
GUNNON, James 4
GUSTON, Catharine 33
GYME, Jacob 25
GYRE, Catrina 27
  Sarah Eliza 27
HACKER, -- 106
  Alexander 101
  Catharine 101
  Isaac C. 101
  J. C. 101
  Jacob 29
  Marietta 101
  Martha 101
  Miriam 101
  Newton 101, 111
  Robert 101
HAGA, David 90
HAGEE, A. J. 65
HAGY, David 76
  Eliza 65
  Margaret 76
HAIL, Elenor 34
  George I. 34
  J. H. 90
HAILE, Anson, Senr. 36

HAILE (cont.)
  Isabella 29
  Jane 29
  Joseph 29
  Margaret 29
  Polly 29
HAINS, Sally 23
HAIR, Eliza Jane 23
  Isaac 9, 16, 23
  Matilda 23
  Sarah 23
HAIRE, Henry 68
  Samuel C. 68
HAITE, Isaac 32
HALE, Abednego 55
  Allison 55
  Amanda Jane 55
  Amon 13, 16
  Ann 10, 41
  Anne 10
  Archibald 50, 55
  Benjamin 41, 52
  Betty 90
  Cage 16
  Canday 18, 47
  Chambdin 108
  Chamberlain 94
  Chase 30, 50, 54, 90
  Chinowth 75, 93
  Clary 38, 90
  D. Malindy 47
  Darcus 47
  David 55
  Elijah 35
  Elizabeth 10, 16, 18,
    26, 35, 44, 47, 90
    96
  Elizabeth T. 26
  Emeline 55
  F. D. 84
  Fanny 12
  Finley 50
  Finley D. 57
  Franklin 47, 50
  Franklin D. 50, 57
  George 10, 73, 90
  George, Sr. 10
  George C. 56
  George T. 42, 80
  Gideon 12
  Hannah 47, 56, 90
  Hannah Liza 56
  Harriet 35, 50, 57,
    84, 93
  Harvey N. 93
  Henry 18, 19, 26, 48,
    50, 57, 70
  Hiram 56, 73
  Hiram C. 84
  Hiram D. 46, 47, 81
  Hobart 47
  Hunterson 106
  Isabella 41
  Jackson 30, 50
  Jacob 44
  James 87, 112
  James P. 22
  Jane 47
  Jeremiah 31
  John 16, 18, 44, 52, 5
  John B. 56
  Jordan Elbert 47
  Joseph 18, 41, 50, 70
  Joseph H. 57
  Joseph L. 50
  Joseph S. 57
  Joshua 16
  Landon 41
  Lemuel J. 65
  Louisa 41
  Lucinda 55
  Lucy 18, 26, 41
  Lydia 18

HALE (cont.)
Maria 18
Mark 42, 50
Martha 41, 50, 55, 57
Martha E. 57
Mary 12, 41, 50, 55,
56, 64
Mary A. 57
Minerva 52, 55
Nancy 41, 90, 93
Nancy Ruth 79
Nicholas 12, 16, 52
Nicholas, Sr. 10, 16
Polly Ann 90
Rena 93
Richard 16, 47
Robert G. 37, 44
Ruth 16, 55, 90
Samuel 10, 47
Sarah 16, 41, 44, 47,
50, 86
Sarah H. 65
Shadrach 23
Smith H. 49, 57
Solomon 18
Stephen 18
Susan 90
Susanna 41
Susannah 10
T. L. 112
Telema 55
Thomas 86, 93
Widow 50
William 16, 46, 55, 56,
57, 90
William C. 56, 57, 79
William H. 57
William K. 50, 57, 84
HALL, David T. 58
Ebenezer 107
Eliza 30, 49
Eliza Ann 49
Elizabeth 30, 49, 84,
107
Ellen 79
Elvirah 99
George F. 81
Henry 79
Ibby 107
James 30, 49, 107
Jane 79
John 30
Lucinda 30
Margaret 49
Martha 79
Mary 79
Mary Jane 79
Nancy 30
Nancy Ruth 79
Patsy 98
Peggy 30
Polly 30
Robert 107
Samuel 22, 79
Sarah 107
Sarah Jane 107
Thomas 30, 49
Thomas H. 79
William 79, 92
HALTI, Margaret Amanda
100
HAMILTON, -- 54
Elizabeth 97
George 94
Isaac 79
Rebecca 94
HAMMER, Aaron 43
Ann 35
Anna 26
Anne 15
Barbara 15
Barbary 15
Catharine 26, 35

HAMMER (cont.)
Closson 11
Deborah 26, 35
Elizabeth 15, 26
Isaac C. 26, 33
Isaac 11, 15, 26, 35
Jacob 15, 26, 35
John 9, 15, 26
Jonathan 15, 26, 27,
35
Jonathan M. 26
Joseph 15
Margaret 15, 26
Mary 15, 26
Rachel 26
Samuel 35
Samuel B. 26
Sarah 26
HAMMIL, Elizabeth 29
HAMMONDS, Catharine 31
Elizabeth 31
George 31
Jacob 31
John 31
Lydia 31
Mary 31
Nancy 41
Thomas 31
HAMPTON, George 6
Hiram 65
John 6, 25
Mary 6
Robert 6
William 6
HANKAL, Abner 100
B. F. 78
Elizabeth 68
H. B. 86
Hezekiah 68
Jas. C. M. 71
Jephtha 68
Margaret 68
Nancy 68
W. E. 111
HANKEL, John 106
HANKLE, Elizabeth 84
H. B. 103
John 84
M. J. 103
Mary J. 96
HANLEY, Mary 24
HANLY, Mary 24
Samuel 24
HANNAH, A. G. 40
Andrew 4, 10, 24, 40,
47
Ann 40, 47
Emma 84
Esther 47, 72, 98
Esther D. 40
Jane 40, 47
John D. 19, 40
L. F. 98
Lucinda 47
Lucinda F. 40, 98
Lucinda J. 72
Lucinda T. 40
Margaret 47
Nancy 84
Tennessee A. 84
William 47, 84
HANSFORD, Mary 89
HARDEMAN, Thomas 1
HARDIN, J. C. 83
HARLOW, C. M. 98
HARMON, -- 39
Adam 42
Barbara 42, 85
Conrad 42
Elizabeth 42
Jacob 42
John 42
Ira 42

HARMON (cont.)
Margaret 42
Michael 6
Philip 85
Phillip 42
Sally 42
Susannah 42
HARNE, Jane 30
HARPER, Eliza R. 51
Matilda 66
HARR, E. H. 104
Isaac 104, 109
HARRINGTON, Ann 63, 106
Christian 106
Henry 63, 88, 106
James 45, 63
Mary 21, 63, 106
Peter 21, 63, 106
Polly 63
Richardson 106
HARRIS, A. N. 50
Alexander N. 40, 69
C. W. C. 40, 71
Caleb W. C. 40
Crampton 40
Edward 40
J. C. 40
J. C. T. 47
J. E. P. 80
J. E. T. 67, 93
James 40
James A. 40
John C. 11, 20, 39, 40,
105
John E. T. 40
John F. 85
Mary E. 40
Michael 40
Miranda 40
Sarah 40
Sarah Ann H. 40
William 74
William H. 40
HARRISON, Emaline 59
H. M. 98
Michael 5
Nancy L. 90
HART, Simon 11
HARTMAN, Henry 13, 36
J. P. 59
J. W. 77
Jacob 63
Jane 43
Jesse Paine 36
John 36
John Blair 36
Jonathan 36, 91
Levi 13, 27
Margaret Gray 84
Mary 55
Matilda 36
Nelson 36
Polly 36
Senith 36
Thomas H. 55
William 43
HARTSELL, Abraham 7
Cob 40
Cynthia 70
Isabel 70
Isabel W. 69
Jacob 39, 80
Nancy 58, 80
HARVEY, Crampton J. 20
Thomas 58
HARWOOD, J. E. 100
Sally 101
HASHBARGER, Elijah 55
HATCHER, Anna 4
Charles 4
Harris 4
James 4
Jamiston 4

HATCHER (cont.)
  Sarah 4
  Rebecca 4
HATS, Mary 41
HAWK, Catharine 72
HAWKS, Christina 72
HAWS, Amanda Jane 98
  Elizabeth English 62
  J. E. T. 80
  Jane 62
  John C. 31
  John Smith 49
  Lindy 34
  Marietta 98
  Mary 62
  Nancy 49
  Shadrack W. 98
  William 46, 98
HAY, Charles 4
  Hulda 4
  Rebecca 4
  Reuben 4
  Sarah 4
HAYES, George 23
  John H. 60
  Margaret 60
HAYNES, Col. J. G. 110
  Landon C. 66
  Sarah P. 91
HAYS, Charles 5
  Elizabeth 5
  Jane 36
  Thomas 100
HAZLET, Kindler 13
  Nancy 13
HEAD, Margaret 66
HEADRICK, E. W. 48
  Jess 38
  W. A. 112
HEDRICK, Jacob 30
HEISKEL, George 73
  Julia 73
  Rebecca 73
HELIBE, John 21
HELM, Amanda 104
  Ann 16
  John 12, 16
  Matilda 12
  William B. 23
HELMS, Louvena 104
  Nelly 104
HELTON, Catharine 36
HENDERSON, Emaline 66
  Finley 89
  Joseph 89
  Martha H. 89
HENDLEY, Elizabeth V. 28
HENDLY, Nancy 19
HENDREX, Sarah R. 86
HENDRICKS, Mary 8
HENDRY, George 28
HENLEY, Caty 7
  Elizabeth 44
  Isaac 44
  Isaac B. 44
  J. S. 97
  James 7, 72
  John 7, 91
  John S. 91
  Jonathan S. 44
  Joshua 44, 91
  Louisa 44
  Luther R. 44
  Margaret L. 95
  Mary 44
  Rebecca 91
  Sarah 72
  Suaphine 91
  Theodore 91
  Thomas R. 44
HENLY, Florain 32
HENRY, Agnes 4
HENSON, Acksah 81

HENSON (cont.)
  Pinckney 81
  Riley Daniel 81
HERKLBAREA, Henry 22
HETT, Virgie 111
HEYER, George Frazer 83
  Philip 83
  Philip J. 83
HICKMAN, W. H. 107
  William 91
HIDER, Adam 3
  Elizabeth 3
  Jacob 3
  John 3
  Joseph 3
  Michael 3
HIGGINS, Ellis 67
  Mary 67
HIGHSINGER, Mary 40
HILBERT, Easter 45
  Jacob 45
  John 104
HILL, Elinor 5, 6
  Ellenor 12
  James 77
  John 6
HILTON, Charles 36
HINDLEY, Isaac 25
HINKLE, Elizabeth 35
  George 35
  George, Senr. 21
  Hezekiah 68
  J. C. M. 68
HIPPS, Nancy 81
HISE, Anna 95
  Elizabeth 95
  Hannah Jane 95
HISHAW, Hosea 51
HITE, Mary Jane 100
HODGE, James 35
  Maggie 108
  Mary 106
HODGES, -- 113
  Abby Jane 98
  Barbary Ellen 75
  Betsy 11
  Canada 64
  Edmond 46
  Edna P. 98
  Elinor 45
  Elizabeth 61, 110
  Elizabeth M. 98
  Emily 75
  Emily S. 98
  G. F. 107
  G. W. 107
  George W. 98
  Hannah 45, 110
  Harriet 87
  Henry 110
  J. K. 110
  James 45, 61, 85, 110
  John 110
  John C. 98
  John C. C. 107
  Joseph 110
  Joseph K. 110
  Katharine 75
  Kenedy 110
  Louisa 110
  Mahlon M. 98
  Martin 64, 110
  Mary 61, 64, 110
  Micajah 98
  Nancy M. 98
  Orlena Josephine 98
  Polly 45
  Robert G. 98
  Roland 45
  Rollen 110
  Sarah H. 98
  Susan 110
  Susannah 45, 72

HODGES (cont.)
  W. 94, 108
  William 61
  William W. 98
HOLLIDAY, Amos 38
HOLT, Augustus 101
  Elizabeth 25, 43
  Jacob 12, 43
  Usley 43
  William B. 43
HOLTSINGER, John 80
  Nacky 80
HONEYCUT, Sara 46
HOOPER, Philip 24
HOP, William 31
HOPE, William 29
HOPKINS, Benjamin P. 34
  Mary 34
HOPPER, Hardin 103
HORNBARGER, Ann 62
  Emily C. 62
  Jacob 61, 62
  James W. 61
  Maranda E. 61
  Mary E. 62
  Ruth A. 62
  Sarah Ann 61
  Thurza Maria 62
  William M. 62
HORTON, A. 31
  Isaac 25, 29
  Joseph 100
  Malinda 100
  Margaret S. 100
  Mary Ann 78
  William 100
HOSS, A. F. 108
  Abraham 15, 16, 41, 45,
    49, 66
  Ann M. 65
  Benjamin 108
  Calvin 15, 72, 80
  Caroline 15
  Catherine 15
  E. E. 80, 81
  Elizabeth 13, 15, 80
  Emma Jane 108
  Fannie 80
  Fannie C. 80
  Franklin 66
  George 15
  Hannah 21
  Hannah M. 80
  Henry 13, 15, 16, 19,
    26, 41, 54, 56, 57,
    65, 72, 77, 80, 81,
    83, 92
  Henry, Jr. 80
  Henry A. 66
  Hugh D. 92
  Isaac 13, 15
  J. 94
  J. M. 75, 89
  Jacob 13, 15
  Jacob, Senr. 12
  John 14, 15, 45, 55
  John V. 13
  John W. 42
  L. C. 108
  Landon C. 57, 108
  Margaret Ann 66
  Mary 13, 15, 66
  Mont 90
  Montgomery 63, 66, 88
  Nancy 91
  Nathaniel K. 66
  Peter 12, 13, 15
  Polly 20
  Salina 66
  Samuel W. 39
  Sarah 13
  Sarah Laws 80
  Sarah Lewis 80

LYON, Amanda 42, 77, 85
  Ezekiel 20, 42
  Franklin 42, 55
  Joseph D. 98, 111
  M. R. 36
  Mason R. 36
  Nancy J. 111
  Nancy T. 63
  Polly 20, 42
  S. E. 73, 74, 77, 81,
    85, 111
  Samuel E. 42, 111
  W. J. 89
  W. L. 111
  William 55
  Wilson 42
MACKLIN, Robert 22
MACY, Thomas 11
MADDEN, John 41
  Mattie 109
MADEN, John 106
MADISON, Julia 73
MAGGOT, Mary 3
  Sarah 3
MAHONEY, Everett 70
  Maj. G. 76
  J. F. 89
  M. S. 76, 100, 101,
    102
  Dr. M. S. 92
  Margaret 101
  Margaret G. 101
MAINS, David 48
  Hiram 48
  Mary 48
MALLERN, P. H. 80
MALLES, E. S. 89
MALONEY, Dr. M. L. 100
MALVEN, Joseph 34
MANDY, Sary 100
MANSFIELD, Elizabeth 29
MARCH, Hannah 100
  Harry 16
  Samuel 100
MARES, Mack 21
  Mary 25
  Sarah 21, 25
MARILLA, Amanda 90
MARKWOOD, Levi H. 108
MARRS, David 27
  Patience 27
  Reese 27
  Ruth 27
MARSH, Abel 43
  Betsy Ann 43
  Erasmus 43
  George 43
  Elizabeth 43
  Gravener 43
  Hannah 43
  Henry 43
  James 43
  John 43
  Jonas 32
  Rebecca 43
  William 43
MARSHALL, Polly 19
MARTIN, -- 81, 100
  A., Dr. 94
  Alfred 96
  Anna Mary 111
  Betty 16
  Caleb 43
  Cloe 16
  Deborah 29
  Delila 97
  E. S. 43
  Elizabeth 8, 95
  Ellen M. 111
  Ellen W. 111
  Eveline 87
  G. R. W. 104
  Henry 16, 68

MARTIN (cont.)
  Ida E. 105
  J. C. 108
  James 8
  Jesse 100
  John 16, 36, 52
  John A. 111
  Jones Hunt 92
  Joseph 20, 70
  Joseph H. 99, 107
  Juliet E. 111
  Kentucky 43
  Lucinda 29
  Marcellus M. 105
  Mary 43
  Matilda 68
  Michael H. 20
  Richard 16
  S. P. 95, 100, 105,
    106, 114
  Samuel 20
  Sarah 43
  Sue 111
  William H. 105
MASAN, A. G. 65
MASON, A. G. 69, 103
  Angeline E. 69
  James G. 83
MASS, Gus 110
MASTERS, Michael 14
MATHENY, Elijah 13
MATHES, -- 90
  A. H. 69
  Adda M. 110
  Alex 15, 16, 24, 80
  Alex P. 110
  Alexander 29, 69, 73,
    98, 106, 110
  Alexander, Sr. 69
  Alexander L. 69
  Alfred H. 63
  Birtie 110
  Calvin 35
  Daniel 57, 68
  E. E. 53, 73, 75, 84
  E. H. 100
  E. L. 19, 29, 32, 36,
    38, 40, 45, 51, 53,
    54, 57, 59, 62, 63,
    68, 69, 71, 75, 90
  E. S. 69, 75
  E. Smith 69, 110
  Ebenezer 18
    Ebenezer C. 34
  Ebenezer L. 15, 62
  Effie D. 110
  Elenore 107
  Emily 107
  Ez. S. 110
  Euphrasia A. 62
  Frank S. 110
  Graham 35
  H. E. 100
  Isabella 69
  J. S. 103
  James 19
  Jeremiah 24
  Lydia E. 69
  Lydia Eliza 63
  Mack M. 110
  Mamie 110
  Margaret 21
  Mattie 107
  Nancy 34
  Nancy A. 69
  Nora Ruble 97
  Phebe 53
  Polly 69
  Rollee J. 110
  Sarah Estelle 107
  Susan 53
  W. E. 90
  William 65, 107

MATHIS, Alex 10
  Alexander 10, 11
  Alexander, Jr. 10
  Alexander, Sr. 10
  Allen 8, 10
  Anne 10
  Ebenezer L. 10
  George 10
  George L. 10
  Grace 10
  Jeremiah 10
  John 10, 20
  Miriam 10
  Rachel 10
  Rosannah 20
MATLOCK, Catherine 3
  David 3
  Elizabeth 3
  George 3
  Gideon 3
  James 84
  Jerome 84
  Josephine 84
  Margaret 3
  Sarah 3, 84
MATTHEWS, Fannie E. 109
  Fanny S. 109
MAUK, A. F. 112
  Abraham 46
  E. E. 99
  Embree 46
  Jacob 46
  James 52
  James M. 46, 88
  John 88
  Montgomery 46
  Polly 37
  Polly Ann 88
  Samuel 37
MAUPEN, George W. 78
MAUPIN, James Henry 112
  John A. P. 112
  Mary M. 112
  Rev. W. P. 101
MAWHORTER, Elizabeth 54,
    55
  James 54
MAXWELL, -- 53
  Albert 52
  Catharine Allen 52
  Grayson 52
  Hester 52
  Jane 52
  Martha 64
  Rebecca A. E. 52
  Samuel 52
  Samuel Allen 52
  William 52
  William H. 74
  William Henry 52
MAY, C. E. 76
  Cassamer E. 74
  Cassamore E. 76
  David 110
  George W. 74, 76
  Isaac 95
  John 20
  Malinda C. 95
  Margaret 95
  Margaret L. 95
  Martha A. 95
  Mary A. 95
  Mary H. 82
  R. M. 100, 101, 106
  Samuel 95
  Susan B. 62
  William A. 91
MAYBERRY, Barbary 6
MAYS, Casmere 39
  David 110
  Eliza 39
  George 39
  Jacob 82

MAYS (cont.)
    James G. 39
    John 39
    Mary 39, 110
    Mary Anon 39
    Samuel 39
    William 39
MC ADAM, Cynthia 29
    Hugh 13, 29
    Isabella 29
    Jane 29
    John 13
    Joseph D. 65
    Margaret 29
    Polly 29
    Robert 13
    Samuel 29
    Samuel B. 65
    Thomas 13, 29
    Thomas C. 36
MC ADAMS, Ann 63
    Ann S. 65
    Cynthia 48
    Margaret L. 107
    Matthew J. 64
    S. P. 63
    Samuel 74
    Samuel B. 64, 65
    Thomas 52
    Thomas 39, 48, 64
    Thomas M. 46
MC ALISTER, Charles 14
    Eleanor R. 51
    Eliza R. 51
    Fanny 14
    Frances 51
    James 14, 29, 51
    John 14, 18, 20
    Louisa 51
    Margaret C. 51
    Samuel R. 51
    Sarah 14
    Susan 51
MC ALLISTER, James 89
MC AMISH, Martin 70
MC ANDERSON, Sue 111
MC BRIDE, Alexander 31
MC CALEB, Ann 17
    Isaac 17
    John 17
    Mary 17
    Peranah 17
MC CALL, -- 76
    Alexander 91
    J. P. 104
    James 18
    Jane 7
    Jemima 28
    Jenny 18
    John 7, 16, 18
    John, Sr. 18
    Margaret 18
    Margarim 18
    Robert 18, 28
    William 18
MC CARDEL, Emily 26
    Esther 26
    Hannah 26
    John 26
    Nancy 26
    Philip 26
    Rebecca 26
MC CARELE, John 18
MC CARROLL, James 18
MC CHESNEY, Isabella 69
MC CLEARY, Sarah 29
MC CLEES, -- 31
MC CLELLAN, A. 33
    William 76
MC CLOUD, William 13
MC CLURE, E. G. 98
    Emma C. 98
    Ewin 11

MC CLURE (cont.)
    Ewing 19, 34, 71
    Ewing G. 71
    James 11
    John 11, 71
    John F. 71
    Mary 11, 71
    Nancy 11
    R. Antoinette 71
    Rebecca 11
    Robert 11
    William 11
MC CONLEY, R. B. 105
MC CONNELL, John 23
MC CORKLE, Eliza E. 101
    J. J. 101
    Martha J. 101
    Mary C. 101
    Nancy H. 101
    Samuel 101
    Susan M. 101
    William 86
    William M. 101
MC COY, Jane 60
    John 14
    Lydia 22
    Margaret 60
    Malinda 60
    Nancy 60
    Sarah 14
MC CRACKEN, -- 43
    Agnes Kelsey 10
    Ann 10, 62
    Catharine 30
    Elizabeth D. 62
    Henry 30, 41, 45, 49
    John 30, 54, 55, 62
    John B. 30, 33
    John M. 62
    Margaret 30, 62
    Martha 30
    Mary 30
    Mary A. 62
    Mary B. 30
    Matthew C. 62
    Robert 30
    Sally Ann 48
    Samuel 30
    Samuel G. 51
    William 30, 62
    William K. 62
MC CRARY, Charles 7
    John 21
MC CRAY, Charles 5
    Daniel 5, 7, 12, 23
    Henry 21, 23
    Sarah 5, 12
    Thomas 23
MC CREHAN, John 19
MC CULBEE, Zachariah 22
MC CULLEY, Robert 110
MC CUNE, Elizabeth 32
MC CURRY, Jane Anna 90
MC EWEN, Alexander 24
    Ebenezer 24, 37
    Elizabeth 37
    John 24
    Margaret 24
    Robert 24
    Samuel 24
    Sarah 24
MC FALL, Neil 6
MC FARLAND, Jane 71
    Robert 4
MC GEE, William O. 17
MC GHEE, Sarah 32
MC GINNIS, Hannah 75
    John 37
MC GLAUGHLIN, Willis 25
MC GUIRE, Amy 41
    Jemima 41
    Jesse 41
    William 41

MC HEAL, Margaret 42
MC INTURFF, Achy 72
    Daniel 76
    Isaac 9
    Gabriel 72
    Serephina 72
    T. 56
MC KALEB, Ann 17
    Isaac 17
    John 17
    Mary 17
    Peranah 17
MC KASSON, Joseph 89
MC KAY, Lydda 6
MC KEE, Alex 13
    Alexander 13
    Bell Jane 107
    Euphrasia A. 62
    Eveline P. 62
    Ewen Y. 62
    Henry Edgar 107
    James P. 62
    John 13
    John C. 62
    Margaret M. 62
    Perine M. 107
    Phebe J. 107
    Rebecca J. 62
    Robert 13, 14, 50, 62,
      76
    Robert M. 62
    Thompson W. 62
    William 13
    William M. 62, 76, 107
    Willie Van Buren 107
MC KENNEY, S. M. 108
MC KENNY, James 14
    Mary 14
MC KILLOP, Ann 17
    Isaac 17
    John 17
    Mary 17
    Peranah 17
MC LIN, Alexander 9, 17,
      23
    Benjamin 23, 33, 44,
      81
    Elizabeth 81
    Elizabeth Ann 49, 89
    Frances 81
    Frances E. 81
    Isabella 23
    John 23
    John B. 89
    Joseph 23
    Locind 89
    Lucinda 81
    Margaret 61
    Margaret C. 73
    Martha 23
    Rachel 81, 89
    Rachel O. 89
    Richard 33, 44, 81, 89
    Robert 23, 81, 89
    Robert A. 81
    Sarah 61
    Sophiah C. 89
    William 12
MC LINS, Robert 33
MC MASTERS, John 55
MC MULLEN, Henry 4
    Mary 4
MC NABB, Baptist 2
    David 2
    Isabella 2
    Jane 2
    John 2
    Jonathan 2
    Katrin 2
    Margaret 2
    Mary 2
    Nathaniel 29
    William 2

MC NEAL, Elizabeth 85
    James P. 85
    William 85
MC NEEC, Jacob 90
MC NEES, Jacob 86
    Lucinda D. 69
MC NEESE, A. C. 111
    Elizabeth 69
    Martha 77
    Mary Ann 35
MC NEıL, Alexander 67
    Charlie 85
    Elizabeth 67
    Mary 85
MC NUTT, Anthony 16, 23
    Elizabeth 52
    Susanna 52
MC PHERON, Elizabeth 27
    Jonas 33
    Isaac 27
    William M. 27
MC PHERSON, Charles C. 92
    Emely 87
    Isaac 35, 37, 42, 45
    Matthew 37
    Nancy 38
    Virginia 92
MC ROBERTS, Robert Lee
    107
    Rosannah 46
    William 42, 46, 47
MC WHERTER, James 9
    Polly Reaney 9
MC WHORTER, Elizabeth 49
    James 30, 49
    Polly 30
    Polly Reaney 9
    Suzy 30
MEAD, Benjamin 35
    Elenor 35
    Elizabeth 35
    John 35, 36
    Polly 35
    Polly Ann 35
    Rebecca 35
    William 35
MEADE, Elisha B. 53
    Jane 53
MEADEN, John 75
MEADS, Rebecca 40
MEARS, Mark 15
MEEK, Charles 65
    Charles W. 83
    Daniel Kinney 65
    Sarah 44, 65
    Sarah A. 83
MELLONER, John 15
MELTON, Samuel 83
MELVEN, Joseph 15
MELVIN, Hannah 15
    James 15, 21, 63
    James R. 63
    John 15
    Joseph 15
    Mahala 63
    Margaret Ann 96
    Rheba 15
    Rhoda 15
    Stacey 63
    Susan 63
    William 103
    William C. 63
MERRITT, Susannah
METCALF, Joseph 8
    Ulysses G. 84
METTELEL, A. W. 111
MICHELBERRY, -- 83
MIDDLETON, Ann 92
    West 77
    William 48, 92
MILBURN, Alfred J. 70
    Henry N. 70
    James H. 70

MILBURN (cont.)
    John 32
    John W. 70
    Mary Elizabeth 70
MILHORN, H. 50
    Martha 108
MILLER, -- 39, 81
    Abraham 47
    Abraham E. 60
    Alexander 32, 66
    Anderson 32
    Ann 22
    Barbary 23
    Catharine 44, 60, 78,
        80
    Chelnesse 60
    Clara 90, 92
    Daniel Y. 47
    Delila 70
    E. L. 39
    E. S. 94, 96, 102, 108
    E. S., Jr. 106
    E. S., Senr. 106
    Elbert 67, 87
    Elbert S. 67
    Elcany 56
    Eliza 60, 91
    Elizabeth 15, 23, 36,
        47, 60, 67, 78, 79,
        85
    Elizabeth D. 86, 92
    Emma 67
    George 3, 72
    Hannah 58, 60
    Henry 85
    Jacob 16, 22, 38, 60,
        81, 114
    Jacob, Sr. 60
    James 56, 67, 86, 87,
        89, 92
    James A. 47
    James M. 92, 95
    John 13, 38, 60, 78
    John P. 95
    Joseph 56, 114
    K. J. 111
    Lizzie 92
    Louise 72
    Madison 76
    Maggie 111
    Margaret 22, 23, 38
    Marh Ann 70
    Martha 47
    Mary 23, 38, 56, 60,
        67, 70, 78, 87, 92
    Mary A. 92
    Matilda 60
    Matilda C. 92
    Maupin 83
    Melissa 92
    Melissa J. 92
    Nancy 14, 26, 67, 78
    P. A. 107
    Peggy Ann 47
    Peter 20, 22, 30, 51,
        61, 67, 68, 70
    Peter R. 60
    Polly 47
    S., Senr. 105
    S. H. 83, 85, 86, 92,
        103
    S. N. 83
    Sallie Jane 96
    Samuel 66, 67, 87, 92,
        97
    Samuel H. 67
    Sarah 56, 67, 92, 111,
        112
    Sarah C. 92
    Sarah J. 92
    Sarah Jane 47
    Solomon 70, 78, 94
    Sophronia 92

MILLER (cont.)
    Sophronia C. 92
    Susan M. 92
    Susannah 56
    Thomas 56
    Van S. 32
    William 43, 67, 86,
        87, 111, 112
    William E. 94
    William Elija 47
    William R. 85
MILLIKEN, John 24
MILLION, Edward 40
    Elizabeth 40
    Jacob 40
    Jane H. 57
    Jeremiah 58
    John 9, 28, 39, 40
    Mary 39, 58
    Mary Nancy 58
    Nancy 58
    Polly May 40
    Robert 40, 57, 58
    Sarah 40, 57, 58
MITCHELL, Adam 9
    Albert 54
    Chase 90
    David 9, 25
    Eliza 11, 54
    Elizabeth 2, 11, 12,
        54
    Emily H. 48
    Hezekiah 9
    Hezekiah B. 20
    Ibby 9
    J. M. 87
    James 2, 9, 11, 36
    Jenny 9, 11
    Joab 1
    John 9, 38
    John M. 106
    Jonathan C. 48
    Malie 54
    Margaret 2, 9, 38
    Mary 1
    Nancy 87
    Rebecca 9, 54
    Richard 1
    Robert 9, 11
    Ruth 90
    S. S. 79
    Samuel 9
    Samuel D. 59, 87
    Sarah 105
    Serephina 54
    Thomas 2
    W. M. 59
    William 9, 18, 25, 54,
        70, 81, 87
    William H. 87
MIZER, David 92
MOCK, Godfrey 30, 36
MOHLER, William 72
·MOLER, Henry 36
    Margaret 36
    Samuel 36
MONGH, --, Dr. 90
MONTEETH, Jane 58
MONTOGOMERY, James 24
    William 17, 22
MOOMAN, Loucindy N. 86
MOONEY, George 1
MOOR, Murrell 82
    Sarah 67
MOORE, Abrrodla 6
    Alex 69
    Alexander 79, 98
    Amanda 57, 69
    Augusta 79
    Basheba 17
    Catharine 69
    Crawford 69
    Daniel 17, 69

PEOPLES (cont.)
Rachel 59
Rachel T. 59
Ruth 59
PERKENS, Jacob 81
W. H. 81
PERKINS, Jacob 105
Sarah 16
PETERS, Jane Smith 105
PEYTON, Joseph 22
PHELPS, Hannah Emily 100
PHERSON, Ellen 79
PHILIPS, Elizabeth 10
PHILLIPS, Baly 18
Elizabeth 79
George 89
Isaac 79
J. N. 82
John 79
Nancy 79
Sarah 79
Temanda 79
PHINNY, C. H. 64
PICKENS, A. G. 110
PICKERING, Enos 30, 43
PIERCE, A. H. 87
Isaac M. 43
John 96
Virginia 101
William 46
PINNER, Abigail 105
PIPER, A. R. 100
Julia C. 66
PITCOCK, Rebecca 75
PLEMMONS, Juliet E. 111
POINDEXTER, Elbert I. 59
Gar 59
Houston 59
James 59
John 59
Martha E. 59
Sarian 59
Thomas 59
William 59
William M. 59
POLSER, Francis W. 56
PONDER, S. H. 109
POOPLES, Elizabeth 22
Mary 22
Nathan 22
PORCH, W. S. 110
PORTER, John 31
Thomas 48
POTTER, Abraham 3
Elizabeth 3
Hannah 3
John 3
Johnston 3
Nancy 3
Sarah 3
POWELL, Elizabeth 13
Henry 13
John 13
Joseph 13
Samuel D. 45
POWERS, John 1
Sarah 67
PRATER, Rosannah 68
PRATHER, Mary Ann 32
PRESCUTT, Nicholas 41
PRESNELL, Henderson 72
John 63
PRESTON, Ruthaw Henry 50
PRETHERO, Alex 17
PRICE, Emily 58
Gardner L. 58
H. L. 96
J. D. 53
James 31, 60
Joseph 104
Joseph D. 53
M. 53
Madison 58

PRICE (cont.)
Mary 58
Mary Ann 78
Mordiciai 6, 53, 58
Rachel 6
T. T. 96
Tabitha 60
Thomas 31
PRICHETT, Amanda Jane 55
Caroline 42
Elizabeth 42
Emily 42
James 42
John 42
Mark M. 42
Mary 87
Nancy 42
Samuel H. 42
Shepherd 42
Singleton 42
William Hiter 42
PRIMMER, Mary 30
PRING, Elizabeth 61
Nicholas 61
Susan 61
Susanna 61
Taritia 61
PRITCHARD, Harvey 103
PRITCHETT, -- 101
J. A. 103
PROFFITT, Emily 75
Daniel B. 44
Margaret 50
Nancy 50
W. B. 75
William 43
William B. 44, 75
PROPST, Jacob L. 71
PRUET, Catharine 29
PUNY, Nicholas 16
PURROLL, Mary 17
PURSELL, Elizabeth 27
George 27
George, Jr. 27
George, Senr. 27
John 27
Sarah 27
PURSELLY, William 5
PURSLEY, Richard 111
QUILLEN, Charles 25
RACKETT, Francis 110
RADER, -- 94
Adam 11, 12
Ann 12
E. D. 55
Elizabeth 12
RAGAN, Catharine 97
Daniel 97
RAINBOLT, Adam 3
RAMSEY, F. A. 5
RANGE, -- 40
Agnes 74
Ann 35
Anna 26
Barbara 15
Barbary 15
Catharine 65, 74, 90
Elendor 73
Eliza 91
Elizabeth 15, 73, 91
Elizabeth Eve 78
Fathee 38
G. W. 71, 78
George H. 64
Jacob 15, 27, 35, 91, 97
James 62, 73
John 15, 26
John N. 65
Jonathan 38
Louisa 73, 91
Martha 73, 97
Mary 73, 110

RANGE (cont.)
Matilday 73
Nancy 91
Peter 15, 73, 91
Rachel 15
Sarah 15
Susan 91
Susannah 73
W. F. 86
W. J. 74
W. T. 102
William 73
William T. 74
Y. H. 71
RANKIN, Elizabeth 91
Robert J. 98
W. P. 98
RATCLIFF, Eli 60
Ely 60
James 60
Jane 60
Mary 60
Nancy 60
Phoebe 60
Reuben 60
Robert 60
Silas 56, 60
Tabitha 60
READ, Delila 82
Elizabeth 82
George 54
Jane 82
Julius 82
Margaret 82
Marjery 82
Mary 82
Summerfield 82
W. 54
William 50, 51, 82
REANEY, Polly 9
RECTOR, Mary 43
William 43
REED, George 43, 52
J. W. 92
Jacob J. 106
James 26
John 106
Julius 82
Margaret 82
Rebecca 92
Robert 108
William 72, 92
REEDY, John 97
REEP, Anderson 91
REESE, Catharine E. 61
Chelnesse 60
REEVES, E. C. 92, 98, 110
Elbert C. 96
George A. 96
J. M. 106
James M. 86, 96
John D. 86, 96
Lizzie A. 96
Matilda C. 92, 96
Peter M. 47, 49, 92, 96
William P. 47, 92, 96
REGISTER, Archibald G. 48
Deborah 29
Francis 29
Gregg 87
Gregory 29
Hannah Eliza 29
James Archibald 29
Jemima 29
Lucinda 29
Orlena 87
Sarah 29
RENEAU, Thomas 3
RESER, Eliza 30
Jacob 46
REUBUSH, John 73
REYNOLDS, W. B. 75

WRIGHT, George
    Washington 90
   James 48
   Jesse 43
   John 33, 90
   John James 90
   Margaret 90
   Mary 58
   Samuel 39
   Sarah 39, 58
   Thomas 58
   William 58
WYAN, Malinda 77
WYLEY, Abel 16
   Samuel Y. 47
WYLY, Charles H. 89
   Joseph A. 89
   Martha H. 89
   Mary A. 48
   Samuel Y. 49, 54
YATES, -- 40
YEAGER, Cornelius 30
   Daniel 22, 27, 30
   E. F. 63
   Elijah F. 30
   Eliza 30
   J. J. 62, 92
   Jonah J. 30
   Martha E. F. 30
   Salina 66
   Solomon N. 30
   Susanna 22, 30
   Susannah M. 30
YOAKLEY, Endymion 76
   Endymon 91
   John 84
   P. 107, 112
YOKLEY, Benjamin L. 35
YOUNG, Agnes 4
   Amy 11
   Anna 11
   Barbara A. 96
   Betsy 11
   Catharine Emily 31
   Caty 12
   Charles 4, 24
   Deborah 35
   Elizabeth 4, 19, 31,
     96
   Ellen C. 96
   Emeline 96
   Ervery 24
   Esther 19, 38
   George W. 96
   Harriett 88
   Harriett J. 83
   Hugh P. 73, 96
   Isabella 96
   Isbell 24
   James 4, 10, 11, 12
   James P. 31
   James W. 19, 26, 31
   Jane 4, 26, 31
   Jane Eliza 31
   Jemima 11
   Jenny 11, 19
   Jinny 24
   John 4, 7, 10, 24, 96
   John C. 96
   Jonathan 10, 11
   Joseph 4, 7, 10, 11,
     12, 19, 31, 96
   Joseph L. 31
   Julia C. 83
   Julia F. 96
   Latitia M. 96
   Lucinda 78
   Margaret 4
   Margaret Caroline 31
   Marth 4
   Mary 83, 96
   Mary E. 83
   Peggy 19

YOUNG (cont.)
   Phebe 10, 11
   Polly 12, 12
   R. M. 80
   R. S. 67
   Rachel Caroline 88
   Rebecca 24, 31
   Robert 4, 7, 10, 11,
     31, 78, 96
   Robert S. 67
   Robert W. 96
   Rosanna 14
   Sabrina A. 41
   Sarah 31, 96
   Sarah E. 83, 96
   Strobie 88
   Susan 96
   T. A. 103
   T. L. 82
   Thomas 4, 10, 11, 24,
     66, 103
   Thomas A. 83
   Thomas F. 58
   Thomas J. 53
   Thomas T. 39, 41, 48
   Thomas R. 31
   W. F. 108
   W. N. 83
   Wilkins 24, 26
   William 4, 10, 12, 31,
     96
   William H. 26, 31, 83
ZETTY, Barbara 35
   Catharine 46
   Christian 12, 35, 46,
     51
   Christian, Senr. 35
   Christiana 35
   Daniel 46
   Daniel Kenney 46
   Elizabeth 35
   Hannah 35
   Jane 46
   Mary 35
   Sarah 46
ZIMMERMAN, Catharine 60
   Sarah 40
---, Adam 5
   Alex 51
   Alfred 37
   Amy 12
   Barney 74
   Beck 7, 17
   Ben 17
   Bet 20
   Bob 16
   Clary 70
   Daniel 60
   Dinnah 16
   Drag 40
   Edward 82
   Emaline 60
   Fan 70
   Fanny 37, 53
   Frank 54
   Grace 1
   Ham 70
   Harriet 53, 54
   Ira 18
   Jack 70
   James 70
   Joe 70
   Laura 64
   Lee 50
   Madison 70
   Manson 74
   Mary Ann 59
   Milly 70
   Peter 6
   Phoebe 40
   Poll 6
   Polly 51
   Prince 2

--- (cont.)
   Punch 2
   Rachel 8
   Rhoda 6
   Robert 31
   Sal 70, 80
   Samuel 80
   Tom 17